DAVID CRYSTAL

* * *

AS THEY SAY IN ZANZIBAR

When two elephants tussle, it's the grass that suffers

ZANZIBAR

AS THEY SAY IN

ZANZIBAR

* * *

DAVID CRYSTAL

OXFORD

UNIVERSITY PRESS

First published in 2006 by Collins

This edition first published in 2008 by Oxford University Press, Inc.

Published in North America by
Oxford University Press, Inc.
198 Madison Avenue,
New York, NY 10016

www.oup.com/us

Oxford is a registered trademark of
Oxford University Press

Library of Congress Cataloging-in-Publication Data

Crystal, David, 1941–
As they say in Zanzibar / David Crystal.
p.   cm.
Includes indexes.
ISBN 978–0–19–537450–6
1.   Proverbs. I. Title
PN6405.C79 2008
808.88'2—dc22   2008015046

Designed by Mark Thomson

Typeset in FF Nexus by
Rowland Phototypesetting Ltd, Bury St Edmunds, Suffolk

Printed and bound in India by
Thomson Press (India) Ltd

ISBN 9780195374506

CONTENTS

INTRODUCTION

When the occasion comes, the proverb comes
GHANA
If there is falsity in a proverb, then milk can be sour
INDIA

IS THERE still a place for proverbs in the language of the
twenty-first century? When I began to compile this book, I
asked several people what they thought of proverbs, and
encountered a surprising number of negative reactions. One
widely held view maintains that proverbs are clichéd
expressions, used by those who have not bothered to think
clearly. Another sees them as out of date, a reflection of a
bygone age. One person – an Internet geek – told me that he
'wouldn't be seen dead using one', citing *Too many cooks spoil
the broth'* as a case in point.

There is a curious double-think operating. I later heard
that same geek joking with some colleagues about the poor
military intelligence that had led a certain government to
make some bad decisions. *'Garbage in, garbage out'*, said the
geek. The phrase originated in his IT world: if invalid data
(garbage) is entered into a system, the output will also be
invalid. During the 1990s, the expression came to be applied
to an increasingly varied range of situations. Within a decade,
it had taken on proverbial status. My anti-proverbial geek was
using a proverb without realizing it.

Within a few days of that first enquiry, I heard several people dropping proverbs, or fragments of proverbs, into their conversations. 'Needs must', said one. 'Ask a silly question', said another. 'People in glass houses', said a third. None of them bothered to complete the well-known proverbs. They were taken for granted.

People may not quote proverbs in full as much as they used to, or treat them with the high respect of an earlier age, but they certainly allude to them. Anyone looking out for proverbs in everyday situations would quickly be able to add to the following brief selection:

- A university department that was being axed advertised its farewell party under the banner headline: 'Come and Hear the Fat Lady Sing'.
- A TV comedian made a risqué joke based on 'A bird in the hand is worth two in the bush'.
- A US motel trying to attract custom to the claimed comfort of its facilities had a sign outside: 'The early bird only gets the worm'.
- A TV comedy programme called itself 'Birds of a Feather'.

Proverbs continue to fascinate people. Here is a test anyone can do. Choose one of the less familiar proverbs from this book, drop it into a conversation, and see what happens. My favourite is the Irish proverb Never bolt your door with a boiled carrot. There is invariably an interesting discussion about the proverb's origins and use. And one proverb then reminds someone of another. It is a bit like punning: when one person makes a pun, others try to do better. Puns are batted back and forth. Some linguists have called this phenomenon 'ping-pong punning'. There is ping-pong proverbing too. Proverb exchanges and contests have a literary history. You will find one in Shakespeare (see p. 488).

There is something about the proverbs associated with other cultures that allows them to evade the kind of criticism we level at our own native expressions. Whatever else we might say about the following, we would not for one moment call them clichés.

> *A coconut shell full of water is a sea to an ant* (ZANZIBAR)
> *Don't call the alligator a big-mouth till you have crossed the*
>   *river* (BELIZE)
> *An untouched drum does not speak* (LIBERIA)
> *Do not try to borrow combs from shaven monks* (CHINA)

Such proverbs do more than express a general truth or universal belief. Each in its own way adds a tiny bit more to our understanding of the world's linguistic and cultural diversity, and thus helps us grasp more fully what it means to be human.

It is a commonplace of comparative linguistics that every language expresses a unique vision of the world. This is not to say that each language is so different from others that its speakers can never communicate outside their own people. The existence of 'balanced bilinguals' – people who have learned two languages from childhood with equal fluency – and the everyday phenomenon of translating and interpreting proves otherwise. Rather, it is to point out that languages are not identical in the way in which they talk about the world. There is a limit to the amount of exact translation equivalence that can be achieved, and people have to be satisfied with an approximation. And it is in this area of approximate equivalence that fascinating cultural differences can be found.

Commentators over the years have drawn attention to the importance of a comparative linguistic perspective on life. Here is Ezra Pound, in *The ABC of Reading* (1960):

> The sum of human wisdom is not contained in any one language, and no single language is capable of expressing all forms and degrees of human comprehension.

And here is George Steiner, in a 1967 essay ('F R Leavis'):

> Is it not the duty of the critic to avail himself, in some imperfect measure at least, of another language – if only to experience the defining contours of his own?

The ideal, of course, is to learn enough of another language to be able to get a sense of the differences directly – to *feel* the contours, without having to rely on a translating intermediary. The second-best approach is to read, in translation, as much as possible of the culturally distinctive literature of other languages, such as its poems, stories, myths, legends – and proverbs.

A collection of cross-linguistic proverbs is of special interest because it conveys two opposed but equally interesting messages. On the one hand, it draws attention to the differences of expression and perception which characterize the world's communities. On the other hand, it shows that, to a very great extent, these communities are the same. People recognize, admire and worry over similar things. Notions such as 'More haste, less speed' can be found in dozens of cultures. And in such examples as the following, the nuance may vary, but the spirit behind the proverb remains the same:

> *A guest and a fish after three days are poison* (FRANCE)
> *Seven days is the length of a guest's life* (MYANMAR)

However, this common human perspective is a complication when it comes to compiling a book such as this one, which aims to be illustrative of proverbial diversity and not comprehensive. It is not possible, in a short selection, to include a proverb as it appears in every country; nor – if reader interest is to be preserved – is it desirable. To illustrate the point, consider these variations on the *guest* theme – just a few taken from Selwyn Gurney Champion's huge collection of translated cultural proverbs (see Further Reading, p. 595):

> *A fish and a guest go bad on the third day and must be thrown out* (BASQUE)
> *Fish and guests smell at three days old* (DANISH)
> *A guest, like a fish, stinks the third day* (DUTCH)
> *A fish and a guest after three days are poison* (ENGLISH)
> *Guests and fish will get old on the third day* (ESTONIAN)
> *The first day a guest, the second a guest, the third day a calamity* (HINDI)
> *Even a welcome guest becomes a bore on the third day* (JAPANESE)

We need only one example to appreciate the point, but that means grasping the nettle and selecting one country to represent all. I have endeavoured to introduce as wide a range of countries as possible, when making such choices. There are 110 (apart from England) listed in Index 5 (p. 711).

All anthologies are made with particular audiences in mind, and selections inevitably change over time. Until as recently as thirty years ago, it would have been normal to find in any proverb collection a predominantly masculine bias, reflecting traditional male-dominated society. Many items, both those native to English and those in translation, would have begun with 'He who . . .' or 'The man who . . .'. Times have moved on. I have replaced these with a generic usage, unless there is a genuine male v female contrast involved. A remarkable number of proverbs, in many countries, also reflect unpalatable notions, such as the desirability of beating one's wife to ensure obedience. And most countries have proverbs which are extremely rude about the people, politics, or religion of their neighbours, especially those with whom they have been at war. I have not included these either, wishing to provide a selection which reinforces the ideals of a more tolerant and inclusive age. The dismissive attitudes are available in the older literature cited in Further Reading (p. 595), should anyone wish to read them.

From a linguistic point of view, I have adopted a sentence-based notion of proverb, as is usual these days. In earlier times, the notion of a proverbial expression covered a wide range of linguistic features, including idioms, riddles, similes, and everyday phrases. *John Bull, hard cheese, Merry England,* and *I told you so* have all been called 'proverbs' in one collection or another, in times past. All the proverbs in the present collection are sentences, conveying autonomous units of sense in a succinct form. Many display structural balance, parallelism, rhythmic contrast, and other rhetorical features which add to their memorability and help explain their common use. But it is not obligatory for a proverb to have a tightly controlled linguistic structure. What is important is the insight rather than the form.

It is not easy to define proverbs from the point of view of the kinds of insight they express. They are generalizations which express a remarkable range of functions – conveying advice, warning against consequences, predicting likelihoods, and recommending behaviours (such as diplomacy, courtesy, charity, and kindliness). Many are quite literal, such as *An apple a day keeps the doctor away*. The more interesting ones operate at two levels of meaning. Whatever we can say about the meaning of *Don't burn your candle at both ends*, one thing is certain: we are not really talking about candles.

Proverb collections have used many methods of organization, from alphabetical order to a broad thematic classification. For the present book, I felt the most interesting principle would be to organize the material into semantic fields, as it is in these domains that we are likely to encounter interesting cultural comparisons. Semantic fields are ways of organizing words (more strictly, lexemes: see Index 4, p. 633) into related groups, such as 'furniture', 'fruit', and 'parts of the body'.

There is no single way of grouping words (and thus proverbs) semantically. Within the category of 'parts of the body', for example, we can distinguish such contrasts as 'upper' v 'lower', or 'head' v 'trunk' v 'limbs', or 'arms' v 'legs', or 'fingers' v 'hands', and so on. For the present book, I have allowed my depth of detail to be influenced by the nature of the proverbial material. Proverbs talk quite a lot about parts of the body, so I have devoted several sections to them (232–250).

By contrast, there are very few proverbs devoted to musical instruments, so I have grouped all types of instrument under a single heading (272).

But how to organize the semantic fields into a sequence? Some collections adopt an arbitrary solution, listing them alphabetically, beginning with 'Ability' (or some other A-notion) and ending with such categories as 'Year' or 'Youth'. This has the disadvantage of separating groups that we feel should belong together. Others list proverbs according to the 'most significant word' – an approach which is doomed to confusion, faced with the many proverbs that contain words that compete for our attention. Which is the most significant word in *The sweeter the perfume, the uglier the flies which gather round the bottle*? Plainly, all the main words make a contribution to the sense, and all need to be recognized.

I much prefer an approach which sequences proverb categories on the basis of the semantic relationship between them. I could have started from scratch, and devised a new system, but what is the point, when we already have a system of semantic classification that has been in widespread use for the past 150 years? I am referring to Roget's *Thesaurus*, first published in May 1852. Roget has become the standard tool for people who want a thesaurus which organizes words into fields of meaning (as distinct from those thesauruses which list words in alphabetical order along with sets of synonyms and antonyms). I felt the level of generality which Roget used in his approach would be close to that required in a thematic classification of proverbs, so I adopted his logic as a means of sequencing the themes I needed to recognize in this book. Sometimes Roget's categories were too abstract, and I had to break them down into more specific domains. Sometimes they were too narrow, and I had to group them into broader types. But on the whole the exercise was helpful, and many of my themes are in a one-to-one relationship with Roget's. The approach may also help those who wish to take Roget in new directions. I have always regretted the absence of proverbs in that work, and Indexes 2 and 3 of the present book can be used to add a proverbial dimension to it.

How then to handle the complexity of such proverbs as *The sweeter the perfume, the uglier the flies which gather round the bottle?* If one of the constituent words stood out – *flies*, say – it would be possible to place the proverb into the appropriate category ('Insects') and cross-refer all the other words to it. But that would mean five cross references – from *sweet, perfume, ugly, gather round,* and *bottle.* Clearly, such a method of classification would flood a book with cross references, and readers would be forever jumping around with their fingers in different pages.

The alternative is to place the proverb into each of the semantic fields that its constituent words belong to. So, we would locate this proverb once under 'Bottles', once under 'Sweet', and so on. The demerit of this approach is that a single proverb appears several times throughout the book. But this is far outweighed, in my view, by the convenience of seeing each proverb in its appropriate semantic place, without the need for cross reference. The statistics are as follows: the book as a whole has some 7,500 listings, representing 2,015 different proverbs, grouped into 468 semantic fields, representing around 650 themes. For a list of the semantic fields and their order, see the Contents page. For a complete listing of all the themes recognized within these fields, see Index 1 (p. 599).

Anthologies are never finished, only abandoned. In the case of proverbs, one has to recognize very early on that the field is one of extraordinary magnitude. The proverbs of the world are numbered not in thousands but in millions. What is a couple of thousand among so many? I believe that small-scale compilations have their place, for there are still many avenues in the investigation of proverbs which remain to be explored. For this book, I have attempted to integrate just two dimensions – the cross-cultural and the semantic. But they are dimensions which are not usually considered together, and I hope thereby to make a small contribution to the evolution of this fascinating field.

This has also been an exercise in standing on shoulders. My research has taken me from the early classical collections, such as *Ray's Proverbs* of 1767, into modern popular collections, of the 'Thousand Chinese Proverbs' type, and from there into the World Wide Web, where there are now some remarkable intercultural sites. I give some references in Further Reading (p. 595). I warmly acknowledge the help I have had from earlier paremiographers, and hope that this latest anthology does them, and their field, no disservice.

David Crystal

THEMATIC CLASSIFICATION

LIST OF PANELS

1 EXISTENCE

1 *God did not create hurry*   FINLAND

2 *Do not blame God for having created the tiger, but thank Him for not having given it wings*   ETHIOPIA

3 *The face came before the photograph*   USA

4 *Heroism consists in hanging on one minute longer*   NORWAY

5 *Everything comes to those who wait*   ENGLAND

6 *There's a time and a place for everything*   ENGLAND

7 *The existence of the sea means the existence of pirates*   MALAYSIA

8 *Handsome is as handsome does*   ENGLAND

9 *Friendly is as friendly does*   USA

10 *Everything is possible, except to bite your own nose*   NETHERLANDS

11 *Fingers were made before forks*   ENGLAND

12 *The bigger they come, the harder they fall*   USA

13 *When God made the rabbit He made bushes too*   HUNGARY

14 *Let the church stand in the churchyard*   ENGLAND

15 *Everything will perish save love and music*   SCOTLAND

16 *Rules are made to be broken*   ENGLAND

17 *If you aren't what you ain't, then you ain't what you are*
    USA

2 FAMILY

1   *If you have no relatives, get married*   EGYPT

2   *Vultures eat with their blood relations*   SOUTH AFRICA

3   *One family builds the wall; two families enjoy it*   CHINA

4   *In every family's cooking-pot is one black spot*   CHINA

5   *The bazaar knows neither father nor mother*   TURKEY

6   *A hundred aunts is not the same as one mother*
    SIERRA LEONE

7   *If my aunt had wheels, she might be an omnibus*
    NETHERLANDS

8   *Bed is your brother*   ZANZIBAR

9   *Better a neighbour over the wall than a brother over
    the sea*   ALBANIA

10 *Two happy days are seldom brothers*   BULGARIA

11 *Three brothers, three fortresses*   PORTUGAL

12 *Brotherly love for brotherly love, but cheese for money*
    ALBANIA

13 *Children regard their father's guest as a slave*
    REPUBLIC OF CONGO

14 *A father is a banker provided by nature*   FRANCE

15 *It's a wise child that knows its own father*   ENGLAND

16 *The house with an old grandparent harbours a jewel*
CHINA

17 *Those whose mother is naked are not likely to clothe their aunt*   SUDAN

18 *Love and blindness are twin sisters*   UKRAINE

19 *When you are chased by a wolf you call the boar your uncle*   SLOVENIA

20 *The spear of kinship soon pierces the eye*   CAMEROON

21 *Many kiss the child for the nurse's sake*   ENGLAND

22 *Those who gossip about their relatives have no luck and no blessing*   NETHERLANDS

3 SAMENESS

1 *It is not the one way everyone goes mad*   IRELAND

2 *The cry of the hyena and the loss of the goat are one*
NIGERIA

3 *Both legs in the stocks or only one is all the same*
GERMANY

4 *Luck and bad luck are driving in the same sledge*
RUSSIA

* * * * * * * * * * * * * * * * * * *

1 FAMILY MOTTOES

Many Latin family mottoes are no more than single words or phrases, such as *Labora* ('Endeavour'). But a number are sentences with a proverbial character. Some families have even adopted a proverb as their motto. In these examples, an illustrative family surname is given in parentheses.

> *Vivis sperandum* While there is life there is hope (NIVEN)
> *Non est sine pulvere palma* The prize is not won without dust (YARBURGH)
> *Ex vulnere sallus* Health comes from a wound (BORTHWICK)
> *Ales volat propriis* The bird flies to its own (TUFTON)
> *Praemonitas praemunitus* Forewarned, forearmed (RICKART)
> *Virtus omnia vincit* Virtue conquers all (WHITE)
> *Labor omnia vincit* Labour conquers all (BROWN)
> *Spes anchora tuta* Hope is a safe anchor (DUNMURE)
> *Audaces fortuna juvat* Fortune favours the brave (CARPENTER)

Other languages than Latin can be a source. Here are two from French (or Old French):

> *Qui sera sera* What will be will be (BETENSON)
> *Qui s'estime petyt deviendra grand* Who esteems himself little will become great (PETYT)

* * * * * * * * * * * * * * * * * *

5   *Ability and necessity dwell in the same cabin*
NETHERLANDS

6   *Lovers have much to relate – but it is always the same thing*   GERMANY

7   *Those who stumble twice over the same stone are fools*
LATIN

8   *It is the hyenas of the same den that hate one another*
KENYA

9   *Straps come from the same leather*   ARGENTINA

10   *A bad thing that does no harm is the same as a good one that does no good*   GERMANY

11   *There are many paths to the top of the mountain – but the view is always the same*   CHINA

12   *A hole here and there is not the same as a window*
KENYA

13   *You cannot jump over two ditches at the same time*
NETHERLANDS

14   *If you climb up a tree, you must climb down the same tree*   SIERRA LEONE

15   *Thin ice and thick ice look the same from a distance*
USA

16   *No one can blow and swallow at the same time*
GERMANY

17   *No one can paddle two canoes at the same time*
SOUTH AFRICA

18   *You can never get all the possums up the same tree*   USA

19   *Lightning never strikes twice in the same place*
       ENGLAND

20   *Love and blindness are twin sisters*   UKRAINE

21   *Crows everywhere are equally black*   CHINA

22   *The water is the same on both sides of the boat*
       FINLAND

23   *Not even a bell always rings the same way*   SERBIA

24   *When it rains, the roof always drips the same way*
       LIBERIA

25   *Great minds think alike*   ENGLAND

26   *One beetle knows another*   IRELAND

27   *Before God and the bus-conductor we are all equal*
       GERMANY

28   *The nail suffers as much as the hole*   NETHERLANDS

29   *Don't run too far; you will have to come back the same distance*   FRANCE

30   *Your fingers can't be of the same length*   CHINA

31   *A hundred aunts is not the same as one mother*
       SIERRA LEONE

32   *A bird in the hand is worth two in the bush*   ENGLAND

33   *A dollar in the bank is worth two in the hand*   USA

34   *The game is not worth the candle*   ENGLAND

35 *Beans are not equal to meat*   NAMIBIA

36 *A child is more than a chip*   ESTONIA

37 *Two wrongs do not make a right*   ENGLAND

38 *The more things change the more they remain the same*
     FRANCE

4 DIFFERENCE

1 *Do not put each foot on a different boat*   CHINA

2 *What makes one abbot glad makes another abbot sad*
     SCOTLAND

3 *Many people are like clocks, they show one hour and
     strike another*   DENMARK

4 *When it rains on one it only drips on another*
     NETHERLANDS

5 *The broad-minded see the truth in different religions;
     the narrow-minded see only the differences*   CHINA

6 *Different holes have different fish*   MALAYSIA

7 *You cannot take one part of a fowl for cooking and leave
     the other part to lay eggs*   INDIA

8 *Look the other way when the girl in the tea-house smiles*
     JAPAN

9 *The exception proves the rule*   ENGLAND

10 *A frog beneath a coconut shell believes there is no other world* MALAYSIA

11 *Other people's books are difficult to read* NETHERLANDS

12 *The toughest broncs is always them you've rode some other place* USA

13 *Fools seldom differ* ENGLAND

14 *Raindrops can't tell broadcloth from jeans* USA

15 *One generation plants the trees; another gets the shade* CHINA

16 *Other trees, other woodcutters* LITHUANIA

17 *Variety is the spice of life* ENGLAND

18 *When one door shuts, another opens* SCOTLAND

5 SMALL AMOUNT

1 *To the ant, a few drops of rain is a flood* JAPAN

2 *The sea is made bigger even by one drop* RUSSIA

3 *Better a handful of bees than a basketful of flies* MOROCCO

4 *Every little helps* ENGLAND

5 *Those who want the last drop out of the can get the lid on their nose* NETHERLANDS

6 *Even a small star shines in the darkness* FINLAND

7   *A bit of fragrance always clings to the hand that gives you roses*   CHINA

8   *A little wood will heat a little oven*   ENGLAND

9   *A sip at a time empties the cask*   NORWAY

10   *The biggest help is help, and even the smallest help is help*   IRELAND

11   *Those who do not wish little things do not deserve big things*   BELGIUM

12   *An indispensable thing never has much value*   GEORGIA

13   *Be always a little afraid so that you never have need of being much afraid*   FINLAND

14   *Cabbage is the best invalid, it needs only a little water*   SERBIA

15   *A good driver turns in a small space*   FRANCE

16   *Errands are small on a spring day*   ICELAND

17   *Every blade of grass gets its own drop of dew*   SCOTLAND

18   *Falling hurts least those who fly low*   CHINA

19   *Generally one loses less by being known too little than by being known too much*   LATIN

20   *If you haven't much to do, start cleaning your own backyard*   USA

21   *It takes little effort to watch someone carry a load*   CHINA

22 *To part is to die a little*   FRANCE

23 *It's a small world*   ENGLAND

24 *A little drop of water silences a boiling pot*   GERMANY

25 *Small cares make many words, great ones are mute*
    GERMANY

26 *When the bed is small lie in the centre*   SPAIN

27 *A small bed will not hold two persons*   NIGERIA

28 *A tree with ripe fruit needs little shaking*   SWITZERLAND

29 *Least said, soonest mended*   ENGLAND

30 *Little said is easy mended; nothing said needs no
    mending*   IRELAND

31 *Great consolation may grow out of the smallest saying*
    SWITZERLAND

6 LARGE AMOUNT

1 *Much treasure, many moths*   ESTONIA

2 *A big crop is best, but a little crop will do*   SCOTLAND

3 *The bird can drink much, but the elephant drinks more*
    SENEGAL

4 *The peace-maker gets two-thirds of the blows*
    MONTENEGRO

5 *They that love most speak least*   SCOTLAND

6   *Discretion is the better part of valour*   ENGLAND

7   *A fox knows much; a hedgehog one great thing*   GREECE

8   *Lovers have much to relate – but it is always the same thing*   GERMANY

9   *Many donkeys need much straw*   SPAIN: BASQUE

10 *Many drops make a puddle*   NETHERLANDS

11 *Too much courtesy is discourtesy*   JAPAN

12 *Too much discussion will lead to a row*   CÔTE D'IVOIRE

13 *What is inflated too much will burst into fragments*   ETHIOPIA

14 *Where there is most mind there is least money*   LATIN

15 *Who sieves too much, keeps the rubbish*   BELGIUM

16 *Think much, say little, write less*   FRANCE

17 *The fish said, 'I have much to say, but my mouth is full of water.'*   GEORGIA

18 *Those who speak much must either know a lot or lie a lot*   GERMANY

19 *Drinking a little too much is drinking a great deal too much*   GERMANY

20 *Genius is one percent inspiration, ninety-nine percent perspiration*   USA

21 *The roughest stone becomes smooth when it is much rolled*   SWITZERLAND

22   *Too much tying loosens*   SYRIA

23   *Who knows much, mistakes much*   ARMENIA

24   *If you engrave it too much it will become a hole*   INDIA

25   *A reasonable amount of fleas is good for a dog; they keep him from broodin' on being a dog*   USA

7 INCREASE – DECREASE

1   *Little by little grow the bananas*   REPUBLIC OF CONGO

2   *The first stage of folly is to consider oneself wise*
     BELGIUM

3   *Friendship is steps*   KENYA

4   *Add caution to caution*   JAPAN

5   *Is it necessary to add acid to the lemon?*   INDIA

6   *Quick work – double work*   MONTENEGRO

7   *Be not afraid of growing slowly, be afraid only of standing still*   CHINA

8   *No matter how full the river, it still wants to grow*
     REPUBLIC OF CONGO

9   *One good turn deserves another*   ENGLAND

10   *The sea is made bigger even by one drop*   RUSSIA

11   *Two things make one either greater or smaller, praise and shadows*   GERMANY

12   *The more one sleeps the less one lives*   PORTUGAL

13   *More haste, less speed*   ENGLAND

14   *Another day, another dollar*   USA

15   *A bald-headed man cannot grow hair by getting excited about it*   REPUBLIC OF CONGO

16   *The more you stroke a cat, the more it lifts its tail*
     ESTONIA

17   *A rolling stone gathers no moss*   ENGLAND

18   *A stationary stone gathers moss*   RUSSIA

8 ONE ALONE

1   *One dog can't fight*   IRELAND

2   *Once is no custom*   NETHERLANDS

3   *The wise person is cheated only once*   FINLAND

4   *No stone ever falls alone*   BELGIUM

5   *In every family's cooking-pot is one black spot*   CHINA

6   *We boil our rice only once*   INDIA

7   *Who hears but one bell hears but one sound*   FRANCE

8   *Who hears music feels his solitude*   FRANCE

9   *Solitude is full of God*   SERBIA

10 *Hit one ring and the whole chain will resound*
     SOUTH AFRICA

11   *One link broken, the whole chain is broken*   GERMANY

12   *One spot spots the whole dress*   BELGIUM

13   *One bad pipe ruins the entire organ*   NETHERLANDS

14   *One rotten egg spoils the whole pudding*   GERMANY

15   *One rotten apple spoils the whole barrel*   ENGLAND

16   *The eyes have one language everywhere*   ENGLAND

17   *Heroism consists in hanging on one minute longer*
        NORWAY

18   *Rather once cry your heart out than always sigh*   CHINA

19   *The person who steals once is always a thief*   SPAIN

20   *Between two points one cannot draw more than one
        straight line*   DENMARK

21   *Empty gossip jumps with one leg*   ESTONIA

22   *It is better to be once in the church sleigh than always in
        the back runners*   FINLAND

23   *Those who have only one bow should be content with one
        fiddle*   GERMANY

24   *One bell serves a parish*   ITALY

25   *A single bracelet doesn't jingle*   GUINEA

26   *Those who have once had luck cannot always call
        themselves unlucky*   BELGIUM

27   *A hundred aunts is not the same as one mother*
        SIERRA LEONE

28   *One thread for the needle, one love for the heart*   SUDAN

29   *Once a crook, always a crook*   USA

30   *Beware the man with only one gun*   USA

31   *When a single hair has fallen from your head, you are not yet bald*   SIERRA LEONE

32   *A fox knows much; a hedgehog one great thing*   GREECE

33   *Never less alone than when alone*   LATIN

34   *If you play alone, you will win*   SYRIA

9   ONE OF TWO

1   *One hand washes the other; both hands wash the face*
     ALBANIA

2   *If a string has one end, then it has another end*   CHINA

3   *If you have two loaves of bread, sell one and buy a lily*
     CHINA

4   *Never try to catch two frogs with one hand*   CHINA

5   *You cannot hold two water melons in one hand*   IRAN

6   *The story is only half told when one side tells it*
     ICELAND

7   *When two ride on one horse, one must sit behind*
     ENGLAND

8   *Too many affairs are like pumpkins in water; one pops up while you try to hold down the other*   CHINA

9   *One family builds the wall; two families enjoy it*   CHINA

10   *One generation plants the trees; another gets the shade*
     CHINA

11   *One foot is better than two stilts*   FRANCE

12   *Both legs in the stocks or only one is all the same*
     GERMANY

13   *In one stable there may be a steed and an ass*   BELGIUM

14   *A lie stands upon one leg, but truth upon two*   ENGLAND

15   *When one door shuts, another opens*   SCOTLAND

16   *To learn costs you one effort, to unlearn, two*   BULGARIA

17   *One beetle knows another*   IRELAND

18   *If two people tell you you are blind, shut one eye*
     GEORGIA

19   *You cannot take one part of a fowl for cooking and leave
     the other part to lay eggs*   INDIA

20   *One hand can't tie a bundle*   LIBERIA

21   *Justice becomes injustice when it makes two wounds on a
     head which only deserves one*   REPUBLIC OF CONGO

22   *Those who have two garments do not wear one only*
     ZANZIBAR

23   *Two crocodiles don't live in one pond*   GAMBIA

24   *You can't dance at two weddings with one pair of feet*
     USA

25   *When you pick up a stick at one end, you also pick up the other end*   USA

26   *Two heads are better than one*   ENGLAND

27   *Better ask twice than go wrong once*   GERMANY

28   *Once bitten, twice shy*   ENGLAND

29   *Measure twice, cut once*   SLOVAKIA

30   *Those who cheat me once, shame fall them; those who cheat me twice, shame fall me*   SCOTLAND

31   *Someone with a watch knows what time it is; someone with two watches is never sure*   FRANCE

   See also: **12 TWO – TWICE – BOTH**

10   ONE OF SEVERAL

1   *Rain does not fall only on one roof*   CAMEROON

2   *Better one living word than a hundred dead ones*   GERMANY

3   *A hat is not made for one shower*   ENGLAND

4   *Before going to war say one prayer; before going to sea, two; before getting married, three*   POLAND

5   *The spider does not weave its web for one fly*   SLOVENIA

6   *The sea is made bigger even by one drop*   RUSSIA

7   *One buffalo brings mud and all the herd are smeared with it*   MALAYSIA

8 *If one finger is gashed, all the fingers are covered with blood* REPUBLIC OF CONGO

9 *A basket-maker who makes one basket makes a hundred* BRAZIL

10 *It's a poor mouse that has but one hole* NETHERLANDS

11 *An elephant does not die from one broken rib* KENYA

12 *Don't tell all of your jokes on one program* USA

13 *One bird in the dish is better than a hundred in the air* GERMANY

14 *If you want one year of prosperity, grow grain. If you want ten years of prosperity, grow trees. If you want a hundred years of prosperity, grow people* CHINA

15 *Life is just one damned thing after another* USA

16 *One accident is one too many* CANADA

17 *One loose pebble can start a landslide* USA

18 *One broken rail will wreck a train* USA

19 *Don't keep all your tongs in one fire* CANADA

20 *Don't put all your eggs in one basket* ENGLAND

21 *There are more ways than one to kill a cat* ENGLAND

22 *A cloth is not woven from a single thread* CHINA

23 *One servant is a servant; two servants are half a servant; three servants are no servant at all* POLAND

24 *It takes a whole village to raise one child* NIGERIA

25 *One actor cannot make a play* USA

26 *Where water has once flowed it will flow again*
MONTENEGRO

27 *Troubles never come singly* ENGLAND

11 ACCOMPANIMENT

1 *When you have no companion, consult your walking-stick* ALBANIA

2 *Misery loves company* ENGLAND

3 *Two's company; three's a crowd* ENGLAND

4 *When a blind person carries the banner, woe to those who follow* FRANCE

5 *Where the needle goes the thread must follow* POLAND

6 *Pull the ear, the head follows* BANGLADESH

7 *When one sheep is over the dam, the rest will follow*
NETHERLANDS

8 *Every flood will have an ebb* SCOTLAND

9 *Who has God for his friend has all the saints in his pocket* ITALY

10 *The reverse side has its reverse side* JAPAN

11 *Adam must have an Eve, to blame for his own faults*
GERMANY

12 *A misty morning may have a fine day*   ENGLAND

13 *A pessimist is a person who has lived with an optimist*
USA

14 *Follow the river and you will reach the sea*   FRANCE

15 *Beware of a person's shadow and a bee's sting*
MYANMAR

16 *Nobody can rest in their own shadow*   HUNGARY

17 *A shadow is a feeble thing but no sun can drive it away*
SWEDEN

18 *A road has no shadow*   SENEGAL

19 *Even a hair has a shadow*   CZECH REPUBLIC

20 *Two things make one either greater or smaller, praise and shadows*   GERMANY

21 *Every Sunday brings a week with it*   SCOTLAND

22 *The one who has taken the bear into the boat must cross over with him*   SWEDEN

12 TWO – TWICE – BOTH

1 *The one who seeks revenge should remember to dig two graves*   CHINA

2 *It's the tortoise that discounts the value of a pair of fast legs*   JAPAN

* * * * * * * * * * * * * * * * * * *

2 GROUPS OF THREE

A long-standing rhetorical tradition – found for example in the language of the Bible – presents warnings in groups of three. Proverbs often display the same rhetoric, beginning with an emphatic 'Three things / kinds . . .'. They are not common in native English proverbs, but they are popular in some other parts of Europe, notably Germany.

> *Three kinds of men fail to understand women – young men, old men, and middle-aged men.*
> *Three sorts of people are always to be found, soldiers, professors, and women.*

Occasionally, a fourth factor is introduced:

> *Three glasses of wine drive away the evil spirits, but with the fourth they return.*

* * * * * * * * * * * * * * * * * *

3   *It is hard to swim between two stretches of bad water*
      NETHERLANDS

4   *To build, one must have two purses*   BELGIUM

5   *It takes two blows to make a battle*   ENGLAND

6   *Go fishing for three days and dry the nets for two*
      CHINA

7   *Every mile is two in winter*   ENGLAND

8   *There's a puddle at every door, and before some doors there are two* SCOTLAND

9   *Two happy days are seldom brothers* BULGARIA

10   *If you try to sit on two chairs, you'll sit on the floor* USA

11   *'Virtue in the middle,' said the devil as he sat between two lawyers* NORWAY

12   *A bird in the hand is worth two in the bush* ENGLAND

13   *One servant is a servant; two servants are half a servant; three servants are no servant at all* POLAND

14   *Every road has two directions* UKRAINE

15   *Two barrels of tears will not heal a bruise* CHINA

16   *Between two points one cannot draw more than one straight line* DENMARK

17   *Two things make one either greater or smaller, praise and shadows* GERMANY

18   *Three are too many and two are too few* BELGIUM

19   *There must be a valley between two hills* GERMANY

20   *Everything has two handles* GREECE

21   *It takes two hands to clap* INDIA

22   *The basket that has two handles can be carried by two* EGYPT

23   *Two pieces of meat confuse the mind of the fly* NIGERIA

24   *A bull does not enjoy fame in two herds* ZAMBIA

25   *When two elephants struggle, it is the grass that suffers*
ZANZIBAR

26   *A loaded gun frightens one; an unloaded one two*
MONTENEGRO

27   *Take a second look; it costs you nothing*   CHINA

28   *It takes two to make a quarrel*   ENGLAND

29   *Two's company; three's a crowd*   ENGLAND

30   *You cannot jump over two ditches at the same time*
NETHERLANDS

31   *Before going to war say one prayer; before going to sea,*
two; before getting married, three   POLAND

32   *A small bed will not hold two persons*   NIGERIA

33   *No one can paddle two canoes at the same time*
SOUTH AFRICA

34   *The only insurance against fire is to have two houses*
NIGERIA

35   *A needle cannot hold two threads or a mind two thoughts*
ETHIOPIA

36   *The one who hunts two rats will catch neither*   UGANDA

37   *The one who hunts two hares will catch neither*
FRANCE

38   *A dollar in the bank is worth two in the hand*   USA

39   *Two swords cannot be kept in one sheath*   INDIA

40   *Two wrongs do not make a right*   ENGLAND

41 *The second word makes the fray* JAPAN

42 *The first blow does not hurt like the second* ZANZIBAR

43 *To read a book for the first time is to make the acquaintance of a new friend; to read it a second time is to meet an old one* CHINA

44 *A fault denied is twice committed* FRANCE

45 *Who lends to a friend loses twice* FRANCE

46 *The one who strikes first, strikes twice* BELGIUM

47 *Those who see the wolf shout; those who see it not, shout twice* BULGARIA

48 *A good song can be sung twice* ESTONIA

49 *Those who stumble twice over the same stone are fools* LATIN

50 *Under trees it rains twice* SWITZERLAND

51 *They give twice who give quickly* TURKEY

52 *Dawn does not come twice to wake us* SOUTH AFRICA

53 *Those who cut their own firewood have it warm them twice* USA

54 *Don't chew your tobacco twice* USA

55 *Lightning never strikes twice in the same place* ENGLAND

56 *You can't expect both ends of a sugar cane to be as sweet* CHINA

57   *The water is the same on both sides of the boat*
      FINLAND

58   *It's a poor rule that doesn't work both ways*   ENGLAND

59   *The sun shines on both sides of the hedge*   ENGLAND

60   *No needle is sharp at both ends*   CHINA

61   *You can't look into a bottle with both eyes*   TOGO

62   *A canoe is paddled on both sides*   NIGERIA

63   *Only a fool tests the depth of the water with both feet*
      NAMIBIA

64   *Don't burn your candle at both ends*   ENGLAND

65   *The rat has a double stomach*   NEW ZEALAND

     See also: **9 ONE OF TWO**

13 THREE – THIRD

1   *A sly rabbit will have three openings to its den*   CHINA

2   *A guest and a fish after three days are poison*   FRANCE

3   *Three glasses of wine drive away the evil spirits, but with the fourth they return*   GERMANY

4   *Three are too many and two are too few*   BELGIUM

5   *Every word has three explanations and three interpretations*   IRELAND

6 *Three kinds of men fail to understand women – young men, old men, and middle-aged men* IRELAND

7 *If they do not open after three knocks, do not wait* POLAND

8 *After three days without reading, talk becomes flavourless* CHINA

9 *One servant is a servant; two servants are half a servant; three servants are no servant at all* POLAND

10 *Three brothers, three fortresses* PORTUGAL

11 *Three sorts of people are always to be found, soldiers, professors, and women* GERMANY

12 *Go fishing for three days and dry the nets for two* CHINA

13 *Let the guests at table be three or four – at the most five* GREECE

14 *God preserve us from pitch-forks, for they make three holes* SWITZERLAND

15 *Before marrying live wildly for three years* POLAND

16 *A kind word warms for three winters* CHINA

17 *The dog on three legs ain't always lame* USA

18 *Two's company; three's a crowd* ENGLAND

19 *Before going to war say one prayer; before going to sea, two; before getting married, three* POLAND

20 *No doctor is better than three* GERMANY

21 *Transgressions should never be forgiven a third time*
CHINA

22 *The third strand makes the cable* NETHERLANDS

14 FOUR OR MORE

1 *Those who can read and write have four eyes* ALBANIA

2 *Four horses cannot overtake the tongue* CHINA

3 *Let the guests at table be three or four – at the most five*
GREECE

4 *Three glasses of wine drive away the evil spirits, but with the fourth they return* GERMANY

5 *A fifth wheel in the wagon hinders more than helps*
FRANCE

6 *The one who asks a question is a fool for five minutes; the one who does not ask a question is a fool forever*
CHINA

7 *If you want to be acquainted with the past and the present, you must read five cartloads of books* CHINA

8 *It is better to follow no saint than six* INDIA

9 *Poverty is the sixth sense* GERMANY

10 *Seven days is the length of a guest's life* MYANMAR

11 *Turn your tongue seven times before speaking* FRANCE

12 *For the diligent, a week has seven days; for the slothful, seven tomorrows* GERMANY

13 *Fall down seven times, get up eight* JAPAN

14 *A stitch in time saves nine* ENGLAND

15 *If bravery is ten, nine is strategy* TURKEY

16 *A smile will gain you ten more years of life* CHINA

17 *Those who have to go ten miles must regard nine as only halfway* GERMANY

18 *Among the ten fingers there are long and short* CHINA

19 *Truth is greater than ten goats* NIGERIA

20 *If you want one year of prosperity, grow grain. If you want ten years of prosperity, grow trees. If you want a hundred years of prosperity, grow people* CHINA

21 *Eleven don't make a dozen* USA

22 *The best time to plant a tree was twenty years ago; the second-best time is now* CHINA

23 *Of all the thirty-six alternatives, running away is the best* CHINA

24 *Misfortunes come by forties* WALES

25 *Gossip lasts but seventy-five days* JAPAN

26 *One can study calligraphy at eighty* JAPAN

27 *Genius is one percent inspiration, ninety-nine percent perspiration* USA

28 *Better one living word than a hundred dead ones*
GERMANY

29 *A bad word whispered will echo a hundred miles*
CHINA

30 *One bird in the dish is better than a hundred in the air*
GERMANY

31 *A basket-maker who makes one basket makes a hundred*
BRAZIL

32 *A hundred aunts is not the same as one mother*
SIERRA LEONE

33 *A hundred men may make an encampment, but it needs
a woman to make a home*   CHINA

34 *A worn-out boat still has three thousand nails in it*
CHINA

35 *A good child has several names*   ESTONIA

36 *Beware of the door which has several keys*   INDIA

15   NEXT TO NOTHING

1 *Take a second look; it costs you nothing*   CHINA

2 *Little said is easy mended; nothing said needs no
mending*   IRELAND

3 *Nothing should be done in a hurry except catching fleas*
GERMANY

63

4   *Nothing enters into a closed hand*   SCOTLAND

5   *Nothing dries sooner than a tear*   LATIN

6   *Nothing kills like doing nothing*   DENMARK

7   *Nothing venture, nothing gain*   ENGLAND

8   *When the sun shines the moon has nothing to do*
FRANCE

9   *Those who are silent do not say nothing*   SPAIN

10   *When in doubt, do nothing*   ENGLAND

11   *Someone who stands behind a wall can see nothing else*
JAPAN

12   *What costs nothing is worth nothing*   NETHERLANDS

13   *One servant is a servant; two servants are half a servant;
three servants are no servant at all*   POLAND

14   *The one who hunts two rats will catch neither*   UGANDA

15   *The one who hunts two hares will catch neither*
FRANCE

16   *Who does not understand half a word will not be wiser
for a whole word*   FINLAND

17   *Half a loaf is better than no bread*   ENGLAND

16 MULTITUDE

1   *A reasonable amount of fleas is good for a dog; they keep
him from broodin' on being a dog*   USA

2 *When rats infest the palace a lame cat is better than the swiftest horse* CHINA

3 *Many donkeys need much straw* SPAIN: BASQUE

4 *You are as many a person as languages you know* ARMENIA

5 *Many books do not use up words; many words do not use up thoughts* CHINA

6 *Too many affairs are like pumpkins in water; one pops up while you try to hold down the other* CHINA

7 *Three are too many and two are too few* BELGIUM

8 *Many kiss the child for the nurse's sake* ENGLAND

9 *Many lose when they win, and others win when they lose* GERMANY

10 *One may as well lose the game by a card too much as a card too few* SPAIN

11 *Much treasure, many moths* ESTONIA

12 *The frightened person has many voices* FINLAND

13 *Many speak a word which if it were a florin they would put back in their purse* GERMANY

14 *If pride were an art, how many graduates we should have* ITALY

15 *Those who read many epitaphs, lose their memory* LATIN

16 *Many a true word is spoken in jest* ENGLAND

17 *The rose that is smelt by many loses its fragrance*
SPAIN

18 *There are many paths to the top of the mountain – but the view is always the same* CHINA

19 *On a green tree there are many parrots* INDIA

20 *Many have bees and buy wax* GERMANY

21 *Many drops make a puddle* NETHERLANDS

22 *Too many cooks spoil the broth* ENGLAND

23 *Too many cooks oversalt the porridge* NETHERLANDS

24 *Too many hands spoil the pie* USA

25 *There's many a slip between cup and lip* ENGLAND

26 *Words will pay for most things* SPAIN

27 *Goods held in common mostly get lost* GERMANY

28 *Charity covers a multitude of sins* ENGLAND

29 *Numerous calls confuse the dog* TANZANIA

30 *Small cares make many words, great ones are mute*
GERMANY

31 *Gossips always suspect that others are talking about them*
NIGERIA

32 *When people praise, few believe it, but when they blame, all believe it* BELGIUM

17 BETTER – WORSE

1   *If he calls it a silly and childish game, that means his wife can beat him at it*   USA

2   *'Tis a good word that can better a good silence*
     NETHERLANDS

3   *Beyond black there is no colour*   IRAN

4   *There is always a boss above the boss*   NETHERLANDS

5   *Great minds think alike*   ENGLAND

6   *They are truly superior who can look upon a game of chess in silence*   CHINA

7   *Good painters need not give a name to their pictures; bad ones must*   POLAND

8   *If you can't beat 'em, join 'em*   USA

9   *The more servants, the worse service*   NETHERLANDS

10 *Good things sell themselves; bad things have to be advertised*   ETHIOPIA

11 *Good is good, but better is better*   NETHERLANDS

12 *Mediocrity is climbing molehills without sweating*
     ICELAND

13 *There is no such thing as a pretty good omelette*
     FRANCE

14 *One bad pipe ruins the entire organ*   NETHERLANDS

15 *There are dregs in the best bottle of wine*   FRANCE

16 *Count not what is lost but what is left* CHINA

17 *When one sheep is over the dam, the rest will follow*
NETHERLANDS

18 *Pretty near ain't quite* USA

19 *One rotten egg spoils the whole pudding* GERMANY

20 *One rotten apple spoils the whole barrel* ENGLAND

21 *Rotten wood cannot be carved* CHINA

22 *'If I rest, I rust', says the key* GERMANY

23 *The best time to plant a tree was twenty years ago; the
second-best time is now* CHINA

18 UNITING

1 *Those who mix themselves with the mud will be eaten by
the swine* NETHERLANDS

2 *If you get mixed with bran, you'll soon be pecked by
chickens* LIBYA

3 *Tangled hair needs a wide comb* SERBIA

4 *When the hands and the feet are bound, the tongue runs
faster* GERMANY

5 *Oil and water will not mix* ENGLAND

6 *Drinking and thinking don't mix* USA

7 *An ox is bound with ropes and a person with words*
ITALY

8   *Slices of bread do not grow together*   ESTONIA

9   *The thinnest bread finds itself married to bread*
     ALGERIA

10   *Straps come from the same leather*   ARGENTINA

11   *A gummed thing soon ungums*   JAPAN

12   *When walking through your neighbour's melon-patch,
don't tie your shoe*   CHINA

13   *Too much tying loosens*   SYRIA

14   *The string of our sack of patience is generally tied with a
slip knot*   JAPAN

15   *One hand can't tie a bundle*   LIBERIA

16   *You cannot tie up another's wound while your own is
still bleeding*   ESTONIA

17   *Everyone buckles their belt their own way*   SCOTLAND

18   *One missing button strikes the eye more than one missing
day*   ESTONIA

19   *Coupled sheep drown each other*   NETHERLANDS

20   *A feather does not stick without gum*   AFGHANISTAN

21   *Sweat makes good mortar*   GERMANY

22   *A stitch in time saves nine*   ENGLAND

23   *Kick an attorney downstairs and he'll stick to you for life*
     SCOTLAND

24 *There is no grace in a benefit that sticks to the fingers*
    ENGLAND

25 *The postage stamp's usefulness lies in the ability to stick*
    USA

26 *Let the cobbler stick to his last*   ENGLAND

19 SEPARATING

1 *One link broken, the whole chain is broken*   GERMANY

2 *United we stand; divided we fall*   USA

3 *The tighter the string, the sooner it will break*   WALES

4 *The one on whose head we would break a coconut never stands still*   NIGERIA

5 *Courteous asking breaks even city walls*   UKRAINE

6 *Luck and glass soon break*   GERMANY

7 *When you give a child a nut, give it also something to break it with*   GEORGIA

8 *You do not know who is your friend or who is your enemy until the ice breaks*   ICELAND

9 *Fortune is glass; just when it is bright it is broken*
   LATIN

10 *Carrying-poles which bend easily do not break*   CHINA

11 *Every plate that is made breaks*   AFGHANISTAN

12 *If you are building a house and a nail breaks, do you stop building or do you change the nail?*
RWANDA AND BURUNDI

13 *A broken glass can't be hurt* ENGLAND

14 *All's lost that's put in a broken dish* SCOTLAND

15 *One broken rail will wreck a train* USA

16 *Where the drum is burst is the place to mend it*
REPUBLIC OF CONGO

17 *A basket with its bottom burst is useless* NIGERIA

18 *What is inflated too much will burst into fragments*
ETHIOPIA

19 *In the choicest vase are found the ugliest cracks* CHINA

20 *If you pick the fluff from a blanket it comes to pieces*
INDIA

21 *Flies never visit an egg that has no crack* CHINA

22 *Cut bread cannot be put together again* LATVIA

23 *It is easy to steal from a cut loaf* ENGLAND

24 *Those who cannot cut the bread evenly cannot get on well with people* CZECH REPUBLIC

25 *Dull scissors can't cut straight* USA

26 *Measure twice, cut once* SLOVAKIA

27 *The axe forgets, but the cut log does not* ZIMBABWE

28 *Those who cut their own firewood have it warm them twice* USA

29 *There is always something to be cut off young trees if they are to grow well* GERMANY

30 *Everyone must skin their own skunk* USA

31 *You cannot take one part of a fowl for cooking and leave the other part to lay eggs* INDIA

32 *A fool and his money are soon parted* ENGLAND

33 *The end of separation is meeting again* TURKEY

34 *One loose pebble can start a landslide* USA

35 *A smooth way makes the foot slip* ESTONIA

36 *Don't look where you fell, but where you slipped* LIBERIA

37 *When a single hair has fallen from your head, you are not yet bald* SIERRA LEONE

38 *An egg on bread is slippery* SCOTLAND

39 *No matter how you slice it, it's still baloney* USA

20 CHAIN – ROPE – STRING

1 *Hit one ring and the whole chain will resound* SOUTH AFRICA

2 *A chain is as strong as its weakest link* ENGLAND

3   *One link broken, the whole chain is broken*   GERMANY

4   *Pull gently at a weak rope*   NETHERLANDS

5   *An ox is bound with ropes and a person with words*
    ITALY

6   *Men hold the buffalo by its rope, a ruler by his word*
    INDONESIA

7   *If a string has one end, then it has another end*   CHINA

8   *The string of our sack of patience is generally tied with a
    slip knot*   JAPAN

9   *If the string is long the kite will fly high*   CHINA

10 *The tighter the string, the sooner it will break*   WALES

11 *There is bound to be a knot in a very long string*   KENYA

21 WHOLE – PART

1   *One rotten egg spoils the whole pudding*   GERMANY

2   *One rotten apple spoils the whole barrel*   ENGLAND

3   *One spot spots the whole dress*   BELGIUM

4   *Those who seek the entrance should also think of the exit*
    GERMANY

5   *When luck offers a finger one must take the whole hand*
    SWEDEN

6   *Who does not understand half a word will not be wiser
    for a whole word*   FINLAND

7   *Every art requires the whole person*   FRANCE

8   *One link broken, the whole chain is broken*   GERMANY

9   *One needn't devour the whole chicken to know the flavour of the bird*   CHINA

10   *Hit one ring and the whole chain will resound*
      SOUTH AFRICA

11   *Better lose the anchor than the whole ship*
      NETHERLANDS

12   *It is better to be entirely without a book than to believe it entirely*   CHINA

13   *One bad pipe ruins the entire organ*   NETHERLANDS

14   *You cannot take one part of a fowl for cooking and leave the other part to lay eggs*   INDIA

15   *The first thread is not part of the yarn*   IRELAND

16   *Discretion is the better part of valour*   ENGLAND

17   *To get out a rusty nail you must take away a piece of the wall*   MALTA

18   *What is inflated too much will burst into fragments*
      ETHIOPIA

19   *The town that parleys is half surrendered*   FRANCE

20   *The story is only half told when one side tells it*
      ICELAND

21   *Chop, and you will have splinters*   DENMARK

22 *For the diligent, a week has seven days; for the slothful,*
seven tomorrows   GERMANY

23 *If a string has one end, then it has another end*   CHINA

22 FULL – ENTIRE

1 *A coconut shell full of water is a sea to an ant*
   ZANZIBAR

2 *The hollow of the ear is never full*   SENEGAL

3 *Full of courtesy, full of craft*   ENGLAND

4 *Solitude is full of God*   SERBIA

5 *No matter how full the river, it still wants to grow*
   REPUBLIC OF CONGO

6 *The fuller the cask, the duller its sound*   GERMANY

7 *The fuller the cup, the sooner the spill*   CHINA

8 *A full cup must be carried steadily*   ENGLAND

9 *The fish said, 'I have much to say, but my mouth is full*
of water.'   GEORGIA

10 *Idle curiosity sometimes fills the mousetrap*
   NETHERLANDS

11 *To fill a ditch a mound must come down*   ARMENIA

12 *While it rains, fill the jar*   TURKEY

13 *Do not fill your basket with useless shells of coconuts*
   KENYA

* * * * * * * * * * * * * * * * * *

3 PROVERBS IN SHAKESPEARE

There are a large number of proverbial expressions in Shakespeare – which is hardly surprising, given the important role played by proverbs in Elizabethan schools (see p. 425). Many are traditional proverbs, sometimes acknowledged to be so. John Hume, in *Henry VI Part Two* (I.ii.100) reflects:

They say 'A crafty knave does need no broker'

and in *The Comedy of Errors* (II.ii.45) Dromio of Syracuse comments:

they say every why hath a wherefore.

'They say'. This is tradition, not Shakespeare, talking. And Shakespeare explicitly refers to 'proverbs' on a number of occasions (see p. 488).

On the other hand, many of the proverbs in Shakespeare are rephrasings, often adapted to suit the metrical demands of a poetic line. Hume's reference is a case in point, for the traditional expression is 'A crafty knave needs no broker'. Proverbial allusions may also reflect the personality of a character. 'Comparisons are odorous', says Dogberry malapropistically (in *Much Ado About Nothing*, III.v.15).

Some are original to Shakespeare: thanks to Polonius, for example, we have 'Neither a borrower nor a lender be' (*Hamlet*, I.iii.75) and 'Brevity is the soul of wit' (*Hamlet*, II.ii.90). Here, as elsewhere, there is a thin line between a quotation and a proverb. Is 'All the world's a stage' (*As You Like It*, II.vii.140) proverbial?

A small selection . . .

Care's an enemy to life (*Twelfth Night*, I.iii.2)

Sweet are the uses of adversity (*As You Like It*, II.i.12)

A rose by any other name would smell as sweet (*Romeo and Juliet*, II.ii.43)

A fool's bolt is soon shot (*Henry V*, III.vii.119)

There's small choice in rotten apples (*The Taming of the Shrew*, I.i.132)

All that glisters is not gold (*The Merchant of Venice*, II.vii.65)

Talkers are no good doers (*Richard III*, I.iii.350)

Blunt wedges rive hard knots (*Troilus and Cressida*, I.iii.316)

Good counsellors lack no clients (*Measure for Measure*, I.ii.106)

He that dies pays all debts (*The Tempest*, III.ii.132)

The better part of valour is discretion (*Henry IV Part One*, V.iv.118)

Pitchers have ears (*Richard III*, II.iv.37)

Every cloud engenders not a storm (*Henry VI Part Three*, V.iii.13)

Give the devil his due (*Henry IV Part One*, I.ii.118)

A light heart lives long (*Love's Labour's Lost*, V.ii.18)

All hoods make not monks (*Henry VIII*, III.i.23)

There is no virtue like necessity (*Richard II*, I.iii.278)

Better three hours too soon than a minute too late (*The Merry Wives of Windsor*, II.ii.296)

Sad hours seem long (*Romeo and Juliet*, I.i.161)

SEE ALSO 'Proverbs' in Shakespeare (p. 488)

* * * * * * * * * * * * * * * * * *

14 *The laden almond-tree by the wayside is sure to be bitter*
JAPAN

15 *Eleven don't make a dozen*   USA

16 *One actor cannot make a play*   USA

17 *There is no hill without a slope*   WALES

18 *It takes a whole village to raise one child*   NIGERIA

19 *Add legs to the snake after you have finished drawing it*
CHINA

20 *How can there be a forest without a crooked tree?*
BULGARIA

21 *There is no bridge without a place the other side of it*
WALES

22 *You may light another's candle at your own without loss*
DENMARK

23   EMPTY – LACKING

1 *The empty nut is the hardest*   WALES

2 *The bell is loud because it is empty*   POLAND

3 *An empty bag cannot stand upright*   ENGLAND

4 *An empty sack can't stand, nor a dead cat walk*
IRELAND

5 *Beauty is an empty calabash*   CAMEROON

6 *Empty barns need no thatch* ENGLAND

7 *A full cabin is better than an empty castle* IRELAND

8 *One missing button strikes the eye more than one missing day* ESTONIA

9 *The best neighbors are vacant lots* USA

10 *It is better to be entirely without a book than to believe it entirely* CHINA

11 *Someone without a friend is like the right hand without the left* BELGIUM

12 *No land without stones, or meat without bones*
    ENGLAND

13 *God, what things we see when we go out without a gun!*
    SOUTH AFRICA

14 *One should not board a ship without an onion*
    NETHERLANDS

15 *Life without literature is death* LATIN

16 *Walls hear without warnings* ENGLAND

17 *Why should someone without a head want a hat?*
    CHILE

18 *Without fingers the hand would be a spoon* SENEGAL

19 *A nation without a language is a nation without a heart*
    WALES

20 *Those who go to sea without biscuits return without teeth*
    FRANCE: CORSICA

21   *A sip at a time empties the cask*   NORWAY

22   *A well without a bucket is no good*   USA

24   SEQUENCE – ORDER

1   *Life is just one damned thing after another*   USA

2   *A beautiful disorder is an effect of art*   FRANCE

3   *Those who place their ladder too steeply will easily fall backwards*   CZECH REPUBLIC

4   *A proverb places the words in one's mouth*   SWITZERLAND

5   *The greatest love is mother-love; after that comes a dog's love; and after that the love of a sweetheart*   POLAND

6   *If a string has one end, then it has another end*   CHINA

7   *Eve is nearer to us than Adam*   SERBIA

8   *Those who want the last drop out of the can get the lid on their nose*   NETHERLANDS

9   *That which goes last into the sack comes out first*   SWEDEN

10   *The game's not over until the last man strikes out*   USA

11   *Those who laugh last laugh loudest*   ENGLAND

12   *It ain't over till the fat lady sings*   USA

13   *The loom that's awry is best handled patiently*   SCOTLAND

14   *What's the good of a spoon after the meal is over?*

       LATVIA

15   *When the date-crop is over, everyone mocks at the palm-tree*   ETHIOPIA

16   *Even a drill goes in from the tip*   KOREA

17   *When you eat a round cake, do you begin at the centre?*

       NIGERIA

18   *You can only go halfway into the darkest forest; then you are coming out the other side*   CHINA

19   *Those who have to go ten miles must regard nine as only halfway*   GERMANY

20   *Those that begin the play must continue it*   TURKEY

21   *Don't start economizing when you are down to your last dollar*   USA

22   *Don't put the cart before the horse*   ENGLAND

25   ASSEMBLAGES

1   *Birds of a feather flock together*   ENGLAND

2   *Call out a name in a crowd and somebody is sure to answer*   CHINA

3   *If you cross in a crowd, the crocodile won't eat you*

       MADAGASCAR

4   *Two's company; three's a crowd*   ENGLAND

5   *It don't need a genius to spot a goat in a flock of sheep*
USA

6   *A cask of wine works more miracles than a church full of saints*   ITALY

7   *A young doctor makes a full graveyard*   CHINA

8   *A full cabin is better than an empty castle*   IRELAND

9   *The sweeter the perfume, the uglier the flies which gather round the bottle*   CHINA

10   *One buffalo brings mud and all the herd are smeared with it*   MALAYSIA

11   *A bull does not enjoy fame in two herds*   ZAMBIA

12   *Goats cannot live in a herd of leopards*   MALI

13   *If you get into the pack you need not bark, but wag your tail you must*   RUSSIA

14   *Hit one ring and the whole chain will resound*
SOUTH AFRICA

15   *One hand can't tie a bundle*   LIBERIA

16   *Sticks in a bundle are unbreakable*   KENYA

17   *If we knew where we would fall, we would spread straw there first*   FINLAND

18   *One sprinkles the most sugar where the tart is burnt*
NETHERLANDS

26 CONTENTS

18   *Not every abyss has a parapet*   GERMANY

19   *The basket that has two handles can be carried by two*
     EGYPT

20   *Every song has its end*   SLOVENIA

27   KINDS

1   *A beautiful bird is the only kind we cage*   CHINA

2   *Three kinds of men fail to understand women – young
men, old men, and middle-aged men*   IRELAND

3   *It isn't every kind of wood that can make a whistle*
     LATVIA

4   *Not every sort of wood is fit to make an arrow*   FRANCE

5   *Three sorts of people are always to be found, soldiers,
professors, and women*   GERMANY

28   ALWAYS HAPPENING

1   *There is always a boss above the boss*   NETHERLANDS

2   *The cork is always bigger than the mouth of the bottle*
     ESTONIA

3   *The cobbler always wears the worst shoes*   FRANCE

4   *Lovers have much to relate – but it is always the same
thing*   GERMANY

21 *The toughest broncs is always them you've rode some other place* USA

22 *The grass always looks greener on the other side of the fence* ENGLAND

23 *Those in love always know the time* GERMANY

24 *Error is always in a hurry* ENGLAND

25 *The tongue always goes to the aching tooth* BULGARIA

26 *There is always something to be cut off young trees if they are to grow well* GERMANY

27 *Stars shine always in a clear sky* ESTONIA

28 *The other side of the road always looks cleanest*
     ENGLAND

29 *However long the procession, it always returns to the church* PHILIPPINES

30 *The string of our sack of patience is generally tied with a slip knot* JAPAN

31 *Abundance does not spread, famine does* SOUTH AFRICA

32 *Once a crook, always a crook* USA

33 *A bit of fragrance always clings to the hand that gives you roses* CHINA

34 *Those who have once had luck cannot always call themselves unlucky* BELGIUM

35 *Boldness, and again boldness, and always boldness*
     FRANCE

36   *Not even Apollo keeps his bow always at full stretch*
     LATIN

37   *A debt is always new*   ESTONIA

38   *Be always a little afraid so that you never have need of being much afraid*   FINLAND

39   *To always win brings suspicion, to always lose brings contempt*   GERMANY

40   *Those who have lost their oxen are always hearing bells*
     SPAIN

41   *Rather once cry your heart out than always sigh*   CHINA

42   *It is better to be once in the church sleigh than always in the back runners*   FINLAND

43   *The world will not conquer him who is always rubbing his beard*   INDIA

29   CONFORMITY

1   *Example is a great orator*   CZECH REPUBLIC

2   *A white cloth and a stain never agree*   NIGERIA

3   *Not every sort of wood is fit to make an arrow*   FRANCE

4   *Donkey's lips do not fit onto a horse's mouth*   CHINA

5   *If the cap fits, wear it*   ENGLAND

6   *If the shoe fits, wear it*   ENGLAND

7   *Words shake but examples attract*   SERBIA

8   *Strange bread makes the cheeks red*   SWITZERLAND

9   *It is not common for hens to have pillows*   SCOTLAND

30   REPETITION

1   *Shut your door in such a way that you can open it again*
    DENMARK

2   *A whitewashed crow soon shows black again*   CHINA

3   *No one can call again yesterday*   ENGLAND

4   *Cut bread cannot be put together again*   LATVIA

5   *Where water has once flowed it will flow again*
    MONTENEGRO

6   *As one calls in the wood, so comes the echo back again*
    ESTONIA

7   *Those who run away will fight again*   GREECE

8   *The end of separation is meeting again*   TURKEY

9   *Boldness, and again boldness, and always boldness*
    FRANCE

10   *By trying often, the monkey learns to jump from the tree*
    CAMEROON

11   *Friends are lost by calling often and calling seldom*
    SCOTLAND

12   *The wise make proverbs but fools repeat them*   ENGLAND

31 TIME

1   *There is time enough to yawn in the grave*   ESTONIA

2   *A stitch in time saves nine*   ENGLAND

3   *Truth is the daughter of time*   GERMANY

4   *The best time to plant a tree was twenty years ago; the second-best time is now*   CHINA

5   *You cannot jump over two ditches at the same time*   NETHERLANDS

6   *No one can blow and swallow at the same time*   GERMANY

7   *It takes a long time to sharpen a hammer made of wood*   NETHERLANDS

8   *Time heals all wounds*   ENGLAND

9   *Seconds are the gold dust of time*   USA

10   *Those who wait long at the ferry will get across some time*   SCOTLAND

11   *Those who wait for roast duck to fly into their mouth must wait a very, very long time*   CHINA

12   *Procrastination is the thief of time*   ENGLAND

13   *What greater crime than loss of time?*   GERMANY

* * * * * * * * * * * * * * * * * *

4 COUNTRY VARIATIONS – CLIMATE

Some of the most noticeable contrasts between the proverbs of different countries relate to the differences in their climate and weather. References to the seasons are especially common.

> *A padded jacket is an acceptable gift, even in summer* (JAPAN)
> *In December and January have mercy on the poor* (LEBANON)
> *Every mile is two in winter* (ENGLAND)
> *No more leaves can fall in autumn than were grown in spring*
> (GERMANY)
> *You do not know who is your friend or who is your enemy until*
> *the ice breaks* (ICELAND)
> *The autumn chill is the first thing felt by a thin person* (CHINA)
> *After a typhoon there are pears to gather up* (CHINA)

SEE ALSO Country variations – artefacts (p. 151); animals
(p. 302); plants (p. 323); beliefs and behaviour (p. 562)

* * * * * * * * * * * * * * * * *

14   *Time and tide wait for no one*   ENGLAND

15   *Money cannot buy time*   CHINA

16   *Time is anger's medicine*   GERMANY

17   *If they do not open after three knocks, do not wait*
      POLAND

18   *Make hay while the sun shines*   ENGLAND

19 *Time to catch bears is when they're out*   USA

20 *One should not ask the time of a rusty clock*
   NETHERLANDS

21 *Those in love always know the time*   GERMANY

22 *Someone with a watch knows what time it is; someone
   with two watches is never sure*   FRANCE

32 YEARS – SEASONS – MONTHS – WEEKS

1 *A weasel comes to say Happy New Year to the chickens*
   CHINA

2 *Errands are small on a spring day*   ICELAND

3 *A padded jacket is an acceptable gift, even in summer*
   JAPAN

4 *One swallow does not make a summer*   ENGLAND

5 *The autumn chill is the first thing felt by a thin person*
   CHINA

6 *No more leaves can fall in autumn than were grown in
   spring*   GERMANY

7 *Every mile is two in winter*   ENGLAND

8 *A kind word warms for three winters*   CHINA

9 *In December and January have mercy on the poor*
   LEBANON

10   *No annual fair without a thief*   NETHERLANDS

11   *An hour of play discovers more than a year of conversation*   PORTUGAL

12   *If you want one year of prosperity, grow grain. If you want ten years of prosperity, grow trees. If you want a hundred years of prosperity, grow people*   CHINA

13   *A smile will gain you ten more years of life*   CHINA

14   *The best time to plant a tree was twenty years ago; the second-best time is now*   CHINA

15   *Before marrying live wildly for three years*   POLAND

16   *A dog last year is a dog this year*   SERBIA

17   *A day of sorrow is longer than a month of joy*   CHINA

18   *For the diligent, a week has seven days; for the slothful, seven tomorrows*   GERMANY

19   *Seven days is the length of a guest's life*   MYANMAR

20   *Those who lose Monday lose all the week*   GEORGIA

21   *Every Sunday brings a week with it*   SCOTLAND

33   DAYS – NIGHTS

1   *Every day cannot be a feast of lanterns*   CHINA

2   *An apple a day keeps the doctor away*   ENGLAND

3   *A hug a day keeps the demons at bay*   GERMANY

4   *Errands are small on a spring day*   ICELAND

5   *A good day is that in which to lay by cold porridge*
   MALAWI

6   *Another day, another dollar*   USA

7   *The better the day, the better the deed*   ENGLAND

8   *Those who lose Monday lose all the week*   GEORGIA

9   *Those who spend a night with a chicken will cackle in the
morning*   TUNISIA

10   *Sunday plans never stand*   CANADA

11   *Every Sunday brings a week with it*   SCOTLAND

12   *The absent get farther off every day*   JAPAN

13   *After three days without reading, talk becomes flavourless*
   CHINA

14   *Seven days is the length of a guest's life*   MYANMAR

15   *A guest and a fish after three days are poison*   FRANCE

16   *A day of sorrow is longer than a month of joy*   CHINA

17   *Every dog has its day*   ENGLAND

18   *Every day is not Friday; there is also Thursday*   USA

19   *Friday begun, never done*   USA

20   *Who teaches me for a day is my father for a lifetime*
   CHINA

21   *For the diligent, a week has seven days; for the slothful,
seven tomorrows*   GERMANY

22 *Go fishing for three days and dry the nets for two*
     CHINA

23 *Two happy days are seldom brothers*   BULGARIA

24 *One missing button strikes the eye more than one missing day*   ESTONIA

25 *There are more days than sausage*   USA

26 *The most wasted of all days is the day when we have not laughed*   FRANCE

27 *The night washes what the day has soaped*
     SWITZERLAND

28 *Gossip lasts but seventy-five days*   JAPAN

29 *Rome was not built in a day*   ENGLAND

30 *Birds hear talk in daytime, rats hear talk at night*
     KOREA

31 *Old countries don't disappear overnight; they stay for breakfast*   EGYPT

32 *Have patience, fleas, the night is long*   NICARAGUA

34 MORNINGS – AFTERNOONS – EVENINGS

1 *Dawn does not come twice to wake us*   SOUTH AFRICA

2 *The darkest hour is just before the dawn*   ENGLAND

3 *We can never see the sun rise by looking into the west*
JAPAN

4 *A misty morning may have a fine day* ENGLAND

5 *The morning is the mother of trades and the evening the mother of thoughts* ITALY

6 *Those who spend a night with a chicken will cackle in the morning* TUNISIA

7 *The afternoon knows what the morning never suspected*
SWEDEN

8 *No day so long but has its evening* FRANCE

9 *The evening crowns the day* SWEDEN

10 *A clear conscience never fears midnight knocking* CHINA

11 *It cannot be later than midnight* MYANMAR

12 *An apple at night puts the dentist to flight* ENGLAND

13 *The later in the evening, the nicer the people*
NETHERLANDS

14 *Even the moon does not shine before it rises* FINLAND

35 HOURS – MINUTES – SECONDS

1 *Many people are like clocks, they show one hour and strike another* DENMARK

2 *The one who asks a question is a fool for five minutes;*

the one who does not ask a question is a fool forever
CHINA

3   *Heroism consists in hanging on one minute longer*
NORWAY

4   *There's one born every minute*   USA

5   *Where the minute-hand suffices the hour-hand is not
needed*   NETHERLANDS

6   *Seconds are the gold dust of time*   USA

7   *God works in moments*   FRANCE

8   *God listens to short prayers*   ITALY

36 LONG TIME

1   *Who teaches me for a day is my father for a lifetime*
CHINA

2   *As long as life lasts, the cow never stops moving its tail*
NIGERIA

3   *Gossip lasts but seventy-five days*   JAPAN

4   *It takes a long time to sharpen a hammer made of wood*
NETHERLANDS

5   *If the bucket has been long in the well, it ought to come
out with water*   NIGERIA

6   *No matter how long a log floats on the river it will never
be a crocodile*   MALI

7 *A day of sorrow is longer than a month of joy* CHINA

8 *The longest chant has an end* SCOTLAND

9 *If you follow a crow long enough you light on carrion*
ALBANIA

10 *An apothecary ought not to be long a cuckold* FRANCE

11 *The one who asks a question is a fool for five minutes;
the one who does not ask a question is a fool forever*
CHINA

12 *No day so long but has its evening* FRANCE

13 *Longest at the fire soonest finds cold* SCOTLAND

14 *Heroism consists in hanging on one minute longer*
NORWAY

15 *One generation plants the trees; another gets the shade*
CHINA

16 *The rod that will hang him is still growing* IRELAND

17 *Who goes around the village long enough will get either a
dog-bite or a dinner* SERBIA

18 *It is the prudent hyena that lives long* ZAMBIA

19 *Those who wait long at the ferry will get across some
time* SCOTLAND

20 *Those who wait for roast duck to fly into their mouth
must wait a very, very long time* CHINA

21 *Creaking wagons are long in passing* NETHERLANDS

22 *Want a thing long enough, and you don't* CHINA

37 NEVER

1 *Sunday plans never stand* CANADA

2 *Driftwood never goes upstream* USA

3 *An elephant never forgets* ENGLAND

4 *Friday begun, never done* USA

5 *Better late than never* ENGLAND

6 *Tomorrow never comes* ENGLAND

38 CLOCKS – WATCHES

1 *Many people are like clocks, they show one hour and strike another* DENMARK

2 *One should not ask the time of a rusty clock* NETHERLANDS

3 *If it were not for the hands the clock would be useless* POLAND

4 *The clock must be the master in the house* SWEDEN

5 *The clock ticks nowhere as it ticks at home* NETHERLANDS

6 *Someone with a watch knows what time it is; someone with two watches is never sure* FRANCE

39 BEGINNINGS – ENDINGS

1 *Communities begin by building their kitchen*   FRANCE

2 *Those who sing worst, let them begin first*   ENGLAND

3 *Those that begin the play must continue it*   TURKEY

4 *When you eat a round cake, do you begin at the centre?*
NIGERIA

5 *When an old barn begins to burn, it is hard to put out*
NETHERLANDS

6 *Friday begun, never done*   USA

7 *Sooner begun, sooner done*   ENGLAND

8 *Charity begins at home*   ENGLAND

9 *The beginning of wisdom is to call things by their right names*   CHINA

10 *Applause is the beginning of abuse*   JAPAN

11 *In eating and scratching, everything is in the beginning*
COLOMBIA

12 *Fish begin to stink from the head*   ALBANIA

13 *If you know the beginning well, the end will not trouble you*   SENEGAL

14 *Meeting is the beginning of parting*   JAPAN

15 *It is the first shower that wets*   ITALY

16 *To read a book for the first time is to make the*

acquaintance of a new friend; to read it a second time is to meet an old one   CHINA

17   *Those who make the first bad move always lose the game*
JAPAN

18   *The first blow does not hurt like the second*   ZANZIBAR

19   *The autumn chill is the first thing felt by a thin person*
CHINA

20   *If you find yourself in a hole, the first thing to do is stop digging*   USA

21   *It is only the first bottle that is dear*   FRANCE

22   *The first stage of folly is to consider oneself wise*
BELGIUM

23   *Ideas start with 'I'*   USA

24   *The first thread is not part of the yarn*   IRELAND

25   *If you want an audience, start a fight*   CHINA

26   *One loose pebble can start a landslide*   USA

27   *When you sweep the stairs, you start at the top*
GERMANY

28   *It is not enough to run; one must start in time*   FRANCE

29   *When the fox starts preaching, look to the hens*
SPAIN: BASQUE

30   *When one starts the song too high it isn't finished*
GERMANY

31 *Don't start economizing when you are down to your last dollar* USA

32 *New officials introduce strict measures* CHINA

33 *Every cackling hen was an egg at first*
      RWANDA AND BURUNDI

34 *Your liberty ends where my nose begins* USA

40 BEFOREHAND

1 *Never say 'whoopee' before you jump* CANADA

2 *Before you go, think of your return* BELGIUM

3 *Honour physicians before you have need of them*
      ENGLAND

4 *The face came before the photograph* USA

5 *The fruit must have a stem before it grows* LIBERIA

6 *Open your mouth before you eat* MAURITANIA

7 *Don't holler before you're hurt* USA

8 *Don't get off the merry-go-round before it stops* USA

9 *Don't get on the streetcar before it stops* CANADA

10 *Don't count your chickens before they're hatched*
      ENGLAND

11 *A skunk smells its own hole first* USA

12 *You have to learn to crawl before you can walk*
    ENGLAND

13 *Fingers were made before forks*   ENGLAND

14 *Even the moon does not shine before it rises*   FINLAND

15 *Those who have free seats at a play hiss first*   CHINA

16 *The darkest hour is just before the dawn*   ENGLAND

17 *The one who strikes first, strikes twice*   BELGIUM

18 *Don't take the antidote before the poison*   LATIN

19 *Don't shout before the birch-rod falls*   LATVIA

20 *Look before you leap*   ENGLAND

21 *Before marrying live wildly for three years*   POLAND

22 *Before going to war say one prayer; before going to sea, two; before getting married, three*   POLAND

23 *All things are difficult before they are easy*   SPAIN

24 *Pride goes before a fall*   ENGLAND

25 *You have no wisdom if you go to sleep before you make your bed*   UGANDA

26 *First lay the egg, then cackle*   ESTONIA

27 *That which you would say to another, say to yourself first*
    ESTONIA

28 *People are not trodden on unless they lie down first*
    GERMANY

29 *The first in the boat has the choice of oars*   ENGLAND

30 *Warm a frozen serpent, and it will sting you first*
ARMENIA

31 *Sweep off your own back porch first* USA

32 *Those who sing worst, let them begin first* ENGLAND

41 AFTERWARDS

1 *What's the good of a spoon after the meal is over?*
LATVIA

2 *It ain't over till the fat lady sings* USA

3 *The game's not over until the last man strikes out* USA

4 *If they do not open after three knocks, do not wait*
POLAND

5 *The greatest love is mother-love; after that comes a dog's love; and after that the love of a sweetheart* POLAND

6 *Why feed a bullock after it is sold?* INDIA

7 *It's no good locking the stable door after the horse is stolen* ENGLAND

8 *If power can be bought, then sell your mother to get it; you can always buy her back later* GHANA

9 *Don't quote your proverb until you bring your ship to port* SCOTLAND

10 *Sell not your bearskin until you have the bear* USA

11 *Don't cross a bridge until you come to it* ENGLAND

* * * * * * * * * * * * * * * * * * *

5 PRESENT TENSE

Proverbs, being the expression of general truths, are usually in the present tense. But occasionally we find them looking backwards and forwards in time.

Past time

A barren sow was never good to pigs.

Because we concentrated on the snake, we missed the scorpion.

A big nose never spoiled a handsome face.

Bacchus has drowned more people than Neptune.

Some have been thought brave because they were afraid to run away.

I gave an order to a cat, and the cat gave it to its tail.

Future time

Go abroad and you'll hear news of home.

An old cat will not learn how to dance.

A dog in desperation will leap over a wall.

A red-nosed man may not be a drinker, but he will find nobody to believe it.

Two barrels of tears will not heal a bruise.

If we knew where we would fall, we would spread straw there first.

* * * * * * * * * * * * * * * * * *

12   *Don't quit until the hearse comes round*   USA

13   *When the face is washed, you finish at the chin*
      NIGERIA

42 PAST – PRESENT – FUTURE

1   *No one can call again yesterday*   ENGLAND

2   *No one thinks of the snow that fell last year*   SWEDEN

3   *It is in vain to look for yesterday's fish in the house of
     the otter*   INDIA

4   *The best time to plant a tree was twenty years ago; the
     second-best time is now*   CHINA

5   *A dog last year is a dog this year*   SERBIA

6   *There's no time like the present*   ENGLAND

7   *Water will run where it ran before*   BULGARIA

8   *Better an egg today than a hen tomorrow*   USA

9   *For the diligent, a week has seven days; for the slothful,
     seven tomorrows*   GERMANY

10 *If you want to be acquainted with the past and the
     present, you must read five cartloads of books*   CHINA

11 *Never put off till tomorrow what can be done today*
      ENGLAND

12 *Here today and gone tomorrow*   ENGLAND

13   *Speak, lest tomorrow you be prevented*   KENYA

14   *Tomorrow blows the wind of tomorrow*   JAPAN

15   *Tomorrow never comes*   ENGLAND

16   *Today is the tomorrow that you worried about yesterday*
   USA

43 SOONER OR LATER

1   *A whitewashed crow soon shows black again*   CHINA

2   *Short hair is soon brushed*   GERMANY

3   *Longest at the fire soonest finds cold*   SCOTLAND

4   *They that think no ill are soonest beguiled*   ENGLAND

5   *The tighter the string, the sooner it will break*   WALES

6   *Nothing dries sooner than a tear*   LATIN

7   *Little kettles soon boil over*   ESTONIA

8   *Honest men marry soon; wise men never*   ENGLAND

9   *Luck and glass soon break*   GERMANY

10   *The fuller the cup, the sooner the spill*   CHINA

11   *A gummed thing soon ungums*   JAPAN

12   *A fool and his money are soon parted*   ENGLAND

13   *Punctuality is the politeness of princes*   FRANCE

14   *If you wish to be angry, pay for something in advance*
      MONTENEGRO

15   *That which is to become a good nettle must sting early*
      SWEDEN

16   *Least said, soonest mended*   ENGLAND

17   *Clumsy birds need early flight*   CHINA

18   *If your neighbour is an early riser, you will become one*
      ALBANIA

19   *It is not economical to go to bed early to save the candles if the result is twins*   CHINA

20   *The early bird catches the worm*   ENGLAND

21   *Strawberries ripen sooner in a low wood than in a high one*   ESTONIA

22   *Sooner begun, sooner done*   ENGLAND

23   *It cannot be later than midnight*   MYANMAR

24   *The later in the evening, the nicer the people*
      NETHERLANDS

25   *Those who are in a hurry are always late*   GEORGIA

26   *Those who come too late find the platter turned over*
      NETHERLANDS

27   *Better late than never*   ENGLAND

44 NEWNESS

1 *New brooms sweep clean*   ENGLAND

2 *A new broom sweeps clean, but the old brush knows the corners*   IRELAND

3 *Even in the freshest of milk you will still find hairs*   MALI

4 *Necessity teaches new arts*   NORWAY

5 *A debt is always new*   ESTONIA

6 *Beware of old streets and new inns*   GERMANY

7 *To read a book for the first time is to make the acquaintance of a new friend; to read it a second time is to meet an old one*   CHINA

8 *An old story does not open the ear as a new one does*   NIGERIA

9 *New clothes have no lice*   NAMIBIA

10 *Out of old fields come new grain*   USA

11 *You can't teach an old dog new tricks*   ENGLAND

12 *Only with a new ruler do you appreciate the value of the old*   MYANMAR

13 *New lords, new laws*   FRANCE

14 *New laws, new frauds*   ENGLAND

15 *New officials introduce strict measures*   CHINA

16   *There is always something to be cut off young trees if they are to grow well*   GERMANY

17   *Better keep under an old hedge than creep under a new furze-bush*   ENGLAND

45 OLDNESS

1   *Old purses shut badly*   NETHERLANDS

2   *Everything ancient is to be respected*   GREECE

3   *Custom is rust that mocks at every file*   BOHEMIA

4   *Once is no custom*   NETHERLANDS

5   *An old story does not open the ear as a new one does*   NIGERIA

6   *When an old barn begins to burn, it is hard to put out*   NETHERLANDS

7   *Old countries don't disappear overnight; they stay for breakfast*   EGYPT

8   *Old droppings don't stink*   KENYA

9   *Out of old fields come new grain*   USA

10   *The older the buck, the harder his horn*   SCOTLAND

11   *The older the ginger, the more it bites*   CHINA

12   *Old sayings contain no lies*   SPAIN: BASQUE

13   *Better keep under an old hedge than creep under a new furze-bush*   ENGLAND

14　*An old moon's mist never died of thirst* IRELAND

15　*Even a young foot finds ease in an old slipper*
　　SCOTLAND

16　*Money is never old-fashioned* NETHERLANDS

17　*To get out a rusty nail you must take away a piece of the
　　wall* MALTA

18　*A new broom sweeps clean, but the old brush knows the
　　corners* IRELAND

19　*An old broom still sweeps the room* ESTONIA

20　*Beware of old streets and new inns* GERMANY

21　*If you want to go fast, go the old road* MYANMAR

22　*There is no better looking-glass than an old friend*
　　ENGLAND

23　*To read a book for the first time is to make the
　　acquaintance of a new friend; to read it a second time
　　is to meet an old one* CHINA

24　*Only with a new ruler do you appreciate the value of the
　　old* MYANMAR

25　*You must go behind the door to mend old breeches*
　　ENGLAND

26　*Hunger doesn't say, 'Stale bread,' and cold doesn't say
　　'Old coat.'* GEORGIA

27　*One should not ask the time of a rusty clock*
　　NETHERLANDS

46 AGE

1 *New-born calves don't fear tigers* CHINA

2 *The baby who does not cry does not get fed*
PHILIPPINES

3 *A frog's baby is a frog* JAPAN

4 *A burnt bairn dreads the fire* SCOTLAND

5 *A child learns quicker to talk than to be silent* NORWAY

6 *Parents who are afraid to put their foot down will have children who step on their toes* CHINA

7 *Many kiss the child for the nurse's sake* ENGLAND

8 *Wine and children speak the truth* ROMANIA

9 *A good child has several names* ESTONIA

10 *To understand your parents' love, bear your own children*
CHINA

11 *A child is more than a chip* ESTONIA

12 *When you give a child a nut, give it also something to break it with* GEORGIA

13 *Children regard their father's guest as a slave*
REPUBLIC OF CONGO

14 *It's a wise child that knows its own father* ENGLAND

15 *Those who have no children do not understand love*
ITALY

16 *It takes a whole village to raise one child* NIGERIA

17 *When you show the moon to a child, it sees only your finger* ZAMBIA

18 *More precious than our children are the children of our children* EGYPT

19 *Spare the rod and spoil the child* ENGLAND

20 *If he calls it a silly and childish game, that means his wife can beat him at it* USA

21 *A young doctor makes a full graveyard* CHINA

22 *Three kinds of men fail to understand women – young men, old men, and middle-aged men* IRELAND

23 *Even a young foot finds ease in an old slipper* SCOTLAND

24 *A young saint, an old devil* ITALY

25 *The house with an old grandparent harbours a jewel* CHINA

26 *An old rat is a brave rat* FRANCE

27 *It is a hard job to make old monkeys pull faces* BELGIUM

28 *An old cat will not learn how to dance* MOROCCO

29 *You can't teach an old dog new tricks* ENGLAND

30 *The mind does not grow old* WALES

31 *An old horse doesn't fear the whip* SWITZERLAND

32 *The head is older than the book* BELGIUM

33 *Age before beauty* USA

34 *You do not teach the paths of the forest to an old gorilla*
REPUBLIC OF CONGO

35 *There are old pilots, and there are bold pilots, but there are no old, bold pilots* USA

36 *Old soldiers never die* ENGLAND

37 *Where paper speaks, beards are silent* FRANCE

38 *To grow is to see* SOUTH AFRICA

39 *Those who do not lie never grow up* UGANDA

47 A TIME AND A PLACE

1 *There's a time and a place for everything* ENGLAND

2 *A good day is that in which to lay by cold porridge*
MALAWI

3 *Although the river is broad there are times when boats collide* CHINA

4 *When the occasion comes, the proverb comes* GHANA

5 *Turn your tongue seven times before speaking* FRANCE

6 *Every time we laugh a nail is removed from our coffin*
ITALY

7 *There is a time to squint, and a time to look straight*
SCOTLAND

8 *Transgressions should never be forgiven a third time*
CHINA

9 *Fall down seven times, get up eight*   JAPAN

10 *To read a book for the first time is to make the acquaintance of a new friend; to read it a second time is to meet an old one*   CHINA

11 *It is not enough to run; one must start in time*   FRANCE

12 *There's no time like the present*   ENGLAND

48 SOMETIMES

1 *A blind hen can sometimes find her corn*   FRANCE

2 *The saddest dog sometimes wags its tail*   ENGLAND

3 *Idle curiosity sometimes fills the mousetrap*
NETHERLANDS

4 *The devil makes pots, but not always lids*
ITALY: SARDINIA

5 *The dog on three legs ain't always lame*   USA

6 *Thunder-clouds do not always give rain*   ARMENIA

7 *Pilgrims seldom come home saints*   GERMANY

8 *Friends are lost by calling often and calling seldom*
SCOTLAND

9 *Where they like you, do not go often*   SPAIN

10 *Even the best smith sometimes hits his thumb*
NETHERLANDS

11 *Two happy days are seldom brothers* BULGARIA

12 *Sometimes one must let turnips be pears* GERMANY

13 *Fools seldom differ* ENGLAND

14 *Not even a bell always rings the same way* SERBIA

49 LASTING

1 *What one writes remains* NETHERLANDS

2 *Accomplishments remain with oneself* JAPAN

3 *A contented mind is a continual feast* ENGLAND

4 *A cat may go to a monastery, but she still remains a cat*
ETHIOPIA

5 *The more things change the more they remain the same*
FRANCE

6 *Someone may learn and learn and yet remain a fool*
GREECE

7 *Even if water flows in all directions, the sand will remain
at the bottom* GEORGIA

8 *Rain which does not fall remains in the sky* ITALY

9 *To fall is no shame, but to remain fallen is* SWEDEN

10 *The eyes close in sleep, but the pillow remains awake*
MALAYSIA

11 *Nobody can rest in their own shadow* HUNGARY

12 *Those who look fixedly at gold lose their sight*
NETHERLANDS

13 *Who marches fast remains on the road* ALBANIA

14 *If you want to keep your milk sweet, leave it in the cow*
LIBERIA

15 *Old countries don't disappear overnight; they stay for breakfast* EGYPT

16 *To open a shop is easy; to keep it open is an art* CHINA

17 *As long as life lasts, the cow never stops moving its tail*
NIGERIA

18 *Those who seek a constant friend go to the cemetery*
RUSSIA

50 CEASING

1 *Your liberty ends where my nose begins* USA

2 *All good things come to an end* ENGLAND

3 *The person who says it cannot be done should not interrupt the one doing it* CHINA

4 *Those who deal in onions no longer smell them*
GERMANY

5 *If you find yourself in a hole, the first thing to do is stop digging* USA

6   *If you are building a house and a nail breaks, do you stop building or do you change the nail?*
RWANDA AND BURUNDI

7   *It is not clever to play but to stop playing*   USA

8   *Time and tide wait for no one*   ENGLAND

9   *Don't quit until the hearse comes round*   USA

51   CHANGING

1   *In the middle of the river do not change horses*   PERU

2   *It is no advantage for someone in a fever to change their bed*   ENGLAND

3   *We cannot direct the wind, but we can adjust the sails*   GERMANY

4   *No matter how much the world changes, cats will never lay eggs*   MALI

5   *When the music changes, so does the dance*   NIGERIA

6   *A change is as good as a rest*   ENGLAND

7   *Rain doesn't remain in the sky*   ESTONIA

8   *If you engrave it too much it will become a hole*   INDIA

9   *Even if you cannot climb the mountain do not remain in the valley*   GERMANY

10   *If your neighbour is an early riser, you will become one*   ALBANIA

11 *The more things change the more they remain the same*
FRANCE

12 *That which is to become a good nettle must sting early*
SWEDEN

13 *The roughest stone becomes smooth when it is much rolled* SWITZERLAND

14 *The dragon in shallow water becomes the butt of shrimps*
CHINA

15 *What falls into salt becomes salt* INDIA

16 *The leopard cannot change its spots* ENGLAND

17 *The smaller the lizard, the greater its hope of becoming a crocodile* ETHIOPIA

18 *Justice becomes injustice when it makes two wounds on a head which only deserves one* REPUBLIC OF CONGO

19 *The twig that falls in the water will never become a fish*
CÔTE D'IVOIRE

20 *A blanket becomes heavier as it becomes wetter* INDIA

21 *Those who change their trade make soup in a basket*
ENGLAND

22 *The wolf changes his hair, but not his skin* ALBANIA

23 *If you are building a house and a nail breaks, do you stop building or do you change the nail?*
RWANDA AND BURUNDI

24 *A bald-headed man cannot grow hair by getting excited about it* REPUBLIC OF CONGO

25 *Even deep water-holes may get dry* SOUTH AFRICA

26 *Those who do not eat cheese will go mad* FRANCE

27 *The mind does not grow old* WALES

28 *The broth from a distance grows cool on the road*
    KENYA

29 *The feathers make the fowl big* CÔTE D'IVOIRE

30 *Puttin' feathers on a buzzard won't make it no eagle*
    USA

31 *Grass must turn to hay* LATIN

32 *What is done cannot be undone* ENGLAND

33 *Luck and glass soon break* GERMANY

34 *You never know your luck till the wheel stops* USA

52 HAPPENINGS

1 *Bad is called good when worse happens* NORWAY

2 *Take the ball as it bounces* FRANCE

3 *Education don't come by bumping against the school-
   house* USA

4 *Everything comes to those who wait* ENGLAND

5 *The thinnest bread finds itself married to bread*
   ALGERIA

* * * * * * * * * * * * * * * * * *

6 BELONGING TOGETHER

A widely used stylistic trick is for a proverb to ascribe a
particular quality to two very different entities. The device
makes us momentarily pause before we see the point.

> *Wine and children speak the truth.* (ROMANIA)
> *Beware of a person's shadow and a bee's sting.* (MYANMAR)
> *Two things make one either greater or smaller, praise and
> shadows.* (GERMANY)
> *In buying horses and in taking a wife, shut your eyes tight and
> commend yourself to God.* (ITALY)
> *Time and tide wait for no one.* (ENGLAND)
> *All is fair in love and war.* (ENGLAND)
> *Eggs and vows are easily broken.* (JAPAN)
> *A guest and a fish after three days are poison.* (FRANCE)
> *Words and feathers are taken by the wind.* (SPAIN: BASQUE)
> *Loving and singing are not to be forced.* (GERMANY)
> *Priests and women never forget.* (GERMANY)
> *A rich person's sickness and a poor person's pancake are smelt a
> long way off.* (BELGIUM)
> *Before God and the bus-conductor we are all equal.*
> (GERMANY)
> *Rhubarb and patience work wonders.* (GERMANY)
> *Mad folks and proverbs reveal many truths.* (USA)

SEE ALSO Contrasts (p. 347)

* * * * * * * * * * * * * * * * * *

6   *If you don't want the gun to go off, don't cock the trigger*
    REPUBLIC OF CONGO

7   *Accidents will happen*   ENGLAND

8   *To read a book for the first time is to make the
    acquaintance of a new friend; to read it a second time
    is to meet an old one*   CHINA

9   *A gardener's flirtations take place outside the garden*
    AFGHANISTAN

10 *Life is just one damned thing after another*   USA

11 *Things don't turn up; they must be turned up*   ENGLAND

12 *Those who simultaneously eat and sing rise up fools*
    PHILIPPINES

13 *The end of an ox is beef, and the end of a lie is grief*
    MADAGASCAR

14 *What reliance can be placed on a sneeze?*   INDIA

15 *One accident is one too many*   CANADA

16 *When luck offers a finger one must take the whole hand*
    SWEDEN

17 *All good things come to an end*   ENGLAND

18 *Buzzards do not sing in bleak regions*   PERU

53 CAUSE – EFFECT

1   *The sign-board brings the custom*   FRANCE

2 *A bad thing that does no harm is the same as a good one that does no good* GERMANY

3 *The big toe never does the ear any harm* NIGERIA

4 *We get the note by striking the string* INDIA

5 *A waiting appetite kindles many a spite* ENGLAND

6 *Too much discussion will lead to a row* CÔTE D'IVOIRE

7 *Justice becomes injustice when it makes two wounds on a head which only deserves one* REPUBLIC OF CONGO

8 *Many drops make a puddle* NETHERLANDS

9 *One pebble doesn't make a floor* NIGERIA

10 *Money makes the world go round* USA

11 *Familiarity breeds contempt* ENGLAND

12 *To always win brings suspicion, to always lose brings contempt* GERMANY

13 *Revolutions are not made by men in spectacles* USA

14 *What makes one abbot glad makes another abbot sad* SCOTLAND

15 *Practice makes perfect* ENGLAND

16 *Cheese and bread make the cheeks red* GERMANY

17 *It takes two blows to make a battle* ENGLAND

18 *The second word makes the fray* JAPAN

19 *Beauty does not make the pot boil* IRELAND

20   *A smooth way makes the foot slip*   ESTONIA

21   *Good words make us laugh; good deeds make us silent*
       FRANCE

22   *One swallow does not make a summer*   ENGLAND

23   *There's nothing like being bespattered for making
someone defy the gutter*   FRANCE

24   *A fire in the heart makes smoke in the head*   GERMANY

25   *The art of being a merchant consists more in getting paid
than in making sales*   SPAIN

26   *Strange bread makes the cheeks red*   SWITZERLAND

27   *It takes two to make a quarrel*   ENGLAND

28   *Two things make one either greater or smaller, praise and
shadows*   GERMANY

29   *God preserve us from pitch-forks, for they make three
holes*   SWITZERLAND

30   *It is the turning of the mill that makes the flour heap*
       INDIA

31   *Peace makes money and money makes war*   FRANCE

32   *Small cares make many words, great ones are mute*
       GERMANY

33   *A coward's fear makes a brave man braver*   SCOTLAND

34   *A fall into a ditch makes you wiser*   CHINA

35   *From fried eggs come no chickens*   USA

36 *A young doctor makes a full graveyard* CHINA

37 *Absence makes the heart grow fonder* ENGLAND

38 *A crooked log makes a good fire* FRANCE

39 *The sweetest wine makes the sharpest vinegar*
  GERMANY

40 *A borrowed drum never makes good dancing* HAITI

41 *At birth we cry – at death we see why* BULGARIA

42 *Straps come from the same leather* ARGENTINA

43 *Good juice from fruit comes without squeezing* IRAN

44 *Slowness comes from God and quickness from the devil*
  MOROCCO

45 *Out of old fields come new grain* USA

46 *A beautiful disorder is an effect of art* FRANCE

47 *God does not shave – why should I?* BULGARIA

48 *Great consolation may grow out of the smallest saying*
  SWITZERLAND

49 *It is not economical to go to bed early to save the candles
if the result is twins* CHINA

50 *Set a thief to catch a thief* ENGLAND

54 STRENGTH – WEAKNESS

1 *Take away the wife of a strong man only when he is out*
UGANDA

2 *Community is as strong as water, and as stupid as a pig*
RUSSIA

3 *The one who is not strong enough to lift the stone must roll it* ESTONIA

4 *The dog on three legs ain't always lame* USA

5 *Truth is greater than ten goats* NIGERIA

6 *Habit hardens the feet* NETHERLANDS

7 *Pray devoutly but hammer stoutly* ENGLAND

8 *Strong people can spin their top in the sand* JAPAN

9 *Good nature is stronger than tomahawks* USA

10 *The throwers of stones fling away the strength of their own arms* NIGERIA

11 *A chain is as strong as its weakest link* ENGLAND

12 *Sticks in a bundle are unbreakable* KENYA

13 *A habit is first cobwebs, then cables* USA

14 *The third strand makes the cable* NETHERLANDS

15 *Too much tying loosens* SYRIA

16 *A barren sow was never good to pigs* ENGLAND

17 *Pull gently at a weak rope* NETHERLANDS

18   *It's a great life if you don't weaken*   USA

19   *An axe with a loose head is the bane of a man up a tree*
     NIGERIA

20   *A shadow is a feeble thing but no sun can drive it away*
     SWEDEN

55   PRODUCTION

1   *A basket-maker who makes one basket makes a hundred*
     BRAZIL

2   *More than one mother can make tasty soup*   NIGERIA

3   *Crab apples make good jelly too*   USA

4   *No more leaves can fall in autumn than were grown in spring*   GERMANY

5   *Make hay while the sun shines*   ENGLAND

6   *A hundred men may make an encampment, but it needs a woman to make a home*   CHINA

7   *One cannot make soup out of beauty*   ESTONIA

8   *Not every sort of wood is fit to make an arrow*   FRANCE

9   *Sweat makes good mortar*   GERMANY

10   *The wise make proverbs but fools repeat them*   ENGLAND

11   *Words do not make flour*   ITALY

12   *They wouldn't make erasers if we didn't make mistakes*
     USA

13   *Neither break a law nor make one*   IRELAND

14   *A hat is not made for one shower*   ENGLAND

15   *It isn't every kind of wood that can make a whistle*
     LATVIA

16   *It is easy to make pipes sitting amongst bulrushes*
     CZECH REPUBLIC

17   *There's no making apples of plums*   GERMANY

18   *Cooks make their own sauce*   FRANCE

19   *Any wood will do to make a signpost*   GREECE

20   *You can't make a cheap palace*   USA

21   *Every chimney makes its own smoke*   ITALY

22   *The devil makes pots, but not always lids*
     ITALY: SARDINIA

23   *Those who change their trade make soup in a basket*
     ENGLAND

24   *Every plate that is made breaks*   AFGHANISTAN

25   *A maker of idols is never an idol-worshipper*   CHINA

26   *Every work revenges itself on its master*   GERMANY

27   *A father is a banker provided by nature*   FRANCE

28   *Two pieces of meat confuse the mind of the fly*   NIGERIA

29   *Good things sell themselves; bad things have to be
     advertised*   ETHIOPIA

30   *The best things in life are free*   USA

31 *Abundance does not spread, famine does* SOUTH AFRICA

32 *Abundance will make cotton pull a stone* NIGERIA

33 *A fruit-tree that grows on a dunghill is sure to flourish*
NEW ZEALAND

34 *Cut your coat according to your cloth* ENGLAND

56 DESTRUCTION

1 *An ant may well destroy a whole dam* CHINA

2 *Small termites collapse the roof* ETHIOPIA

3 *To fill a ditch a mound must come down* ARMENIA

4 *A candle lights others and consumes itself* ENGLAND

5 *A fallen lighthouse is more dangerous than a reef*
CHINA

6 *Weeds never perish* NETHERLANDS

7 *Feigned laughter ruins the teeth* INDIA

8 *Those who hesitate are lost* ENGLAND

9 *Do not tear down the east wall to repair the west*
CHINA

10 *You cannot damage a wrecked ship* ITALY

11 *One broken rail will wreck a train* USA

12 *Sharp acids corrode their own containers* ALBANIA

57 FORCE

1   *No matter how hard you throw a dead fish in the water,*
    it still won't swim   REPUBLIC OF CONGO

2   *A hungry louse bites hard*   USA

3   *It's not so bad to fall in the gutter, but it's worse to lay*
    there   USA

4   *It takes two blows to make a battle*   ENGLAND

5   *There's no crime in the blow that has not been struck*
    IRELAND

6   *The first blow does not hurt like the second*   ZANZIBAR

7   *The peace-maker gets two-thirds of the blows*
    MONTENEGRO

8   *Those who bring good news knock hard*   ENGLAND

9   *The bigger they come, the harder they fall*   USA

10 *When two elephants struggle, it is the grass that suffers*
    ZANZIBAR

11 *Pull gently at a weak rope*   NETHERLANDS

12 *If you have strings, pull them*   USA

58 PARENTS – CHILDREN

1   *To understand your parents' love, bear your own children*
    CHINA

2   *A crab does not beget a bird*   CÔTE D'IVOIRE

3   *We are all Adam's children*   ENGLAND

4   *Proverbs are the children of experience*   ENGLAND

5   *Who teaches me for a day is my father for a lifetime*
   CHINA

6   *Poets are fathers of lies*   LATIN

7   *A boulder is the father of the rocks*   NIGERIA

8   *Give your love to your wife and your secret to your
mother*   IRELAND

9   *The morning is the mother of trades and the evening the
mother of thoughts*   ITALY

10   *The bazaar knows neither father nor mother*   TURKEY

11   *Those whose mother is naked are not likely to clothe their
aunt*   SUDAN

12   *A hundred aunts is not the same as one mother*
   SIERRA LEONE

13   *More than one mother can make tasty soup*   NIGERIA

14   *If power can be bought, then sell your mother to get it;
you can always buy her back later*   GHANA

15   *Necessity is the mother of invention*   ENGLAND

16   *If you laugh at your mother-in-law, you'll get dirt in
your eye*   KENYA

17   *Parents who are afraid to put their foot down will have
children who step on their toes*   CHINA

18 *It takes a whole village to raise one child*   NIGERIA

19 *It is not economical to go to bed early to save the candles if the result is twins*   CHINA

20 *Admiration is the daughter of ignorance*   SPAIN

21 *Truth is the daughter of time*   GERMANY

22 *An heir also inherits quarrels*   NAMIBIA

23 *It is easier to rule a nation than a son*   CHINA

24 *A child is more than a chip*   ESTONIA

59 LOCATIONS

1 *There's a time and a place for everything*   ENGLAND

2 *There's more room outside than inside*   CANADA

3 *It is hard to swim between two stretches of bad water*   NETHERLANDS

4 *A new broom sweeps clean, but the old brush knows the corners*   IRELAND

5 *The best neighbors are vacant lots*   USA

6 *A good driver turns in a small space*   FRANCE

7 *Where the drum is burst is the place to mend it*   REPUBLIC OF CONGO

8 *It is with its own face that the plate receives the soup*   NIGERIA

9 *Between two points one cannot draw more than one straight line*   DENMARK

10 *If you can't drive your car, park it*   USA

11 *Do not put each foot on a different boat*   CHINA

12 *Precious ointments are put in small boxes*   FRANCE

13 *All's lost that's put in a broken dish*   SCOTLAND

14 *Lightning never strikes twice in the same place*   ENGLAND

15 *The quiet duck puts his foot on the unobservant worm*   CHINA

16 *Puttin' feathers on a buzzard won't make it no eagle*   USA

17 *Many speak a word which if it were a florin they would put back in their purse*   GERMANY

18 *It is easier to throw the load off the cart than to put it on*   CZECH REPUBLIC

19 *Don't put all your goods in your shop window*   USA

20 *A gladiator only takes counsel in the arena*   LATIN

60 STANDING – SITTING – LYING

1 *Standing on top of one mountain, the other mountain is higher*   CHINA

2   *Someone who stands behind a wall can see nothing else*
    JAPAN

3   *A lie stands upon one leg, but truth upon two*   ENGLAND

4   *It is easy to make pipes sitting amongst bulrushes*
    CZECH REPUBLIC

5   *When two ride on one horse one must sit behind*
    ENGLAND

6   *Who sits under a pear-tree will eat pears*   BULGARIA

7   *'Virtue in the middle,' said the devil as he sat between
    two lawyers*   NORWAY

8   *Who sits on the floor, is not afraid of a fall*
    CZECH REPUBLIC

9   *Sparrows clean their beaks against the branch on which
    they sit*   ESTONIA

10 *A bird with a beautiful plumage doesn't sit in the corner*
    CAMEROON

11 *If you try to sit on two chairs, you'll sit on the floor*   USA

12 *Those who have free seats at a play hiss first*   CHINA

13 *At a round table every seat is first*   GERMANY

14 *Don't be breaking your shin on a stool that's not in your
    way*   IRELAND

15 *Judge not the horse by his saddle*   CHINA

16 *Flies never alight on boiling pots*   UKRAINE

17   *If you would climb into the saddle don't despise the stirrup*   GERMANY

18   *Those who lie on the ground have no place from which to fall*   LATIN

19   *When the bed is small lie in the centre*   SPAIN

20   *People are not trodden on unless they lie down first*   GERMANY

61   FINDING

1   *A blind hen can sometimes find her corn*   FRANCE

2   *If you find yourself in a hole, the first thing to do is stop digging*   USA

3   *A red-nosed man may not be a drinker, but he will find nobody to believe it*   CHINA

4   *You can't find a thing except in the place it is*   IRELAND

5   *Three sorts of people are always to be found, soldiers, professors, and women*   GERMANY

6   *In the choicest vase are found the ugliest cracks*   CHINA

7   *The paddle which you find in the canoe is the one that will take you across*   LIBERIA

8   *Even in the freshest of milk you will still find hairs*   MALI

9   *Don't hold the dime so near your eye that you can't see the dollar*   USA

62 HOME – ABROAD

1   *Better do a good deed near at home than go far away to burn incense*   CHINA

2   *Who knows the language is at home everywhere*   NETHERLANDS

3   *Don't shuck your corn till the hogs come home*   USA

4   *Chickens come home to roost*   ENGLAND

5   *Pilgrims seldom come home saints*   GERMANY

6   *Send your charity abroad wrapped in blankets*   ENGLAND

7   *If you haven't much to do, start cleaning your own backyard*   USA

8   *Slowly but surely the excrement of foreign poets will come to your village*   MALI

9   *The crossroads always confuse the stranger*   NIGERIA

10   *There is no bridge without a place the other side of it*   WALES

11   *Go abroad and you'll hear news of home*   ENGLAND

12   *The toughest broncs is always them you've rode some other place*   USA

* * * * * * * * * * * * * * * * * * *

7 CHILDREN PLAY WITH PROVERBS

Proverbs become a part of children's linguistic consciousness quite early in life. This is partly because of their frequency in everyday domestic conversation and partly because they are quite commonly mentioned in children's story-books. As a result, children play with proverbs as they do with every other aspect of language.

Teachers can rely on this experience to help develop their students' linguistic awareness. One teacher gave a class of seven-year-olds a list of proverbs, left out the final word or phrase, and asked them to finish it off in their own way. Here are some of the results.

> *As you make your bed so you must . . . mess it up.*
> *Don't bite the hand that . . . looks dirty.*
> *You can't teach an old dog new . . . maths.*
> *Where there's smoke, there's . . . pollution.*
> *A penny saved is . . . not much.*
> *Children should be seen and not . . . grounded.*

SEE ALSO Adults play with proverbs (p. 541)

* * * * * * * * * * * * * * * * * * *

13   *Buzzards do not sing in bleak regions*   PERU

14   *Keep your chickens in your own backyard*   USA

15   *Don't stand by the water and long for fish; go home and weave a net*   CHINA

16 *One sits best on one's own bench*   NORWAY

17 *The saints of the home work no miracles*   ITALY

18 *When the cat's not home, the mice jump on the table*
   NETHERLANDS

19 *Charity begins at home*   ENGLAND

20 *The clock ticks nowhere as it ticks at home*
   NETHERLANDS

21 *Home is where the heart is*   ENGLAND

63 COUNTRIES

1 *The hyena of your own country does not break your bones*
   KENYA

2 *All countries are frontiers*   SOUTH AFRICA

3 *It is easy to lie about a far-off country*   ETHIOPIA

4 *Old countries don't disappear overnight; they stay for
   breakfast*   EGYPT

5 *It is a fine thing to die for one's fatherland, but a still
   finer thing to live for it*   HUNGARY

6 *Fear the Greeks even when they bring gifts*   LATIN

7 *The skin creaks according to the country*   ETHIOPIA

8 *All the keys in the land do not hang from one girdle*
   SCOTLAND

64 CITIES – TOWNS – VILLAGES

1   *Do not dwell in a city where a horse does not neigh nor a dog bark*   ENGLAND

2   *Courteous asking breaks even city walls*   UKRAINE

3   *You may read Pompeii in some people's faces*   ITALY

4   *When in Rome do as the Romans do*   ENGLAND

5   *Those who wish to live at Rome must not quarrel with the pope*   FRANCE

6   *All roads lead to Rome*   ENGLAND

7   *Rome was not built in a day*   ENGLAND

8   *Not everyone can be the pope of Rome*   NETHERLANDS

9   *He who never leaves Paris will never be pope*   FRANCE

10 *The town that parleys is half surrendered*   FRANCE

11 *The moon moves slowly, but it gets across the town*   CÔTE D'IVOIRE

12 *The village that can be seen needs no signpost*   ALBANIA

13 *Don't snap your fingers at the dogs before you are outside the village*   FRANCE

14 *It is not good to be the poet of a village*   GERMANY

15 *Obey the customs of the village you enter*   JAPAN

16 *Who goes around the village long enough will get either a dog-bite or a dinner*   SERBIA

17 *A village in sight does not require a guide*   TURKEY

18 *The medicine man is not esteemed in his own village*
    KENYA

19 *It takes a whole village to raise one child*   NIGERIA

20 *Slowly but surely the excrement of foreign poets will come
    to your village*   MALI

21 *The hindermost ox also reaches the kraal*
    SOUTH AFRICA

65 WHERE TO LIVE

1 *A little nest is warmer than a big nest*   IRELAND

2 *Empty barns need no thatch*   ENGLAND

3 *Ability and necessity dwell in the same cabin*
   NETHERLANDS

4 *Every priest praises his convent*   PHILIPPINES

5 *Don't praise a cottage in which you haven't yet slept*
   SOUTH AFRICA

6 *You cannot catch a tiger cub unless you enter the tiger's
   den*   JAPAN

7 *When an old barn begins to burn, it is hard to put out*
   NETHERLANDS

8 *It is the hyenas of the same den that hate one another*
   KENYA

9   *A hundred men may make an encampment, but it needs a woman to make a home*   CHINA

10   *Draw the snake from its hole by someone else's hand* SPAIN

11   *A skunk smells its own hole first*   USA

12   *Beware of old streets and new inns*   GERMANY

13   *Better keep under an old hedge than creep under a new furze-bush*   ENGLAND

14   *Never follow a beast into its lair*   SOUTH AFRICA

15   *Insects do not nest in a busy door-hinge*   CHINA

16   *Every cabin has its mosquito*   JAMAICA

17   *Two crocodiles don't live in one pond*   GAMBIA

18   *An artist lives everywhere*   ENGLAND

19   *A sly rabbit will have three openings to its den*   CHINA

20   *Those who wish to live at Rome must not quarrel with the pope*   FRANCE

21   *Goats cannot live in a herd of leopards*   MALI

22   *All hillbillies don't live in the hills*   CANADA

23   *A full cabin is better than an empty castle*   IRELAND

24   *A chattering bird builds no nest*   CAMEROON

25   *It is a cunning mouse which nests in the cat's ear* ENGLAND

26   *You cannot prevent the birds of sadness from flying over*

your head, but you can prevent them from nesting in your hair CHINA

27   *A clever bird builds its nest with other birds' feathers*
ZIMBABWE

28   *When rats infest the palace a lame cat is better than the swiftest horse* CHINA

29   *You can't make a cheap palace* USA

30   *In one stable there may be a steed and an ass* BELGIUM

66   HOUSES

1   *In every house there are always cobwebs* SERBIA

2   *A word flies away like a sparrow and returns to the house like a crow* GERMANY

3   *The clock must be the master in the house* SWEDEN

4   *When the house is built the carpenter is forgotten* INDIA

5   *A quarrel in a neighbouring house is refreshing* INDIA

6   *Little houses have fat mice* TANZANIA

7   *A book holds a house of gold* CHINA

8   *When the bee comes to your house, let her have beer; you may want to visit the bee's house some day*
REPUBLIC OF CONGO

9   *Woe to the house where there is no chiding* ENGLAND

10   *A house is not built on earth, but on a woman*   SERBIA

11   *Look the other way when the girl in the tea-house smiles*
     JAPAN

12   *A little dog is really brave in front of his master's house*
     HAITI

13   *Those who haven't seen a church bow before a fireplace*
     POLAND

14   *It is in vain to look for yesterday's fish in the house of the otter*   INDIA

15   *A long beard does not prevent a house going to bed hungry*   CAMEROON

16   *The only insurance against fire is to have two houses*
     NIGERIA

17   *If you are building a house and a nail breaks, do you stop building or do you change the nail?*
     RWANDA AND BURUNDI

18   *The house with an old grandparent harbours a jewel*
     CHINA

19   *An old broom still sweeps the room*   ESTONIA

20   *People who live in glass houses shouldn't throw stones*
     ENGLAND

21   *Those who live in the attic know where the roof leaks*
     NIGERIA

22   *Do not jump high under a low ceiling*   CZECH REPUBLIC

23   *Rain does not fall only on one roof*   CAMEROON

24 *When it rains, the roof always drips the same way*
LIBERIA

25 *Small termites collapse the roof* ETHIOPIA

26 *Communities begin by building their kitchen* FRANCE

27 *It is no use standing with an open mouth in front of an
oven* DENMARK

28 *Insects do not nest in a busy door-hinge* CHINA

29 *Sweep off your own back porch first* USA

30 *Only the sweep knows what is up the chimney* ITALY

31 *Every chimney makes its own smoke* ITALY

67 DOORS – WINDOWS – KEYS

1 *They must stoop who have a low door* SCOTLAND

2 *A door must either be open or shut* FRANCE

3 *Teachers open the door; you enter by yourself* CHINA

4 *When one door shuts, another opens* SCOTLAND

5 *Never bolt your door with a boiled carrot* IRELAND

6 *Shut your door in such a way that you can open it again*
DENMARK

7 *Why seek the key of an open door?* INDIA

8 *Let everyone sweep before their own door* GERMANY

9 *You must go behind the door to mend old breeches*
ENGLAND

10 *There's a puddle at every door, and before some doors there are two* SCOTLAND

11 *On going into a church leave the world behind the door* SPAIN

12 *A hole here and there is not the same as a window* KENYA

13 *It is no use applying eye-medicine from a two-storey window* JAPAN

14 *Don't put all your goods in your shop window* USA

15 *'If I rest, I rust', says the key* GERMANY

16 *The used key is always bright* ENGLAND

17 *Those who would enter paradise must have a good key* ENGLAND

18 *Beware of the door which has several keys* INDIA

19 *All the keys in the land do not hang from one girdle* SCOTLAND

20 *The key that opens is also the key that locks* REPUBLIC OF CONGO

68 GUESTS

1 *Seven days is the length of a guest's life* MYANMAR

2 *A guest and a fish after three days are poison* FRANCE

3 *Let the guests at table be three or four – at the most five*
   GREECE

4 *Children regard their father's guest as a slave*
   REPUBLIC OF CONGO

5 *Aching teeth are ill tenants* ENGLAND

6 *The later in the evening, the nicer the people*
   NETHERLANDS

69 ABSENT – PRESENT

1 *Absence makes the heart grow fonder* ENGLAND

2 *You cannot shave a man's head in his absence* NIGERIA

3 *The absent get farther off every day* JAPAN

4 *The absent always bear the blame* NETHERLANDS

5 *Whose presence does no good, their absence does no harm*
   ENGLAND

6 *Easy come, easy go* ENGLAND

7 *Away from the battle all are soldiers* GERMANY

8 *An apple a day keeps the doctor away* ENGLAND

9 *Take away the wife of a strong man only when he is out*
UGANDA

10 *Time to catch bears is when they're out* USA

11 *Here today and gone tomorrow* ENGLAND

12 *Present to the eye, present to the mind* CHINA

13 *While the cat's away, the mice will play* ENGLAND

14 *A proverb characterizes nations, but must first dwell among them* SWITZERLAND

70 BAGS – SACKS

1 *Don't rely on the label of the bag* FRANCE

2 *An empty bag cannot stand upright* ENGLAND

3 *At the bottom of the bag one finds the bill*
NETHERLANDS

4 *It is folly to put flour into a bag facing the wind*
GERMANY

5 *After the game the king goes into the sack like the pawn*
ITALY

6 *If you look in a chief's bag you will always find something* UGANDA

7 *That which goes last into the sack comes out first*
SWEDEN

8   *The string of our sack of patience is generally tied with a slip knot*   JAPAN

9   *An empty sack can't stand, nor a dead cat walk*
    IRELAND

71   BARRELS – CASKS

1   *Never argue with someone who buys ink by the barrel*
    CHINA

2   *One rotten apple spoils the whole barrel*   ENGLAND

3   *Two barrels of tears will not heal a bruise*   CHINA

4   *A sip at a time empties the cask*   NORWAY

5   *The fuller the cask, the duller its sound*   GERMANY

6   *A cask of wine works more miracles than a church full of saints*   ITALY

72   BASKETS

1   *A pretty basket does not prevent worries*
    REPUBLIC OF CONGO

2   *Those who change their trade make soup in a basket*
    ENGLAND

3   *The basket that has two handles can be carried by two*
    EGYPT

4   *A basket-maker who makes one basket makes a hundred*
BRAZIL

5   *A basket with its bottom burst is useless*   NIGERIA

6   *Do not fill your basket with useless shells of coconuts*
KENYA

7   *Even the bottom of a basket finds something to hold*
MADAGASCAR

8   *Don't put all your eggs in one basket*   ENGLAND

9   *Better a handful of bees than a basketful of flies*
MOROCCO

73   BOTTLES – CANS

1   *The sweeter the perfume, the uglier the flies which gather round the bottle*   CHINA

2   *You can't look into a bottle with both eyes*   TOGO

3   *The one who has put an egg into a bottle can easily take it out*   NIGERIA

4   *Save your bottles; it may rain whiskey*   USA

5   *Those who want the last drop out of the can get the lid on their nose*   NETHERLANDS

6   *Every alley has its own tin can*   USA

74 CUPS – GLASSES

1   *There's many a slip between cup and lip*   ENGLAND

2   *The fuller the cup, the sooner the spill*   CHINA

3   *A full cup must be carried steadily*   ENGLAND

4   *Three glasses of wine drive away the evil spirits, but with the fourth they return*   GERMANY

5   *A broken glass can't be hurt*   ENGLAND

6   *You don't have to buy a dairy just because you want a glass of milk*   USA

75 DISHES – PLATES

1   *One bird in the dish is better than a hundred in the air* GERMANY

2   *All's lost that's put in a broken dish*   SCOTLAND

3   *Enjoy your ice-cream while it's on your plate*   USA

4   *Every plate that is made breaks*   AFGHANISTAN

5   *It is with its own face that the plate receives the soup* NIGERIA

6   *It's a poor crust that can't grease its own plate*   USA

7   *Those who come too late find the platter turned over* NETHERLANDS

76 POTS – BOWLS – JUGS

1 *Beauty does not make the pot boil*   IRELAND

2 *Flies never alight on boiling pots*   UKRAINE

3 *A little drop of water silences a boiling pot*   GERMANY

4 *The devil makes pots, but not always lids*
ITALY: SARDINIA

5 *I can tell by my own pot how the others are boiling*
FRANCE

6 *When the beans get too thick, the pot burns*   USA

7 *A watched pot never boils*   ENGLAND

8 *It is the pot that boils, but the dish gets the credit*
CAMEROON

9 *Those who were surprised by a turtle are surprised by a pot cover*   KOREA

10 *The sun cannot shine into an inverted bowl*   CHINA

11 *The basin must hold what the cauldron cooks*   ESTONIA

12 *While it rains, fill the jar*   TURKEY

13 *Whether the stone bumps the jug, or the jug bumps the stone, it is bad for the jug*   USA

* * * * * * * * * * * * * * * * * * *

8 COUNTRY VARIATIONS – ARTEFACTS

Vehicles, games, money, musical instruments, and other
artefacts often give a proverb some local colouring.

> *Every day cannot be a feast of lanterns* (CHINA)
> *Don't hold the dime so near your eye that you can't see the dollar*
> (USA)
> *If you don't toot your own horn, nobody else will* (USA)
> *A love-letter sometimes costs more than a three-cent stamp* (USA)
> *Good nature is stronger than tomahawks* (USA)
> *Learn to handle a writing-brush, and you'll never handle a*
> *begging-bowl* (CHINA)
> *Those who do not know how to squander their money – buy*
> *some porcelain and drop it* (NETHERLANDS)
> *In chess the fools are nearest the kings* (FRANCE)
> *Carrying-poles which bend easily do not break* (CHINA)
> *A canoe is paddled on both sides* (NIGERIA)
> *If all get into the palanquin, who will be the bearers?* (INDIA)
> *The wife of the amber-turner wears pearls of glass* (IRAN)
> *An untouched drum does not speak* (LIBERIA)
> *Straps come from the same leather* (ARGENTINA)
> *The woman who sells fans often shades her eyes with her hands* (CHINA)
> *Beauty is an empty calabash* (CAMEROON)
> *Those who cannot build the dyke should hand over the land*
> (NETHERLANDS)

SEE ALSO Country variations – climate (p. 90); animals
(p. 302); plants (p. 323); beliefs and behaviour (p. 562)

* * * * * * * * * * * * * * * * * * *

77 SPOONS – LADLES

1 *What's the good of a spoon after the meal is over?*
LATVIA

2 *God gives the wideness of the mouth according to the bigness of the spoon*   POLAND

3 *A dry spoon scratches the mouth*   RUSSIA

4 *The spoon is prized when the soup is being eaten*
CZECH REPUBLIC

5 *Food tastes best when one eats it with one's own spoon*
DENMARK

6 *If in the pot, it will come into the spoon*   INDIA

7 *Without fingers the hand would be a spoon*   SENEGAL

8 *Until the soup boils over, the ladle has no value*
TURKEY

9 *When is a cook's ladle hungry or a beer jug thirsty?*
ESTONIA

78 WELLS

1 *Painting the pump will not clean out the well*   ENGLAND

2 *Dig a well before you are thirsty*   CHINA

3 *Cast no dirt into the well that has given you water*
ENGLAND

4   *Well water does not invade river water*   CHINA

5   *If the bucket has been long in the well, it ought to come out with water*   NIGERIA

6   *A well without a bucket is no good*   USA

79 OTHER CONTAINERS

1   *Sharp acids corrode their own containers*   ALBANIA

2   *Precious ointments are put in small boxes*   FRANCE

3   *A coconut shell full of water is a sea to an ant*
    ZANZIBAR

4   *Beauty is an empty calabash*   CAMEROON

5   *A beautiful maiden is a devil's pocket*   PHILIPPINES

6   *Even in the sheath the knife must be sharp*   FINLAND

7   *Two swords cannot be kept in one sheath*   INDIA

8   *The pig dreams of his trough*   FINLAND

9   *In the choicest vase are found the ugliest cracks*   CHINA

80 LOADS

1   *There is no light burden on a long road*   CHINA

2   *On a level road a small stone upsets the cartload*
    ESTONIA

3 *If you want to be acquainted with the past and the present, you must read five cartloads of books*   CHINA

4 *It takes little effort to watch someone carry a load*   CHINA

5 *It is easier to throw the load off the cart than to put it on*   CZECH REPUBLIC

6 *Not the load, but the overload kills*   SPAIN

7 *Let every pedlar carry his own pack*   GERMANY

8 *The label is bigger than the package*   GREECE

9 *Dynamite comes in small packages*   USA

81   BIG SIZE

1 *Big tree but no shade*   PHILIPPINES

2 *A fly before one's own eye is bigger than an elephant in the next field*   CHINA

3 *A big nose never spoiled a handsome face*   FRANCE

4 *The big toe never does the ear any harm*   NIGERIA

5 *A big head, a big headache*   BULGARIA

6 *Those who jump over a big stone often stumble over a pebble*   NETHERLANDS

7 *The cork is always bigger than the mouth of the bottle*   ESTONIA

8   *The sea is made bigger even by one drop*   RUSSIA

9   *The label is bigger than the package*   GREECE

10   *The feathers make the fowl big*   CÔTE D'IVOIRE

11   *A big fish is caught with big bait*   SIERRA LEONE

12   *Never marry a woman who has bigger feet than you*
        MOZAMBIQUE

13   *When the going is rough, big potatoes come to the top*
        USA

14   *Stretch your legs according to the length of your
        bedspread*   LIBYA

15   *God gives the wideness of the mouth according to the
        bigness of the spoon*   POLAND

16   *The mouse is not crushed under the haystack*
        SCOTLAND

17   *Little houses have fat mice*   TANZANIA

18   *Those who have a great nose think everyone speaks of it*
        SCOTLAND

19   *The longer the spoke, the greater the tire*   USA

20   *Little crows have the largest beaks*   BELGIUM

21   *The more naked the jackal the larger the tail*
        SOUTH AFRICA

22   *Your fingers can't be of the same length*   CHINA

23   *The cobra knows its length*   NAMIBIA

24   *It ain't over till the fat lady sings*   USA

82   LITTLE SIZE

1   *Every little bird has a long beak*   NAMIBIA

2   *A little spark shines in the dark*   FRANCE

3   *A little dog is really brave in front of his master's house*
HAITI

4   *A little wood will heat a little oven*   ENGLAND

5   *Little kettles soon boil over*   ESTONIA

6   *Proverbs are little gospels*   SPAIN

7   *Precious ointments are put in small boxes*   FRANCE

8   *On a level road a small stone upsets the cartload*
ESTONIA

9   *Dynamite comes in small packages*   USA

10   *Small termites collapse the roof*   ETHIOPIA

83   BIG v LITTLE

1   *A big crop is best, but a little crop will do*   SCOTLAND

2   *Big hammers don't play with little nails*   GERMANY

3   *The biggest help is help, and even the smallest help is help*
IRELAND

4   *A viper is a viper, whether big or small*   SLOVENIA

5   *Big oaks from little acorns grow*   ENGLAND

6   *Law is a spider's web; big flies break through but the little ones are caught*   HUNGARY

7   *Little crows have the largest beaks*   BELGIUM

8   *Little houses have fat mice*   TANZANIA

9   *The smaller the lizard, the greater its hope of becoming a crocodile*   ETHIOPIA

10   *A little nest is warmer than a big nest*   IRELAND

11   *Those who do not wish little things do not deserve big things*   BELGIUM

12   *The more you squeeze a nettle the less it stings*
      GERMANY

13   *You must take the little potato with the big potato*
      IRELAND

84 DISTANCE

1   *The broth from a distance grows cool on the road*
      KENYA

2   *Thin ice and thick ice look the same from a distance*
      USA

3   *Better do a good deed near at home than go far away to burn incense*   CHINA

4   *The apple does not fall far from the apple-tree*   ALBANIA

5   *Far waters cannot quench near fires*   CHINA

6   *The seagull sees furthest who flies highest*   FRANCE

7   *The absent get farther off every day*   JAPAN

8   *It is easy to lie about a far-off country*   ETHIOPIA

9   *One must draw back in order to leap further*   FRANCE

10   *The sigh goes further than the shout*   SCOTLAND

11   *Pride only goes the length one can spit*
     REPUBLIC OF CONGO

12   *A bad word whispered will echo a hundred miles*
     CHINA

13   *Every mile is two in winter*   ENGLAND

14   *Don't believe those who come from afar, but those who return from it*   SPAIN

15   *Don't run too far; you will have to come back the same distance*   FRANCE

16   *Those who have to go ten miles must regard nine as only halfway*   GERMANY

17   *A rich person's sickness and a poor person's pancake are smelt a long way off*   BELGIUM

85 NEARNESS

1 *Don't snuff the light too close, or you will burn your fingers* DENMARK

2 *The world is dark an inch ahead* JAPAN

3 *The higher the castle the nearer to the lightning* RUSSIA

4 *Eve is nearer to us than Adam* SERBIA

5 *In chess the fools are nearest the kings* FRANCE

6 *Far waters cannot quench near fires* CHINA

7 *Better do a good deed near at home than go far away to burn incense* CHINA

8 *Don't hold the dime so near your eye that you can't see the dollar* USA

9 *Pretty near ain't quite* USA

10 *The nearer the bone, the sweeter the meat* ENGLAND

11 *A quarrel in a neighbouring house is refreshing* INDIA

12 *They that get the next best are not ill off* SCOTLAND

13 *Cleanliness is next to godliness* ENGLAND

14 *People scratch where they can reach* KENYA

15 *A fly before one's own eye is bigger than an elephant in the next field* CHINA

16 *Sweetest the grass next to the ground* WALES

86 LONG – SHORT

1   *Among the ten fingers there are long and short*   CHINA

2   *A long beard does not prevent a house going to bed hungry*   CAMEROON

3   *Every little bird has a long beak*   NAMIBIA

4   *Between two points one cannot draw more than one straight line*
          DENMARK

5   *There is bound to be a knot in a very long string*   KENYA

6   *The longer the spoke, the greater the tire*   USA

7   *However long the procession, it always returns to the church*   PHILIPPINES

8   *A rich person's sickness and a poor person's pancake are smelt a long way off*   BELGIUM

9   *There is no light burden on a long road*   CHINA

10   *One must measure to know which is longer*   KOREA

11   *If the string is long the kite will fly high*   CHINA

12   *Stretch your legs according to the length of your bedspread*   LIBYA

13   *Short hair is soon brushed*   GERMANY

14   *Long hair – short brains*   MONTENEGRO

87 MIDDLE – ENDS

1   'Virtue in the middle,' said the devil as he sat between
    two lawyers   NORWAY

2   In the middle of the river do not change horses   PERU

3   From the midst of the wood the hatchet gets its handle
    GERMANY

4   When the bed is small lie in the centre   SPAIN

5   No needle is sharp at both ends   CHINA

6   Give to no one the end of the thread   TURKEY

7   If a string has one end, then it has another end   CHINA

8   When you pick up a stick at one end, you also pick up the
    other end   USA

9   Don't burn your candle at both ends   ENGLAND

10 You can't expect both ends of a sugar cane to be as sweet
    CHINA

88 WIDE – NARROW

1   Wider will the cow-dung be for trampling on it   WALES

2   Although the river is broad there are times when boats
    collide   CHINA

3   Not even Apollo keeps his bow always at full stretch
    LATIN

4   *Thin ice and thick ice look the same from a distance*
     USA

5   *The autumn chill is the first thing felt by a thin person*
     CHINA

6   *Tangled hair needs a wide comb*   SERBIA

7   *God gives the wideness of the mouth according to the bigness of the spoon*   POLAND

8   *The cow which has the loudest bellowing has the slenderest tail*   IRELAND

9   *The thinnest bread finds itself married to bread*
     ALGERIA

10   *Only thin dogs become wild*   MADAGASCAR

89   HAIRS – THREADS

1   *Abundance will make cotton pull a stone*   NIGERIA

2   *Even a hair has a shadow*   CZECH REPUBLIC

3   *Even in the freshest of milk you will still find hairs*
     MALI

4   *The third strand makes the cable*   NETHERLANDS

5   *Give to no one the end of the thread*   TURKEY

6   *A hot needle burns the thread*   CÔTE D'IVOIRE

7   *A cloth is not woven from a single thread*   CHINA

* * * * * * * * * * * * * * * * * * *

9 SUCCINCTNESS

The succinctness of a proverb derives from a number of features – length of sentence, length of word, and structural balance.

Proverbs are typically short: the average number of words per proverb in this collection is 8.7. There are several of just four words:

> *Still waters run deep.*
> *Waste not, want not.*

And sometimes fewer:

> *Pigs might fly.*
> *Money talks.*

Most English proverbs contain four main units of sense – a trend which is also found in the translated items:

> *There's **many** a **slip** between **cup** and **lip**.*
> ***Speech** is **silver**; **silence** is **golden**.*
> *A **stitch** in **time saves nine**.*
> *A **rolling stone gathers** no **moss**.*
> *What you **lose** on the **swings** you **gain** on the **roundabouts**.*
> *That **miller** is **honest** who has **hair** on his **teeth**.*

There is a heavy reliance on monosyllabic words:

> *If the shoe fits, wear it.*
> *A black hen can lay a white egg.*
> *Those who bring good news knock hard.*

Words of two or three syllables are common enough, but it is very unusual to find longer words:

Procrastination is the thief of time.
Familiarity breeds contempt.

Longer proverbs usually break down into a series of short components with parallel structure:

If you want one year of prosperity, grow grain. If you want ten years of prosperity, grow trees. If you want a hundred years of prosperity, grow people.
The best time to plant a tree was twenty years ago; the second-best time is now.

* * * * * * * * * * * * * * * * * *

8   *The first thread is not part of the yarn*   IRELAND

9   *Where the needle goes the thread must follow*   POLAND

10   *One thread for the needle, one love for the heart*   SUDAN

11   *A needle cannot hold two threads or a mind two thoughts*
ETHIOPIA

90 HIGH – LOW

1   *Ambition and fleas jump high*   GERMANY

2   *If the string is long the kite will fly high*   CHINA

3   *There is no slope above without a slope below*   SPAIN

4   *Only when all contribute their firewood can they build up a good fire*   CHINA

5   *The higher the castle the nearer to the lightning*   RUSSIA

6   *Do not jump high under a low ceiling*   CZECH REPUBLIC

7   *The seagull sees furthest who flies highest*   FRANCE

8   *Do not lift the club too high, it may fall on your head*   FINLAND

9   *You won't help shoots grow by pulling them up higher*   CHINA

10   *When you sweep the stairs, you start at the top*   GERMANY

11   *A frog beneath a coconut shell believes there is no other world*   MALAYSIA

12   *Even if water flows in all directions, the sand will remain at the bottom*   GEORGIA

13   *Those who lie on the ground have no place from which to fall*   LATIN

14   *If you bow at all, bow low*   CHINA

15   *A low stump upsets the sledge*   FINLAND

16   *Falling hurts least those who fly low*   CHINA

17   *They must stoop who have a low door*   SCOTLAND

18   *Everyone leaps the dyke where it's lowest*   SCOTLAND

19   *Strawberries ripen sooner in a low wood than in a high one*   ESTONIA

20   *Who sits under a pear-tree will eat pears*   BULGARIA

21   *Under trees it rains twice*   SWITZERLAND

22   *Never look an auto bargain under the hood*   USA

23   *The mouse is not crushed under the haystack* SCOTLAND

24   *Not every abyss has a parapet*   GERMANY

25   *When in love, a cliff becomes a meadow*   ETHIOPIA

91   DEPTH

1   *Even deep water-holes may get dry*   SOUTH AFRICA

2   *Only those who have travelled the road know where the holes are deep*   CHINA

3   *Still waters run deep*   ENGLAND

4   *When you want to test the depth of a stream, don't use both feet*   CHINA

5   *Only a fool tests the depth of the water with both feet* NAMIBIA

6   *The water is shallowest where it babbles*   WALES

7   *The dragon in shallow water becomes the butt of shrimps*
     CHINA

8   *Thin ice and thick ice look the same from a distance*
     USA

9   *People carrying elephant's flesh on their head should not look for crickets underground*   NIGERIA

10   *Every flood will have an ebb*   SCOTLAND

92 HILLS – MOUNTAINS

1   *There is no hill without a slope*   WALES

2   *The more one walks the more hills one sees*   FINLAND

3   *There must be a valley between two hills*   GERMANY

4   *A horse never goes straight up a hill*   USA

5   *Anyone may laugh on a hillside*   SCOTLAND

6   *All hillbillies don't live in the hills*   CANADA

7   *The highest hill is usually covered with clouds*
     SCOTLAND

8   *Those who think they are building a mound may only in reality be digging a pit*   CHINA

9   *Mediocrity is climbing molehills without sweating*
     ICELAND

10   *To fill a ditch a mound must come down*   ARMENIA

11   *If you don't scale the mountain, you can't see the plain*
     CHINA

12   *Mountains cannot meet, people can*   BULGARIA

13   *Standing on top of one mountain, the other mountain is
     higher*   CHINA

14   *Even if you cannot climb the mountain do not remain in
     the valley*   GERMANY

15   *There are many paths to the top of the mountain – but
     the view is always the same*   CHINA

16   *The boat of affection ascends even mountains*
     BANGLADESH

17   *Rein in the horse at the edge of the cliff*   CHINA

18   *It is no use trying to tug the glacier backwards*   CHINA

93 TOP – BOTTOM

1   *In rivers and bad government, the lightest things swim at
    the top*   USA

2   *There are many paths to the top of the mountain – but
    the view is always the same*   CHINA

3   *When the going is rough, big potatoes come to the top*
    USA

4   *At the bottom of the bag one finds the bill*
NETHERLANDS

5   *A basket with its bottom burst is useless*   NIGERIA

6   *Even the bottom of a basket finds something to hold*
MADAGASCAR

7   *One pebble doesn't make a floor*   NIGERIA

8   *If you try to sit on two chairs, you'll sit on the floor*   USA

9   *At the foot of the lighthouse it is dark*   JAPAN

94 HOLDING

1   *Everything has two handles*   GREECE

2   *From the midst of the wood the hatchet gets its handle*
GERMANY

3   *The basket that has two handles can be carried by two*
EGYPT

4   *A handleless axe does not scare the forest*   BULGARIA

5   *You cannot hold two water melons in one hand*   IRAN

6   *A small bed will not hold two persons*   NIGERIA

7   *A needle cannot hold two threads or a mind two thoughts*
ETHIOPIA

8   *Whoever holds the ladder is as bad as the thief*
GERMANY

9   *When you pick up a stick at one end, you also pick up the other end*   USA

10   *When you have no companion, consult your walking-stick*   ALBANIA

95   SUPPORT

1   *Failures are the pillars of success*   WALES

2   *The eyes close in sleep, but the pillow remains awake*   MALAYSIA

3   *It is not common for hens to have pillows*   SCOTLAND

4   *The rod that will hang him is still growing*   IRELAND

5   *All the keys in the land do not hang from one girdle*   SCOTLAND

6   *Some hang out more than they wash*   USA

7   *Bread is the staff of life, but the pudding makes a good crutch*   SCOTLAND

8   *Promise is a bridge of words, unsafe to walk across*   GERMANY

96   TABLES – CHAIRS

1   *When the cat's not home, the mice jump on the table*   NETHERLANDS

2   *You can't eat a square meal off a round table* USA

3   *At a round table every seat is first* GERMANY

4   *If you try to sit on two chairs, you'll sit on the floor* USA

5   *Those who have free seats at a play hiss first* CHINA

6   *Don't be breaking your shin on a stool that's not in your way* IRELAND

7   *One sits best on one's own bench* NORWAY

8   *A good buttock finds a bench for itself* ESTONIA

97 UPRIGHT – FALLING

1   *An empty bag cannot stand upright* ENGLAND

2   *An empty sack can't stand, nor a dead cat walk*
     IRELAND

3   *One never falls but on the side towards which one leans*
     FRANCE

4   *Those who place their ladder too steeply will easily fall backwards* CZECH REPUBLIC

5   *A low stump upsets the sledge* FINLAND

6   *On a level road a small stone upsets the cartload*
     ESTONIA

7   *There's no such thing as a horse that can't be rode or a cowboy that can't be throwed* USA

98 OUTSIDE – INSIDE

1 *Don't snap your fingers at the dogs before you are outside the village* FRANCE

2 *A gardener's flirtations take place outside the garden* AFGHANISTAN

3 *The candle is put into the lantern and the moth is left outside fluttering* IRAN

4 *There's more room outside than inside* CANADA

5 *The shell is needed till the bird is hatched* RUSSIA

6 *Do not fill your basket with useless shells of coconuts* KENYA

7 *The beauty of the corn cob is apparent on the inside only* KENYA

8 *When hunger gets inside you, nothing else can* NIGERIA

9 *The sun cannot shine into an inverted bowl* CHINA

10 *Those who come too late find the platter turned over* NETHERLANDS

11 *A frog beneath a coconut shell believes there is no other world* MALAYSIA

12 *There's more room outside than inside* CANADA

99 COVERING

1 *The highest hill is usually covered with clouds*
SCOTLAND

2 *Every cloud has a silver lining* ENGLAND

3 *If one finger is gashed, all the fingers are covered with blood* REPUBLIC OF CONGO

4 *If you go to the wedding you cover up the sledge*
ESTONIA

5 *The one who was surprised by a turtle is surprised by a pot cover* KOREA

6 *One generation plants the trees; another gets the shade*
CHINA

7 *Big tree but no shade* PHILIPPINES

8 *The woman who sells fans often shades her eyes with her hands* CHINA

9 *Send your charity abroad wrapped in blankets*
ENGLAND

10 *That which is said at table should be wrapped up in the tablecloth* ITALY

11 *Paper can't wrap up a fire* CHINA

100 CLOTHING

1   *Even a silk shirt only clothes a naked body*   GERMANY

2   *Those whose mother is naked are not likely to clothe their aunt*   SUDAN

3   *New clothes have no lice*   NAMIBIA

4   *Dress slowly when you are in a hurry*   FRANCE

5   *Those who have two garments do not wear one only*   ZANZIBAR

6   *Only God helps the ill-dressed*   SPAIN

7   *People sell their rags in their own market*   EGYPT

8   *The more naked the jackal the larger the tail*   SOUTH AFRICA

9   *Clothes put on while running come off while running*   ETHIOPIA

101 BODYWEAR

1   *You must go behind the door to mend old breeches*   ENGLAND

2   *A protector is like a cloak*   HAITI

3   *The borrowed cloak never warms*   SYRIA

4   *Hunger doesn't say, 'Stale bread,' and cold doesn't say 'Old coat.'*   GEORGIA

5   *When someone's coat is threadbare, it is easy to pick a hole in it* ENGLAND

6   *Cut your coat according to your cloth* ENGLAND

7   *One spot spots the whole dress* BELGIUM

8   *The forest is the poor person's fur-coat* ESTONIA

9   *A padded jacket is an acceptable gift, even in summer* JAPAN

10   *Raindrops can't tell broadcloth from jeans* USA

11   *A cat with mittens won't catch mice* SCOTLAND

12   *Keep your broken arm inside your sleeve* CHINA

13   *Habit is a shirt that we wear till death* RUSSIA

14   *Even a silk shirt only clothes a naked body* GERMANY

15   *Never trust a fellow that wears a suit* USA

16   *You can't catch trout with dry trousers* USA

17   *Money cries in one's pocket* ESTONIA

18   *Who has God for his friend has all the saints in his pocket* ITALY

19   *A shroud has no pockets* SCOTLAND

20   *Those who have an egg in their pocket do not dance* GABON

21   *Everyone buckles their belt their own way* SCOTLAND

22   *All the keys in the land do not hang from one girdle* SCOTLAND

23   *The wife of the amber-turner wears pearls of glass*   IRAN

102   FOOTWEAR

1   *The boot must put up with the dirt*   GERMANY

2   *The cobbler always wears the worst shoes*   FRANCE

3   *Let the cobbler stick to his last*   ENGLAND

4   *When walking through your neighbour's melon-patch, don't tie your shoe*   CHINA

5   *A handsome shoe often pinches the feet*   FRANCE

6   *Those who wait for a dead person's shoes are in danger of going barefoot*   FRANCE

7   *Walk as your shoes will let you*   SCOTLAND

8   *Better a crease in the shoe than a blister on the toe*
     ESTONIA

9   *One cannot shoe a running horse*   NETHERLANDS

10   *You can get used to anything except a rock in your shoe*
     USA

11   *If the shoe fits, wear it*   ENGLAND

12   *Those who go barefoot aren't pinched by their shoes*
     GERMANY

13   *Even a young foot finds ease in an old slipper*
     SCOTLAND

103 HEADWEAR

1   *Why should someone without a head want a hat?*
     CHILE

2   *A head without a brain has no need of a hat*   SPAIN

3   *A hat is not made for one shower*   ENGLAND

4   *A man's hat in his hand never did him any harm*
     SCOTLAND

5   *The circumstances of people will appear from the
     condition of their hat*   SRI LANKA

6   *If the cap fits, wear it*   ENGLAND

104 WEAVING

1   *The loom that's awry is best handled patiently*
     SCOTLAND

2   *Everyone must spin on their own spinning wheel*
     ESTONIA

3   *A cloth is not woven from a single thread*   CHINA

4   *Don't stand by the water and long for fish; go home and
     weave a net*   CHINA

5   *The spider does not weave its web for one fly*   SLOVENIA

6   *Law is a spider's web; big flies break through but the little
     ones are caught*   HUNGARY

7   *If it weren't for the wind the spiders would web the sky*
    SERBIA

8   *Stretch your legs according to the length of your*
    bedspread   LIBYA

9   *Send your charity abroad wrapped in blankets*
    ENGLAND

10 *If you pick the fluff from a blanket it comes to pieces*
    INDIA

11 *A blanket becomes heavier as it becomes wetter*   INDIA

12 *That which is said at table should be wrapped up in the*
    tablecloth   ITALY

105 BETWEEN

1   *Between two points one cannot draw more than one*
    straight line   DENMARK

2   *'Virtue in the middle,' said the devil as he sat between*
    two lawyers   NORWAY

3   *There must be a valley between two hills*   GERMANY

4   *It is hard to swim between two stretches of bad water*
    NETHERLANDS

5   *There's many a slip between cup and lip*   ENGLAND

106 WALLS

1 *Better a neighbour over the wall than a brother over the sea* ALBANIA

2 *Courteous asking breaks even city walls* UKRAINE

3 *One family builds the wall; two families enjoy it* CHINA

4 *Walls hear without warnings* ENGLAND

5 *Silent worms bore holes in the wall* JAPAN

6 *A dog in desperation will leap over a wall* CHINA

7 *Someone who stands behind a wall can see nothing else* JAPAN

8 *Do not tear down the east wall to repair the west* CHINA

9 *To get out a rusty nail you must take away a piece of the wall* MALTA

107 EDGES

1 *Rein in the horse at the edge of the cliff* CHINA

2 *The grub eats round the edges of the leaves* NEW ZEALAND

3 *It is easy to hurt yourself on a stone that has sharp corners* KOREA

4 *A bird with a beautiful plumage doesn't sit in the corner* CAMEROON

* * * * * * * * * * * * * * * * * *

10 LOCAL WORDS

Proverbs are not known for their lexical inventiveness. They use everyday words and display very few unusual word coinages. If we encounter unfamiliar vocabulary, it is usually because the words are archaic, are from a local dialect, or relate to a culture that has disappeared.

> *Those who will have a cake out of the wheat must tarry the grinding.* (*tarry* = wait for)
> *A burnt bairn dreads the fire.* (Scotland and Northern England)
> *A quick sixpence is better than a slow shilling.* (old money system)

Different international dialects of English sometimes make their presence felt. The distinctive identity of American English can be heard in these examples from the present collection:

> *No matter how you slice it, it's still baloney.*
> *Never look an auto bargain under the hood.*
> *Puttin' feathers on a buzzard won't make it no eagle.*
> *Don't shuck your corn till the hogs come home.*
> *Don't holler before you're hurt.*
> *Every train has a caboose.*

SEE ALSO Nonstandard language (p. 396)

* * * * * * * * * * * * * * * * * *

5   *The dogs will go into the corner that's open*   SCOTLAND

6   *All countries are frontiers*   SOUTH AFRICA

7   *One cannot ski so softly that the traces cannot be seen*
    FINLAND

8   *The laden almond-tree by the wayside is sure to be bitter*
    JAPAN

108   ENCLOSURES

1   *Silence is a fence round wisdom*   GERMANY

2   *There is no fence that does not let the wind through*
    CHINA

3   *Do not protect yourself by a fence, but by your friends*
    CZECH REPUBLIC

4   *Everyone pushes a falling fence*   CHINA

5   *The grass always looks greener on the other side of the fence*   ENGLAND

6   *If you want to catch a wild horse, find a tight corral*
    HAITI

7   *Everyone leaps the dyke where it's lowest*   SCOTLAND

8   *A fly before one's own eye is bigger than an elephant in the next field*   CHINA

9   *The sun shines on both sides of the hedge*   ENGLAND

10   *Those who plant a hedge round their garden invite it to be jumped*   RUSSIA

11   *Love your neighbour, yet pull not down your hedge*   ENGLAND

12   *There is no limit to looking upward*   JAPAN

109 IN FRONT – BEHIND

1   *To know the road ahead, ask those coming back*   CHINA

2   *The world is dark an inch ahead*   JAPAN

3   *Let everyone sweep before their own door*   GERMANY

4   *There's a puddle at every door, and before some doors there are two*   SCOTLAND

5   *Don't put the cart before the horse*   ENGLAND

6   *Those who haven't seen a church bow before a fireplace*   POLAND

7   *Advice should be viewed from behind and not from in front*   SWEDEN

8   *It is no use standing with an open mouth in front of an oven*   DENMARK

9   *It is better to be once in the church sleigh than always in the back runners*   FINLAND

10   *If the swing goes forward it will go backward too*   SRI LANKA

11 *When two ride on one horse one must sit behind*
ENGLAND

12 *Someone who stands behind a wall can see nothing else*
JAPAN

13 *Leave a good name behind in case you return*   KENYA

14 *You must go behind the door to mend old breeches*
ENGLAND

15 *On going into a church leave the world behind the door*
SPAIN

16 *The hindermost ox also reaches the kraal*
SOUTH AFRICA

110 SIDES

1 *The reverse side has its reverse side*   JAPAN

2 *The sun shines on both sides of the hedge*   ENGLAND

3 *You can only go halfway into the darkest forest; then you are coming out the other side*   CHINA

4 *The water is the same on both sides of the boat*
FINLAND

5 *There is no bridge without a place the other side of it*
WALES

6 *One never falls but on the side towards which one leans*
FRANCE

7   *The other side of the road always looks cleanest*
    ENGLAND

8   *A canoe is paddled on both sides*   NIGERIA

9   *The grass always looks greener on the other side of the
    fence*   ENGLAND

10 *It is folly to put flour into a bag facing the wind*
    GERMANY

11 *Practice with the left hand while the right hand is still
    there*   LIBERIA

12 *Someone without a friend is like the right hand without
    the left*   BELGIUM

13 *Don't buy a left-hand monkey-wrench*   CANADA

111   BUILDING

1   *A chattering bird builds no nest*   CAMEROON

2   *One family builds the wall; two families enjoy it*   CHINA

3   *Communities begin by building their kitchen*   FRANCE

4   *To build, one must have two purses*   BELGIUM

5   *A house is not built on earth, but on a woman*   SERBIA

6   *Those who cannot build the dyke should hand over the
    land*   NETHERLANDS

7   *Those who think they are building a mound may only in
    reality be digging a pit*   CHINA

8   *When the house is built the carpenter is forgotten*   INDIA

9   *A clever bird builds its nest with other birds' feathers*
     ZIMBABWE

10   *If you are building a house and a nail breaks, do you
     stop building or do you change the nail?*
     RWANDA AND BURUNDI

11   *Rome was not built in a day*   ENGLAND

12   *You may know a carpenter by his chips*   ENGLAND

112 STRAIGHT – BENT – CROOKED

1   *Between two points one cannot draw more than one
     straight line*   DENMARK

2   *Dull scissors can't cut straight*   USA

3   *There is a time to squint, and a time to look straight*
     SCOTLAND

4   *Carrying-poles which bend easily do not break*   CHINA

5   *Those who know how to bend the fish-hook know how to
     straighten it*   TANZANIA

6   *Those who cannot cut the bread evenly cannot get on well
     with people*   CZECH REPUBLIC

7   *A crooked log makes a good fire*   FRANCE

8 *How can there be a forest without a crooked tree?*
BULGARIA

9 *Think not because the cane is bent the sugar is crooked too* MALAYSIA

10 *In crooked wood one recognizes the artist* TOGO

11 *Crooked furrows grow straight grain* CANADA

12 *One camel does not make fun of another camel's hump*
GUINEA

113 ROUNDNESS

1 *When you eat a round cake, do you begin at the centre?*
NIGERIA

2 *At a round table every seat is first* GERMANY

3 *All that is round is not a cake* LIBYA

4 *You can't eat a square meal off a round table* USA

5 *Grief and joy are a revolving wheel* INDIA

6 *If my aunt had wheels, she might be an omnibus*
NETHERLANDS

7 *Any spoke will lead the ant to the hub* USA

8 *The energy of the dung-beetle is put into rolling its ball of dung* CHINA

114 PROMINENCES

1 *The protruding nail will be pounded down*   JAPAN

2 *Little crows have the largest beaks*   BELGIUM

3 *Sparrows clean their beaks against the branch on which they sit*   ESTONIA

4 *Every little bird has a long beak*   NAMIBIA

5 *Those who are not in the habit of riding forget the spurs*
  IRELAND

6 *A low stump upsets the sledge*   FINLAND

115 HOLES

1 *If it is your own lantern, do not poke holes in the paper*
  CHINA

2 *If you find yourself in a hole, the first thing to do is stop digging*   USA

3 *Dig a well before you are thirsty*   CHINA

4 *The nail suffers as much as the hole*   NETHERLANDS

5 *God preserve us from pitch-forks, for they make three holes*   SWITZERLAND

6 *When someone's coat is threadbare, it is easy to pick a hole in it*   ENGLAND

7 *Those who think they are building a mound may only in reality be digging a pit*   CHINA

8   *If you engrave it too much it will become a hole*   INDIA

9   *Silent worms bore holes in the wall*   JAPAN

10   *Different holes have different fish*   MALAYSIA

11   *Only those who have travelled the road know where the holes are deep*   CHINA

12   *The hollow of the ear is never full*   SENEGAL

13   *The one who seeks revenge should remember to dig two graves*   CHINA

14   *Even a mole may instruct a philosopher on the art of digging*   CHINA

116   SHARP THINGS

1   *Where the needle goes the thread must follow*   POLAND

2   *No needle is sharp at both ends*   CHINA

3   *A hot needle burns the thread*   CÔTE D'IVOIRE

4   *One thread for the needle, one love for the heart*   SUDAN

5   *A needle cannot hold two threads or a mind two thoughts*   ETHIOPIA

6   *Better be stung by a nettle than pricked by a rose*   ENGLAND

7   *The more you squeeze a nettle the less it stings*   GERMANY

8   *That which is to become a good nettle must sting early*
    SWEDEN

9   *Never feed a dog with corn, nor attempt to pick your teeth*
    with a pair of scissors   CHINA

10 *Dull scissors can't cut straight*   USA

11 *Even in the sheath the knife must be sharp*   FINLAND

12 *Have a mouth as sharp as a dagger, but a heart as soft*
    as tofu   CHINA

13 *It is easy to hurt yourself on a stone that has sharp*
    corners   KOREA

14 *It takes a long time to sharpen a hammer made of wood*
    NETHERLANDS

15 *It is very difficult to beat a drum with a sickle*   NIGERIA

16 *Beware of a person's shadow and a bee's sting*
    MYANMAR

17 *Bees that have honey in their mouths have stings in their*
    tails   FRANCE

18 *If you run away from a mosquito the sharper will its*
    sting be   SLOVENIA

19 *Those who want the rose must also take the thorns*
    GERMANY

20 *Use a thorn to extract a thorn*   INDIA

117 ROUGH – SMOOTH

1   *The roughest stone becomes smooth when it is much rolled*   SWITZERLAND

2   *A dry spoon scratches the mouth*   RUSSIA

3   *Short hair is soon brushed*   GERMANY

4   *Custom is rust that mocks at every file*   BOHEMIA

5   *On a level road a small stone upsets the cartload*   ESTONIA

6   *The roughest stone becomes smooth when it is much rolled*   SWITZERLAND

7   *A smooth way makes the foot slip*   ESTONIA

8   *If you pick the fluff from a blanket it comes to pieces*   INDIA

9   *Better a crease in the shoe than a blister on the toe*   ESTONIA

10   *Crooked furrows grow straight grain*   CANADA

118 OPENING – CLOSING

1   *The cork is always bigger than the mouth of the bottle*   ESTONIA

2   *An old story does not open the ear as a new one does*   NIGERIA

* * * * * * * * * * * * * * * * * *

11 PHONETIC STRUCTURE

The memorability of a proverb is considerably enhanced by its phonetic structure, especially in its use of repeated initial sounds (alliteration) and a balanced rhythm. These features are noticeable in the proverbs of all languages, though they are not always translatable. English proverbs on the whole make relatively little use of phonetic features, so that when they do occur, they stand out.

Alliteration
Full of courtesy, full of craft.
There's crust and crumb in every loaf.

Metrical rhythm
Absence makes the heart grow fonder.
Actions speak louder than words.

Rhyme
Pray devoutly but hammer stoutly.
A good cat deserves a good rat.

Rhyme and rhythm combined
An apple a day keeps the doctor away.
No land without stones, or meat without bones.

* * * * * * * * * * * * * * * * * *

3   *To open a shop is easy; to keep it open is an art*   CHINA

4   *If they do not open after three knocks, do not wait*
POLAND

5   *Open your mouth before you eat*   MAURITANIA

6   *The dogs will go into the corner that's open*   SCOTLAND

7   *The eyes close in sleep, but the pillow remains awake*
MALAYSIA

8   *A closed mouth catches no flies*   ENGLAND

9   *Nothing enters into a closed hand*   SCOTLAND

10   *Steal a bell with your ears covered*   CHINA

11   *Those who want the last drop out of the can get the lid
on their nose*   NETHERLANDS

12   *The devil makes pots, but not always lids*
ITALY: SARDINIA

13   *Old purses shut badly*   NETHERLANDS

14   *In buying horses and in taking a wife, shut your eyes
tight and commend yourself to God*   ITALY

15   *All are not asleep who have their eyes shut*   GERMANY

16   *If two people tell you you are blind, shut one eye*
GEORGIA

17   *If you want to catch a wild horse, find a tight corral*
HAITI

18   *It's no good locking the stable door after the horse is
stolen*   ENGLAND

See also: **67 DOORS – WINDOWS – KEYS**

119 MOTION

1 *When a man eats, his own beard moves and not another's* TOGO

2 *As long as life lasts, the cow never stops moving its tail* NIGERIA

3 *Move your neck according to the music* ETHIOPIA

4 *The moon moves slowly, but it gets across the town* CÔTE D'IVOIRE

5 *Pride only goes the length one can spit* REPUBLIC OF CONGO

6 *A boat does not go forward if everyone rows their own way* KENYA

7 *Driftwood never goes upstream* USA

8 *Dead fish go always with the stream* ENGLAND

9 *Where the needle goes the thread must follow* POLAND

10 *If the swing goes forward it will go backward too* SRI LANKA

11 *You must go behind the door to mend old breeches* ENGLAND

12 *The sigh goes further than the shout* SCOTLAND

13 *Money makes the world go round* USA

14 *The tongue always goes to the aching tooth* BULGARIA

15 *The fish does not go after the hook, but after the bait*
CZECH REPUBLIC

16 *Who marches fast remains on the road* ALBANIA

17 *An army marches on its stomach* FRANCE

18 *You can't slide uphill* USA

19 *Parents who are afraid to put their foot down will have
children who step on their toes* CHINA

20 *A wolf does not step on the tail of a wolf* ESTONIA

21 *The rhinoceros which has no calf takes itself to the muddy
pool* SOUTH AFRICA

22 *The paddle which you find in the canoe is the one that
will take you across* LIBERIA

23 *A featherless arrow does not travel very far* ZANZIBAR

24 *Making preparations does not spoil the trip* GUINEA

25 *Words shake but examples attract* SERBIA

26 *When the going is rough, big potatoes come to the top*
USA

27 *A quick nickel is better than a slow dollar* USA

28 *A quick sixpence is better than a slow shilling* ENGLAND

120 STANDING STILL

1 *The one on whose head we would break a coconut never stands still* NIGERIA

2 *Be not afraid of growing slowly, be afraid only of standing still* CHINA

3 *Milk the cow that stands still* ENGLAND

4 *You never know your luck till the wheel stops* USA

5 *Still waters run deep* ENGLAND

6 *In a calm sea everyone is a pilot* ENGLAND

7 *Don't get off the merry-go-round before it stops* USA

8 *Don't get on the streetcar before it stops* CANADA

121 COMING – GOING

1 *Better go than send* CHINA

2 *One only goes to look at the prickly pear-tree when it is bearing fruit* MEXICO

3 *Better ask twice than go wrong once* GERMANY

4 *Let those who do not know what war is go to war*
CHINA

5 *Before going to war say one prayer; before going to sea, two; before getting married, three* POLAND

6   *Those who seek a constant friend go to the cemetery*
RUSSIA

7   *Who goes around the village long enough will get either a dog-bite or a dinner*   SERBIA

8   *When a donkey is well off he goes dancing on ice*
CZECH REPUBLIC

9   *If you go to the wedding you cover up the sledge*
ESTONIA

10   *You can only go halfway into the darkest forest; then you are coming out the other side*   CHINA

11   *Where everyone goes, the grass never grows*   GERMANY

12   *Those who wait for a dead person's shoes are in danger of going barefoot*   FRANCE

13   *Where they like you, do not go often*   SPAIN

14   *Better do a good deed near at home than go far away to burn incense*   CHINA

15   *Signposts only show the road, they don't go along it*
SWITZERLAND

16   *If you want to go fast, go the old road*   MYANMAR

17   *Don't stand by the water and long for fish; go home and weave a net*   CHINA

18   *Going slowly doesn't stop one arriving*   GUINEA

19   *What goes up must come down*   ENGLAND

20   *Conversation is a ladder for a journey*   SRI LANKA

21   *Only those who have travelled the road know where the holes are deep* CHINA

22   *If the swing goes forward it will go backward too* SRI LANKA

23   *Garbage in, garbage out* USA

24   *Every flood will have an ebb* SCOTLAND

25   *One must draw back in order to leap further* FRANCE

26   *Who plays at bowls must expect the ball returned* NETHERLANDS

27   *God, what things we see when we go out without a gun!* SOUTH AFRICA

122 WALKING

1   *Promise is a bridge of words, unsafe to walk across* GERMANY

2   *When walking through your neighbour's melon-patch, don't tie your shoe* CHINA

3   *An empty sack can't stand, nor a dead cat walk* IRELAND

4   *Walk as your shoes will let you* SCOTLAND

5   *The more one walks the more hills one sees* FINLAND

6   *You have to learn to crawl before you can walk* ENGLAND

7   *Knock before crossing even a stone bridge*   KOREA

8   *Don't cross a bridge until you come to it*   ENGLAND

9   *A cat may go to a monastery, but she still remains a cat*
     ETHIOPIA

10   *Those who have to go ten miles must regard nine as only
     halfway*   GERMANY

11   *Those who go barefoot aren't pinched by their shoes*
     GERMANY

12   *Fools rush in where angels fear to tread*   ENGLAND

13   *Wider will the cow-dung be for trampling on it*   WALES

14   *When you have trodden on the cat, what help is it to
     stroke her back?*   SWITZERLAND

123   RIDING

1   *It is not enough for people to know how to ride; they
     must know how to fall*   MEXICO

2   *When two ride on one horse one must sit behind*
     ENGLAND

3   *Sickness comes riding on horseback and goes away on
     foot*   BELGIUM

4   *The toughest broncs is always them you've rode some
     other place*   USA

5   *There's no such thing as a horse that can't be rode or a cowboy that can't be throwed*   USA

6   *Those who are not in the habit of riding forget the spurs*
    IRELAND

7   *A horse never goes straight up a hill*   USA

124 CARRYING

1   *It takes little effort to watch someone carry a load*
    CHINA

2   *When a blind person carries the banner, woe to those who follow*   FRANCE

3   *Let every pedlar carry his own pack*   GERMANY

4   *A full cup must be carried steadily*   ENGLAND

5   *You can't carry what you can't lift*   LATVIA

6   *The dog barks, the wind carries*   ESTONIA

7   *The one who carries the bludgeon owns the buffalo*
    INDIA

8   *The basket that has two handles can be carried by two*
    EGYPT

9   *People carrying elephant's flesh on their head should not look for crickets underground*   NIGERIA

10 *An anchored ship doesn't carry much cargo*   USA

11 *The shrimp that sleeps is carried away by the current*
CHILE

12 *Those who are carried down the stream need not row*
ENGLAND

13 *If you don't hear the story clearly, don't carry it off with you under your arm* THAILAND

14 *Carrying-poles which bend easily do not break* CHINA

15 *The absent always bear the blame* NETHERLANDS

16 *If all get into the palanquin, who will be the bearers?*
INDIA

17 *Those who bring good news knock hard* ENGLAND

18 *Fear the Greeks even when they bring gifts* LATIN

19 *One buffalo brings mud and all the herd are smeared with it* MALAYSIA

125 TRAVEL BY LAND

1 *If you can't drive your car, park it* USA

2 *A good driver turns in a small space* FRANCE

3 *Don't quit until the hearse comes round* USA

4 *Never look an auto bargain under the hood* USA

5 *Before God and the bus-conductor we are all equal*
GERMANY

6   *If you don't have a ticket, you don't ride*   USA

7   *Don't get on the streetcar before it stops*   CANADA

8   *If my aunt had wheels, she might be an omnibus*
     NETHERLANDS

9   *Oats pull the cart out of the mud*   SERBIA

10   *Don't put the cart before the horse*   ENGLAND

11   *It is easier to throw the load off the cart than to put it on*
     CZECH REPUBLIC

12   *If all get into the palanquin, who will be the bearers?*
     INDIA

13   *One broken rail will wreck a train*   USA

14   *Every train has a caboose*   USA

15   *Luck and bad luck are driving in the same sledge*
     RUSSIA

16   *A low stump upsets the sledge*   FINLAND

17   *If you go to the wedding you cover up the sledge*
     ESTONIA

18   *It is better to be once in the church sleigh than always in
     the back runners*   FINLAND

19   *Any spoke will lead the ant to the hub*   USA

20   *A greased cartwheel does not squeak*   ESTONIA

21   *The longer the spoke, the greater the tire*   USA

22 *The wheel that does the squeaking is the one that gets the grease* USA

23 *Creaking wagons are long in passing* NETHERLANDS

24 *A fifth wheel in the wagon hinders more than helps*
FRANCE

25 *The steam that blows the whistle never turns the wheel*
USA

26 *Gossip needs no carriage* RUSSIA

126 TRAVEL BY SEA

1 *Before going to war say one prayer; before going to sea, two; before getting married, three* POLAND

2 *Better lose the anchor than the whole ship*
NETHERLANDS

3 *An anchored ship doesn't carry much cargo* USA

4 *Those who wish to learn to pray must go to sea*
ENGLAND

5 *Those who go to sea without biscuits return without teeth*
FRANCE: CORSICA

6 *Don't quote your proverb until you bring your ship to port* SCOTLAND

7 *We cannot direct the wind, but we can adjust the sails*
GERMANY

8 *It's no wonder that the herring vessel smells of herring*
SCOTLAND

9 *In a calm sea everyone is a pilot* ENGLAND

10 *One should not board a ship without an onion*
NETHERLANDS

11 *You cannot damage a wrecked ship* ITALY

12 *Don't spoil the ship for a ha'porth of tar* ENGLAND

127 TRAVEL BY RIVER

1 *If you cross in a crowd, the crocodile won't eat you*
MADAGASCAR

2 *The hippo blocked up the ford, and no one could cross*
NIGERIA

3 *Don't call the alligator a big-mouth till you have crossed the river* BELIZE

4 *You cannot cross a river without getting wet*
SOUTH AFRICA

5 *The first in the boat has the choice of oars* ENGLAND

6 *Row with the oars you have* NETHERLANDS

7 *A boat does not go forward if everyone rows their own way* KENYA

8 *Those who are carried down the stream need not row*
ENGLAND

9   *No matter how long a log floats on the river it will never be a crocodile*   MALI

10   *Do not put each foot on a different boat*   CHINA

11   *No one can paddle two canoes at the same time*
SOUTH AFRICA

12   *The water is the same on both sides of the boat*
FINLAND

13   *Those who own the boat should give it a name*
NORWAY

14   *The one who has taken the bear into the boat must cross over with him*   SWEDEN

15   *Although the river is broad there are times when boats collide*   CHINA

16   *On a slimy shore it is easy to push a canoe*   CAMEROON

17   *The paddle which you find in the canoe is the one that will take you across*   LIBERIA

18   *A canoe is paddled on both sides*   NIGERIA

19   *When a canoe capsizes, everyone gets wet*   MADAGASCAR

20   *Those who wait long at the ferry will get across some time*   SCOTLAND

21   *A worn-out boat still has three thousand nails in it*
CHINA

22   *The junk capsizes and the shark has its bellyful*
MALAYSIA

128 SWIMMING

1 *Swimmers do not see their own back*   TOGO

2 *Dogs do not know how to swim until the water reaches their ears*   UKRAINE

3 *No matter how hard you throw a dead fish in the water, it still won't swim*   REPUBLIC OF CONGO

4 *It is hard to swim between two stretches of bad water*   NETHERLANDS

5 *In rivers and bad government, the lightest things swim at the top*   USA

129 TRAVEL BY AIR

1 *A featherless arrow does not travel very far*   ZANZIBAR

2 *One bird in the dish is better than a hundred in the air*   GERMANY

3 *Clumsy birds need early flight*   CHINA

4 *The candle is put into the lantern and the moth is left outside fluttering*   IRAN

5 *The fly flutters about the candle until at last it gets burnt*   NETHERLANDS

6 *Falling hurts least those who fly low*   CHINA

7 *The seagull sees furthest who flies highest*   FRANCE

* * * * * * * * * * * * * * * * * *

12 DRAMATIC PROVERBS

During the eighteenth century, a genre of drama based on the proverb emerged in France. The origins of these *proverbes dramatiques* are unclear, but their popularity at the time owes much to the French painter and architect Louis de Carmontelle (1717–1806). The audiences would be presented with a short drama containing clues that pointed to a particular proverb. The game was to guess the proverb. The genre was exploited in several European countries. Catherine the Great of Russia made up her own dramatic proverbs to be acted out by her court. The modern game of charades does something similar.

In the nineteenth century, there was a further development, in the form of *proverbes* – a genre of comedy characterized by dialogue rather than action and with a proverb as its theme. The French poet Alfred de Musset (1810–57) wrote several such pieces, whose names speak for themselves:

> *On ne badine pas avec l'amour* (1834) – There's no trifling with love
> *Il ne faut jurer de rien* (1836) – You can't be sure of anything
> *Il faut qu'une porte soit ouverte ou fermée* (1845) – A door must be open or shut
> *On ne saurait penser à tout* (1853) – You can't think of everything

* * * * * * * * * * * * * * * * * *

8   *Those who wait for roast duck to fly into their mouth must wait a very, very long time*   CHINA

9   *God gives birds their food, but they must fly for it* NETHERLANDS

10   *You cannot prevent the birds of sadness from flying over your head, but you can prevent them from nesting in your hair*   CHINA

11   *If the string is long the kite will fly high*   CHINA

12   *Pigs might fly*   ENGLAND

13   *There are old pilots, and there are bold pilots, but there are no old, bold pilots*   USA

14   *A sparrow in the hand is better than a crane on the wing* FRANCE

15   *A lie has no legs, but a scandal has wings*   ENGLAND

16   *When an ant gets wings it perishes*   SERBIA

17   *Do not blame God for having created the tiger, but thank Him for not having given it wings*   ETHIOPIA

130   FAST

1   *When in doubt, gallop*   FRENCH FOREIGN LEGION

2   *It's the tortoise that discounts the value of a pair of fast legs*   JAPAN

3   *If you want to go fast, go the old road*   MYANMAR

4   *Who marches fast remains on the road*   ALBANIA

5   *Four horses cannot overtake the tongue*   CHINA

6   *A child learns quicker to talk than to be silent*   NORWAY

7   *Quick work – double work*   MONTENEGRO

8   *They give twice who give quickly*   TURKEY

9   *When the hands and the feet are bound, the tongue runs faster*   GERMANY

10   *Slowness comes from God and quickness from the devil*
     MOROCCO

11   *Those who have not seen a hare run, must not speak of fear*   ITALY

12   *Don't run too far; you will have to come back the same distance*   FRANCE

13   *'Tis the one who runs that falls*   IRELAND

14   *Clothes put on while running come off while running*
     ETHIOPIA

15   *One cannot shoe a running horse*   NETHERLANDS

16   *What is the use of running when we are not on the right road?*   GERMANY

17   *More haste, less speed*   ENGLAND

18   *It is not enough to run; one must start in time*   FRANCE

19   *When rats infest the palace a lame cat is better than the swiftest horse*   CHINA

131 SLOW

1   *Be not afraid of growing slowly, be afraid only of
    standing still*   CHINA

2   *The mills of God grind slowly*   ENGLAND

3   *Dress slowly when you are in a hurry*   FRANCE

4   *Going slowly doesn't stop one arriving*   GUINEA

5   *You have to learn to crawl before you can walk*
    ENGLAND

6   *Slowly, slowly makes the slug arrive at the fountain*
    RWANDA

7   *Slowly but surely the excrement of foreign poets will come
    to your village*   MALI

8   *Better keep under an old hedge than creep under a new
    furze-bush*   ENGLAND

9   *Slowness comes from God and quickness from the devil*
    MOROCCO

10 *The moon moves slowly, but it gets across the town*
    CÔTE D'IVOIRE

132 STRIKING

1   *A blow on the purse of another is like a blow on a
    sand-hill*   EGYPT

2   *A good question is like one beating a bell*   CHINA

3 *Although the river is broad there are times when boats collide* CHINA

4 *Chop, and you will have splinters* DENMARK

5 *Don't shout before the birch-rod falls* LATVIA

6 *Education don't come by bumping against the school-house* USA

7 *Even the best smith sometimes hits his thumb* NETHERLANDS

8 *Everything is possible, except to bite your own nose* NETHERLANDS

9 *Hit one ring and the whole chain will resound* SOUTH AFRICA

10 *If you pound palm-nuts, some will stain your cloth* CÔTE D'IVOIRE

11 *It is very difficult to beat a drum with a sickle* NIGERIA

12 *Kick an attorney downstairs and he'll stick to you for life* SCOTLAND

13 *Lightning never strikes twice in the same place* ENGLAND

14 *Many people are like clocks, they show one hour and strike another* DENMARK

15 *Never trust your back to a slap* SCOTLAND

16 *Pelt a dog with a bone and you will not offend him* ITALY

17 *Pray devoutly but hammer stoutly* ENGLAND

18 *Strike a flint and you get fire* USA

19 *The dragon in shallow water becomes the butt of shrimps*
    CHINA

20 *The one who strikes first, strikes twice* BELGIUM

21 *The protruding nail will be pounded down* JAPAN

22 *There's no crime in the blow that has not been struck*
    IRELAND

23 *Upon what tree does the wind not strike?* INDIA

24 *We get the note by striking the string* INDIA

25 *Whether the stone bumps the jug, or the jug bumps the
    stone, it is bad for the jug* USA

133 DIRECTIONS

1 *Every road has two directions* UKRAINE

2 *Do not tear down the east wall to repair the west*
    CHINA

3 *Any spoke will lead the ant to the hub* USA

4 *Easy street never leads anywhere* USA

5 *All roads lead to Rome* ENGLAND

6 *Even if water flows in all directions, the sand will remain
    at the bottom* GEORGIA

7   *A north-easterly wind is heaven's broom*   ESTONIA

8   *When you show the moon to a child, it sees only your finger*   ZAMBIA

9   *One never falls but on the side towards which one leans*   FRANCE

10   *Driftwood never goes upstream*   USA

11   *There is no limit to looking upward*   JAPAN

12   *The stairs are swept downwards, not upwards*   ROMANIA

13   *Look the other way when the girl in the tea-house smiles*   JAPAN

14   *The way of the wheat is through the mill*   AFGHANISTAN

15   *Don't be breaking your shin on a stool that's not in your way*   IRELAND

16   *One does not lose by asking the way*   CHINA

17   *If in the pot, it will come into the spoon*   INDIA

18   *When the going is rough, big potatoes come to the top*   USA

19   *We can never see the sun rise by looking into the west*   JAPAN

20   *You cannot push yourself forward by patting yourself on the back*   CHINA

21   *The wise read a letter backwards*   GERMANY

22   *It is no use trying to tug the glacier backwards*   CHINA

23 *A horse never goes straight up a hill* USA

24 *Take the ball as it bounces* FRANCE

134 THROWING

1 *The throwers of stones fling away the strength of their own arms* NIGERIA

2 *Cast no dirt into the well that has given you water* ENGLAND

3 *No matter how hard you throw a dead fish in the water, it still won't swim* REPUBLIC OF CONGO

4 *Do a good deed and throw it into the sea* BULGARIA

5 *It is no use throwing water on a drowned rat* IRELAND

6 *If you throw cakes at people they will throw cakes at you* KOREA

7 *People who live in glass houses shouldn't throw stones* ENGLAND

8 *It is easier to throw the load off the cart than to put it on* CZECH REPUBLIC

9 *Ashes will always blow back into the face of the thrower* NIGERIA

135 PUSHING – PULLING

1 *Everyone pushes a falling fence*   CHINA

2 *You cannot climb a ladder by pushing others down*
ENGLAND

3 *On a slimy shore it is easy to push a canoe*   CAMEROON

4 *You cannot push yourself forward by patting yourself on the back*   CHINA

5 *Draw the snake from its hole by someone else's hand*
SPAIN

6 *Beauty draws more than oxen*   ENGLAND

7 *Use a thorn to extract a thorn*   INDIA

8 *Oats pull the cart out of the mud*   SERBIA

9 *Pull gently at a weak rope*   NETHERLANDS

10 *Pull the ear, the head follows*   BANGLADESH

11 *Abundance will make cotton pull a stone*   NIGERIA

12 *It is no use trying to tug the glacier backwards*   CHINA

136 ARRIVAL

1 *Going slowly doesn't stop one arriving*   GUINEA

2 *Mountains cannot meet, people can*   BULGARIA

3 *Flies never visit an egg that has no crack*   CHINA

4   *Slowly, slowly makes the slug arrive at the fountain*
RWANDA

5   *Don't quote your proverb until you bring your ship to*
port   SCOTLAND

6   *When the occasion comes, the proverb comes*   GHANA

7   *Dawn does not come twice to wake us*   SOUTH AFRICA

8   *A weasel comes to say Happy New Year to the chickens*
CHINA

9   *You come with a cat and call it a rabbit*   CAMEROON

10   *When the bee comes to your house, let her have beer; you*
may want to visit the bee's house some day
REPUBLIC OF CONGO

11   *If I keep a green bough in my heart, a singing-bird will*
come   CHINA

12   *Pilgrims seldom come home saints*   GERMANY

13   *Sickness comes riding on horseback and goes away on*
foot   BELGIUM

14   *It is no use lifting your leg until you come to the stile*
ENGLAND

15   *Adversity comes with instruction in its hand*   WALES

16   *Tomorrow never comes*   ENGLAND

17   *Don't believe those who come from afar, but those who*
return from it   SPAIN

18   *Holidays come like kings and go like beggars*   ESTONIA

19 *Who knows when death or a customer will come?*
    INDIA

20 *Don't cross a bridge until you come to it*   ENGLAND

21 *Those who come too late find the platter turned over*
    NETHERLANDS

22 *Slowly but surely the excrement of foreign poets will come
    to your village*   MALI

23 *Don't shuck your corn till the hogs come home*   USA

24 *Troubles never come singly*   ENGLAND

25 *Misfortunes come by forties*   WALES

26 *When a severe illness comes, eat bread and onions*
    INDIA

27 *Miracles come to those who believe in them*   FRANCE

28 *The hornet also comes to the sugar-pot*   CHINA

29 *Don't quit until the hearse comes round*   USA

30 *If you follow a crow long enough you light on carrion*
    ALBANIA

31 *The end of separation is meeting again*   TURKEY

32 *Meeting is the beginning of parting*   JAPAN

33 *Dogs do not know how to swim until the water reaches
    their ears*   UKRAINE

34 *Follow the river and you will reach the sea*   FRANCE

35 *The hindermost ox also reaches the kraal*
    SOUTH AFRICA

36 *However long the procession, it always returns to the
    church* PHILIPPINES

37 *Those who go to sea without biscuits return without teeth*
    FRANCE: CORSICA

38 *Priests return to the temple; merchants to the shop*
    CHINA

39 *Leave a good name behind in case you return* KENYA

40 *Beware of a returning arrow* JAPAN

41 *A word flies away like a sparrow and returns to the house
    like a crow* GERMANY

42 *To know the road ahead, ask those coming back* CHINA

43 *Before you go, think of your return* BELGIUM

44 *Chickens come home to roost* ENGLAND

45 *Dynamite comes in small packages* USA

46 *Three glasses of wine drive away the evil spirits, but with
    the fourth they return* GERMANY

137 DEPARTURE

1 *The only victory over love is flight* FRANCE

2 *An apple at night puts the dentist to flight* ENGLAND

3   *Everyone who says goodbye is not gone*   USA

4   *The fly will never leave the confectioner's shop*   INDIA

5   *Before you go, think of your return*   BELGIUM

6   *Holidays come like kings and go like beggars*   ESTONIA

7   *Sickness comes riding on horseback and goes away on foot*   BELGIUM

8   *The one who enters as a whirlwind will depart as an ant*   INDONESIA

9   *A word flies away like a sparrow and returns to the house like a crow*   GERMANY

10   *He who never leaves Paris will never be pope*   FRANCE

11   *To part is to die a little*   FRANCE

12   *Meeting is the beginning of parting*   JAPAN

13   *When the leopard moves away, it takes its tail with it*   NIGERIA

14   *A shadow is a feeble thing but no sun can drive it away*   SWEDEN

15   *Poke a bamboo thicket, drive out a snake*   JAPAN

16   *A soft answer turns away wrath*   ENGLAND

17   *Three glasses of wine drive away the evil spirits, but with the fourth they return*   GERMANY

18   *Don't run too far; you will have to come back the same distance*   FRANCE

138 ENTERING – LEAVING

1   *One should not board a ship without an onion*
NETHERLANDS

2   *A careless watch bids the thief come in*   SCOTLAND

3   *Where the finger-nail will enter, there is no need of iron*
INDIA

4   *Obey the customs of the village you enter*   JAPAN

5   *The one who enters as a whirlwind will depart as an ant*
INDONESIA

6   *You cannot catch a tiger cub unless you enter the tiger's den*   JAPAN

7   *Teachers open the door; you enter by yourself*   CHINA

8   *Nothing enters into a closed hand*   SCOTLAND

9   *When hunger gets inside you, nothing else can*   NIGERIA

10   *If you get into the pack you need not bark, but wag your tail you must*   RUSSIA

11   *If all get into the palanquin, who will be the bearers?*
INDIA

12   *The dogs will go into the corner that's open*   SCOTLAND

13   *What comes from the heart goes to the heart*   ENGLAND

14   *After the game the king goes into the sack like the pawn*
ITALY

15   *On going into a church leave the world behind the door*
SPAIN

16   *A sponge sucks itself full, but when it has to yield anything one has to squeeze it*   GERMANY

17   *Even a drill goes in from the tip*   KOREA

18   *Well water does not invade river water*   CHINA

19   *All is fish that goes into the net*   SCOTLAND

20   *No one can blow and swallow at the same time*
GERMANY

21   *You can only go halfway into the darkest forest; then you are coming out the other side*   CHINA

22   *Enter the mill and you come out floury*   SERBIA

23   *That which goes last into the sack comes out first*
SWEDEN

24   *If the bucket has been long in the well, it ought to come out with water*   NIGERIA

25   *The fuller the cup, the sooner the spill*   CHINA

26   *It is not healthy to swallow books without chewing*
GERMANY

27   *They must have clean fingers who would blow another's nose*   DENMARK

28   *Shed no tears until seeing the coffin*   CHINA

29   *Pride only goes the length one can spit*
REPUBLIC OF CONGO

30 *Those who seek the entrance should also think of the exit*
GERMANY

31 *A sly rabbit will have three openings to its den*   CHINA

139 HUNGER

1 *Hunger doesn't say, 'Stale bread,' and cold doesn't say
'Old coat.'*   GEORGIA

2 *A waiting appetite kindles many a spite*   ENGLAND

3 *The pig dreams of his trough*   FINLAND

4 *To an empty stomach white bread tastes like brown*
ESTONIA

5 *When hunger gets inside you, nothing else can*   NIGERIA

6 *Hungry bellies have no ears*   ENGLAND

7 *When is a cook's ladle hungry or a beer jug thirsty?*
ESTONIA

8 *A long beard does not prevent a house going to bed
hungry*   CAMEROON

9 *A hungry louse bites hard*   USA

10 *Hunger is the best sauce*   ENGLAND

11 *Don't stand by the water and long for fish; go home and
weave a net*   CHINA

12 *A starving crocodile is never pleasant*   MADAGASCAR

140 THIRST

1   *Those who have no thirst have no business at the fountain*   NETHERLANDS

2   *Dig a well before you are thirsty*   CHINA

3   *When is a cook's ladle hungry or a beer jug thirsty?*
    ESTONIA

4   *An old moon's mist never died of thirst*   IRELAND

5   *When the figs are ripe, all the birds want to eat*   KENYA

6   *You don't have to buy a dairy just because you want a glass of milk*   USA

141 EATING

1   *Open your mouth before you eat*   MAURITANIA

2   *While the sheep bleats it loses its mouthful*   BELGIUM

3   *If you get mixed with bran, you'll soon be pecked by chickens*   LIBYA

4   *With patience and saliva, the elephant swallows an ant*
    COLOMBIA

5   *No one can blow and swallow at the same time*
    GERMANY

6   *However much the beetle is afraid, it will not stop the lizard swallowing it*   CAMEROON

7 *The soup is never swallowed as hot as it is cooked*
GERMANY

8 *Insults and pills must not be chewed* GERMANY

9 *Don't chew your tobacco twice* USA

10 *One must chew according to one's teeth* NORWAY

142 FOOD

1 *A greyhound finds its food in its feet* IRELAND

2 *Do not salt other people's food* BULGARIA

3 *Food tastes best when one eats it with one's own spoon*
DENMARK

4 *God gives birds their food, but they must fly for it*
NETHERLANDS

5 *If you are looking for a fly in your food, it means you are
full* SOUTH AFRICA

6 *The horse must graze where it is tethered* BELGIUM

7 *The baby who does not cry does not get fed*
PHILIPPINES

8 *Never feed a dog with corn, nor attempt to pick your teeth
with a pair of scissors* CHINA

9 *Why feed a bullock after it is sold?* INDIA

10 *You can't have your cake and eat it* ENGLAND

11   *Those who simultaneously eat and sing rise up fools*
PHILIPPINES

12   *When eating bamboo sprouts, remember the one who planted them*   CHINA

13   *Eat with the dogs, howl with the wolves*   ALBANIA

14   *Eat not cherries with the great*   ENGLAND

15   *Who sits under a pear-tree will eat pears*   BULGARIA

16   *The cat who frightens the mice away is as good as the cat who eats them*   GERMANY

17   *There never was a persimmon except there was a possum to eat it*   USA

18   *The proof of the pudding is in the eating*   ENGLAND

19   *Those who do not eat cheese will go mad*   FRANCE

20   *The spoon is prized when the soup is being eaten*
CZECH REPUBLIC

21   *The fox believes that everyone eats hens like himself*
FRANCE

22   *When a severe illness comes, eat bread and onions*
INDIA

23   *Eating pears always cleans one's teeth*   KOREA

24   *Vultures eat with their blood relations*   SOUTH AFRICA

25   *Dog does not eat dog*   ENGLAND

26   *When you eat a round cake, do you begin at the centre?*
NIGERIA

27 *When a man eats, his own beard moves and not another's* TOGO

28 *If you cross in a crowd, the crocodile won't eat you* MADAGASCAR

29 *Cleverness eats its owner* SOUTH AFRICA

30 *In eating and scratching, everything is in the beginning* COLOMBIA

31 *The grub eats round the edges of the leaves* NEW ZEALAND

32 *Those who mix themselves with the mud will be eaten by the swine* NETHERLANDS

33 *When the figs are ripe, all the birds want to eat* KENYA

34 *If you had teeth of steel, you could eat iron coconuts* SENEGAL

35 *You can't eat a square meal off a round table* USA

36 *One needn't devour the whole chicken to know the flavour of the bird* CHINA

143 COOKING

1 *Beauty does not make the pot boil* IRELAND

2 *I can tell by my own pot how the others are boiling* FRANCE

3   *It is the pot that boils, but the dish gets the credit*
CAMEROON

4   *A watched pot never boils*   ENGLAND

5   *Little kettles soon boil over*   ESTONIA

6   *Boil a stone in butter and its juice will be drunk*
IRELAND

7   *Until the soup boils over, the ladle has no value*
TURKEY

8   *Never bolt your door with a boiled carrot*   IRELAND

9   *A little drop of water silences a boiling pot*   GERMANY

10   *Flies never alight on boiling pots*   UKRAINE

11   *Cooks make their own sauce*   FRANCE

12   *When is a cook's ladle hungry or a beer jug thirsty?*
ESTONIA

13   *The smartest housewife cannot cook a meal without rice*
CHINA

14   *One should not light a fire unless one wants to cook*
DENMARK

15   *The basin must hold what the cauldron cooks*   ESTONIA

16   *The soup is never swallowed as hot as it is cooked*
GERMANY

17   *You cannot take one part of a fowl for cooking and leave
the other part to lay eggs*   INDIA

18　*If familiarity were useful, water wouldn't cook fish*
　　CAMEROON

19　*Those who have the frying-pan in their hand turn it at
　　will*　NETHERLANDS

20　*A lobster loves water, but not when he's being cooked in
　　it*　SENEGAL

21　*In every family's cooking-pot is one black spot*　CHINA

22　*Even beech leaves are good when they are fried in butter*
　　SERBIA

23　*You can't unscramble eggs*　USA

24　*Too many cooks spoil the broth*　ENGLAND

25　*Too many cooks oversalt the porridge*　NETHERLANDS

144　MEALS

1　*Old countries don't disappear overnight; they stay for
　　breakfast*　EGYPT

2　*Hope is a good breakfast but a bad supper*　ENGLAND

3　*Who goes around the village long enough will get either a
　　dog-bite or a dinner*　SERBIA

4　*Better a free meal of acorns than a honey feast on trust*
　　WALES

5　*Enough is as good as a feast*　ENGLAND

6   *The smartest housewife cannot cook a meal without rice*
CHINA

7   *You can't eat a square meal off a round table*   USA

8   *What's the good of a spoon after the meal is over?*
LATVIA

9   *Let the guests at table be three or four – at the most five*
GREECE

10   *That which is said at table should be wrapped up in the tablecloth*   ITALY

145 FRUIT

1   *A pig won't spare even the most beautiful fruit*   ALBANIA

2   *What matter what blossom it is if there is no fruit?*
SERBIA

3   *Blossoms are not fruits*   NETHERLANDS

4   *A tree with ripe fruit needs little shaking*   SWITZERLAND

5   *The fruit on a creeper is no burden to it*   SRI LANKA

6   *Good juice from fruit comes without squeezing*   IRAN

7   *One only goes to look at the prickly pear-tree when it is bearing fruit*   MEXICO

8   *The fruit must have a stem before it grows*   LIBERIA

9   *A fruit-tree that grows on a dunghill is sure to flourish*
NEW ZEALAND

10   *The laden almond-tree by the wayside is sure to be bitter*
JAPAN

11   *The apple does not fall far from the apple-tree* ALBANIA

12   *An apple a day keeps the doctor away* ENGLAND

13   *An apple at night puts the dentist to flight* ENGLAND

14   *A stone from the hand of a friend is an apple*
MAURITANIA

15   *If you don't like my apples, don't shake my tree* USA

16   *One rotten apple spoils the whole barrel* ENGLAND

17   *Little by little grow the bananas* REPUBLIC OF CONGO

18   *Lower your head modestly while passing, and you will harvest bananas* REPUBLIC OF CONGO

19   *Eat not cherries with the great* ENGLAND

20   *If you had teeth of steel, you could eat iron coconuts*
SENEGAL

21   *The one on whose head we would break a coconut never stands still* NIGERIA

22   *The lot of the coconut shell is to float and the lot of the stone is to sink* INDONESIA

23   *Crab apples make good jelly too* USA

24   *When the date-crop is over, everyone mocks at the palm-tree* ETHIOPIA

25   *When the figs are ripe, all the birds want to eat* KENYA

146 VEGETABLES

1 *If you want one year of prosperity, grow grain. If you want ten years of prosperity, grow trees. If you want a hundred years of prosperity, grow people* CHINA

2 *Ants can attack with a grain of rice* MADAGASCAR

3 *Crooked furrows grow straight grain* CANADA

4 *Out of old fields come new grain* USA

5 *By the stubble you may guess the grain* USA

6 *You won't help shoots grow by pulling them up higher* CHINA

7 *Better a free meal of acorns than a honey feast on trust* WALES

8 *When eating bamboo sprouts, remember the one who planted them* CHINA

9 *Those who fear wild cranes should not sow beans* MALTA

10 *One can't get beans out of wild melons* NAMIBIA

11 *When the beans get too thick, the pot burns* USA

12 *Beans are not equal to meat* NAMIBIA

13 *Even beech leaves are good when they are fried in butter* SERBIA

14 *If you get mixed with bran, you'll soon be pecked by chickens* LIBYA

* * * * * * * * * * * * * * * * * * *

13 TRACING A HISTORY

'If it be true that good wine needs no bush, 'tis true that a good play needs no epilogue.' So says Rosalind, as Epilogue, in Shakespeare's *As You Like It*. The meaning is that good wine needs no sign – that is, no advertising.

The bush in question was the ivy bush. It was used in the manner of a modern inn sign, hung outside taverns, fair booths, and houses to show that beer or wine could be obtained within. But why ivy?

There is an association with Bacchus, the Roman god of wine, who is frequently depicted holding an ivy-entwined drinking cup or wearing an ivy wreath. According to legend, ivy grew abundantly at Nyssa, where Bacchus spent his youth. There was also a belief that ivy was intoxicating, and that the bad effects of wine could be prevented by wreathing the brow with ivy leaves or by boiling them with wine and drinking the resulting potion.

The proverb is first known from Roman times, therefore. In Latin we find it as *Vino vendibili hedera non opus est.* The Romans then brought it into Europe. The French version is *Au vin qui se vend bien, il ne faut point de lierre.* Eventually it arrived in Britain – and, as we see, on the stage.

* * * * * * * * * * * * * * * * * * *

15 *A louse in the cabbage is better than no meat at all*
    NETHERLANDS

16 *Cabbage is the best invalid, it needs only a little water*
    SERBIA

17 *She is a foolish woman who blames her own cabbage*
    DENMARK

18 *Cabbage for cabbage* FRANCE

19 *Never bolt your door with a boiled carrot* IRELAND

20 *To the pig a carrot is a present* GERMANY

21 *A blind hen can sometimes find her corn* FRANCE

22 *If the brain sows not corn, it plants thistles* ENGLAND

23 *Remember the rain that made your corn grow* HAITI

24 *No mill will grind wet corn* ESTONIA

25 *Never feed a dog with corn, nor attempt to pick your teeth with a pair of scissors* CHINA

26 *Don't shuck your corn till the hogs come home* USA

27 *The beauty of the corn cob is apparent on the inside only*
    KENYA

28 *Do not sow groundnuts when the monkey is watching*
    NIGERIA

29 *What good is the hay if the horse is dead?* PHILIPPINES

30 *Why should the cow trouble to think if she has plenty of hay?* SLOVAKIA

31 *The empty nut is the hardest*   WALES

32 *When you give a child a nut, give it also something to break it with*   GEORGIA

33 *Oats pull the cart out of the mud*   SERBIA

34 *One should not board a ship without an onion*
NETHERLANDS

35 *When a severe illness comes, eat bread and onions*
INDIA

36 *Those who deal in onions no longer smell them*
GERMANY

37 *Be it an onion, let it be given graciously*   AFGHANISTAN

38 *An onion shared with a friend tastes like roast lamb*
EGYPT

39 *Never scald your lips with someone else's porridge*
IRELAND

40 *A good day is that in which to lay by cold porridge*
MALAWI

41 *Too many cooks oversalt the porridge*   NETHERLANDS

42 *You must take the little potato with the big potato*
IRELAND

43 *When the going is rough, big potatoes come to the top*
USA

44 *Too many affairs are like pumpkins in water; one pops up while you try to hold down the other*   CHINA

45   *Every pumpkin is known by its stem*   USA

46   *From the radish, radish leaves*   INDIA

47   *Rhubarb and patience work wonders*   GERMANY

48   *The smartest housewife cannot cook a meal without rice*
     CHINA

49   *We boil our rice only once*   INDIA

50   *Where should we pour the gravy if not on the rice?*
     MALAYSIA

51   *Have a mouth as sharp as a dagger, but a heart as soft as tofu*   CHINA

52   *Sometimes one must let turnips be pears*   GERMANY

53   *Those who will have a cake out of the wheat must tarry the grinding*   ENGLAND

54   *The way of the wheat is through the mill*   AFGHANISTAN

147 MEAT

1   *No matter how you slice it, it's still baloney*   USA

2   *It is still a parrot, whether roasted or raw*
     NEW ZEALAND

3   *The end of an ox is beef, and the end of a lie is grief*
     MADAGASCAR

4   *One needn't devour the whole chicken to know the flavour of the bird*   CHINA

5   *The fox believes that everyone eats hens like himself*
FRANCE

6   *People carrying elephant's flesh on their head should not look for crickets underground*   NIGERIA

7   *No land without stones, or meat without bones*
ENGLAND

8   *A louse in the cabbage is better than no meat at all*
NETHERLANDS

9   *Beans are not equal to meat*   NAMIBIA

10   *The soup would be none the worse for more meat*
SUDAN

11   *The nearer the bone, the sweeter the meat*   ENGLAND

12   *Those who wait for roast duck to fly into their mouth must wait a very, very long time*   CHINA

13   *An onion shared with a friend tastes like roast lamb*
EGYPT

14   *There are more days than sausage*   USA

15   *Two pieces of meat confuse the mind of the fly*   NIGERIA

148 SOUP

1   *More than one mother can make tasty soup*   NIGERIA

2   *The broth from a distance grows cool on the road*
KENYA

3   *Too many cooks spoil the broth*   ENGLAND

4   *The spoon is prized when the soup is being eaten*
     CZECH REPUBLIC

5   *The soup would be none the worse for more meat*
     SUDAN

6   *One cannot make soup out of beauty*   ESTONIA

7   *The vulture's foot spoils the soup*   NIGERIA

8   *Those who change their trade make soup in a basket*
     ENGLAND

9   *Of soup and love, the first is the best*   PORTUGAL

10 *Those who have been scalded with hot soup blow on cold water*   UKRAINE

11 *The soup is never swallowed as hot as it is cooked*
     GERMANY

12 *Cheap soup has no taste*   TURKESTAN

13 *It is with its own face that the plate receives the soup*
     NIGERIA

14 *Until the soup boils over, the ladle has no value*
     TURKEY

149 BAKERY

1 *Be not a baker if your head be butter* FRANCE

2 *It isn't in a coal-sack that one finds white flour*
BELGIUM

3 *Words do not make flour* ITALY

4 *It is the turning of the mill that makes the flour heap*
INDIA

5 *It takes dough to have crust* USA

6 *Those who go to sea without biscuits return without teeth*
FRANCE: CORSICA

7 *There's crust and crumb in every loaf* ENGLAND

8 *Those who have not bread to spare should not keep a dog*
CHINA

9 *Cheese and bread make the cheeks red* GERMANY

10 *Bread is the staff of life, but the pudding makes a good crutch* SCOTLAND

11 *Cut bread cannot be put together again* LATVIA

12 *If you have two loaves of bread, sell one and buy a lily*
CHINA

13 *Slices of bread do not grow together* ESTONIA

14 *To an empty stomach white bread tastes like brown*
ESTONIA

15 *It is easy to steal from a cut loaf* ENGLAND

16 *Hunger doesn't say, 'Stale bread,' and cold doesn't say 'Old coat.'* GEORGIA

17 *You cannot fill your belly by painting pictures of bread* CHINA

18 *Strange bread makes the cheeks red* SWITZERLAND

19 *When a severe illness comes, eat bread and onions* INDIA

20 *The thinnest bread finds itself married to bread* ALGERIA

21 *An egg on bread is slippery* SCOTLAND

22 *Half a loaf is better than no bread* ENGLAND

23 *It's a poor crust that can't grease its own plate* USA

24 *Those who will have a cake out of the wheat must tarry the grinding* ENGLAND

25 *If you throw cakes at people they will throw cakes at you* KOREA

26 *When you eat a round cake, do you begin at the centre?* NIGERIA

27 *All that is round is not a cake* LIBYA

28 *A cake on the palm won't toast or burn* SCOTLAND

29 *You can't have your cake and eat it* ENGLAND

30 *Crab apples make good jelly too* USA

31 *A rich person's sickness and a poor person's pancake are smelt a long way off* BELGIUM

32   *Too many hands spoil the pie*   USA

33   *One rotten egg spoils the whole pudding*   GERMANY

34   *The proof of the pudding is in the eating*   ENGLAND

35   *One does not distribute sweetmeats in a fight*   INDIA

36   *One sprinkles the most sugar where the tart is burnt*
     NETHERLANDS

150   DAIRY

1   *What butter or whiskey will not cure, there is no cure for*
    IRELAND

2   *Even beech leaves are good when they are fried in butter*
    SERBIA

3   *Be not a baker if your head be butter*   FRANCE

4   *Boil a stone in butter and its juice will be drunk*
    IRELAND

5   *Cheese and bread make the cheeks red*   GERMANY

6   *Brotherly love for brotherly love, but cheese for money*
    ALBANIA

7   *Those who do not eat cheese will go mad*   FRANCE

8   *You cannot take one part of a fowl for cooking and leave
    the other part to lay eggs*   INDIA

9   *An egg on bread is slippery*   SCOTLAND

10 *Flies never visit an egg that has no crack* CHINA

11 *Better an egg today than a hen tomorrow* ALBANIA

12 *One rotten egg spoils the whole pudding* GERMANY

13 *A wild goose never lays a tame egg* ENGLAND

14 *From fried eggs come no chickens* USA

15 *Eggs and vows are easily broken* JAPAN

16 *A black hen can lay a white egg* SCOTLAND

17 *Those who steal the egg will also steal the hen* MALTA

18 *First lay the egg, then cackle* ESTONIA

19 *Words are good, but fowls lay eggs* GERMANY

20 *The one who has put an egg into a bottle can easily take it out* NIGERIA

21 *You can't unscramble eggs* USA

22 *A kiss without a beard is like an egg without salt*
    NETHERLANDS

23 *No matter how much the world changes, cats will never lay eggs* MALI

24 *Even though chickens don't wash, their eggs are still white* SIERRA LEONE

25 *Every cackling hen was an egg at first*
    RWANDA AND BURUNDI

26 *Those who have an egg in their pocket do not dance*
    GABON

27   *Don't put all your eggs in one basket*   ENGLAND

28   *Enjoy your ice-cream while it's on your plate*   USA

29   *Those who have burnt their mouth with milk blow on ice-cream*   TURKEY

30   *If there is falsity in a proverb, then milk can be sour*   INDIA

31   *If you want to keep your milk sweet, leave it in the cow*   LIBERIA

32   *Black cows give white milk*   GERMANY

33   *Milk the cow that stands still*   ENGLAND

34   *Even in the freshest of milk you will still find hairs*   MALI

35   *You don't have to buy a dairy just because you want a glass of milk*   USA

36   *There is no such thing as a pretty good omelette*   FRANCE

151   SAUCES – CONDIMENTS – SWEETENERS

1   *Cooks make their own sauce*   FRANCE

2   *Hunger is the best sauce*   ENGLAND

3   *Where would the gravy be but for the water?*   ZANZIBAR

4   *Where should we pour the gravy if not on the rice?*
    MALAYSIA

5   *Sauce for the goose is sauce for the gander*   ENGLAND

6   *Do not salt other people's food*   BULGARIA

7   *All good salt stings*   SPAIN

8   *What falls into salt becomes salt*   INDIA

9   *Salt doesn't boast that it is salted*   HAITI

10 *A kiss without a beard is like an egg without salt*
    NETHERLANDS

11 *Friendship does not need pepper to cry*
    REPUBLIC OF CONGO

12 *The older the ginger, the more it bites*   CHINA

13 *Bees that have honey in their mouths have stings in their
    tails*   FRANCE

14 *Why use poison when you can kill with honey?*
    BELGIUM

15 *Though honey is sweet, do not lick it off a briar*
    IRELAND

16 *Where there are bees there is honey*   ENGLAND

17 *It is in sugar that you see the dead ant*   MALAYSIA

18 *Think not because the cane is bent the sugar is crooked
    too*   MALAYSIA

19 *You can't expect both ends of a sugar cane to be as sweet*
    CHINA

20   *One sprinkles the most sugar where the tart is burnt*
      NETHERLANDS

21   *The sweetest wine makes the sharpest vinegar*
      GERMANY

22   *In vinegar, sharpness is a virtue*   RUSSIA

152   ALCOHOLIC DRINKS

1   *When the bee comes to your house, let her have beer; you*
      may want to visit the bee's house some day
      REPUBLIC OF CONGO

2   *Froth is no beer*   NETHERLANDS

3   *When is a cook's ladle hungry or a beer jug thirsty?*
      ESTONIA

4   *There are dregs in the best bottle of wine*   FRANCE

5   *What butter or whiskey will not cure, there is no cure for*
      IRELAND

6   *Gin caresses lungs and liver*   NETHERLANDS

7   *Save your bottles; it may rain whiskey*   USA

8   *The sweetest wine makes the sharpest vinegar*
      GERMANY

9   *The cork is always bigger than the mouth of the bottle*
      ESTONIA

10   *Wine and children speak the truth*   ROMANIA

11 *Three glasses of wine drive away the evil spirits, but with the fourth they return* GERMANY

12 *A cask of wine works more miracles than a church full of saints* ITALY

13 *Drinking and thinking don't mix* USA

153 NON-ALCOHOLIC DRINKS

1 *The lazy ox drinks dirty water* COLOMBIA

2 *Even a hen, when it drinks, looks towards heaven* TURKEY

3 *The bird can drink much, but the elephant drinks more* SENEGAL

4 *Boil a stone in butter and its juice will be drunk* IRELAND

5 *Good juice from fruit comes without squeezing* IRAN

6 *A hasty person drinks tea with a fork* CHINA

7 *Whoever is king, tea is queen* IRELAND

154 EXCRETION

1 *Wider will the cow-dung be for trampling on it* WALES

2 *Old droppings don't stink* KENYA

3   *The energy of the dung-beetle is put into rolling its ball of dung*   CHINA

4   *A fruit-tree that grows on a dunghill is sure to flourish*
NEW ZEALAND

5   *Slowly but surely the excrement of foreign poets will come to your village*   MALI

155   INSERTING – EXTRACTING

1   *If it is your own lantern, do not poke holes in the paper*
CHINA

2   *When someone's coat is threadbare, it is easy to pick a hole in it*   ENGLAND

3   *The spear of kinship soon pierces the eye*   CAMEROON

4   *Endurance pierces marble*   MOROCCO

5   *It is folly to put flour into a bag facing the wind*
GERMANY

6   *If you put your nose into water you will also wet your cheeks*   GEORGIA

7   *The candle is put into the lantern and the moth is left outside fluttering*   IRAN

8   *The one who has put an egg into a bottle can easily take it out*   NIGERIA

9   *The idle person will put the cat in the fire*   SCOTLAND

10   *Don't put all your eggs in one basket*   ENGLAND

11   *To get out a rusty nail you must take away a piece of the
wall*   MALTA

12   *You can't get blood out of a stone*   ENGLAND

13   *If you pick the fluff from a blanket it comes to pieces*
      INDIA

14   *You can't take the grunt out of a pig*   USA

156 PASSING

1   *The hippo blocked up the ford, and no one could cross*
      NIGERIA

2   *The moon moves slowly, but it gets across the town*
      CÔTE D'IVOIRE

3   *Those who wait long at the ferry will get across some
time*   SCOTLAND

4   *Let everyone praise the bridge they go over*   ENGLAND

5   *There is no fence that does not let the wind through*
      CHINA

6   *Lower your head modestly while passing, and you will
harvest bananas*   REPUBLIC OF CONGO

7   *Creaking wagons are long in passing*   NETHERLANDS

8   *The dog barks, but the camel passes on*   SUDAN

9   *On an unknown path every foot is slow*   IRELAND

10 *There are many paths to the top of the mountain – but the view is always the same* CHINA

11 *You do not teach the paths of the forest to an old gorilla*
REPUBLIC OF CONGO

12 *A smooth way makes the foot slip* ESTONIA

157 ASCENT

1 *Looking for fish? Don't climb a tree* CHINA

2 *Even if you cannot climb the mountain do not remain in the valley* GERMANY

3 *When an elephant chases you, you climb a prickly tree*
KENYA

4 *Mediocrity is climbing molehills without sweating*
ICELAND

5 *A horse never goes straight up a hill* USA

6 *They cannot climb up who cannot climb down* NORWAY

7 *The boat of affection ascends even mountains*
BANGLADESH

8 *If you would climb into the saddle don't despise the stirrup* GERMANY

9 *If you climb up a tree, you must climb down the same tree* SIERRA LEONE

10 *You can never get all the possums up the same tree* USA

11 *Whoever holds the ladder is as bad as the thief*
  GERMANY

12 *You cannot climb a ladder by pushing others down*
  ENGLAND

13 *Those who place their ladder too steeply will easily fall*
  backwards CZECH REPUBLIC

14 *If you don't scale the mountain, you can't see the plain*
  CHINA

15 *Don't get on the streetcar before it stops* CANADA

16 *When you sweep the stairs, you start at the top*
  GERMANY

17 *The stairs are swept downwards, not upwards*
  ROMANIA

18 *You can't slide uphill* USA

158 DESCENT

1 *Once on a tiger's back, it is hard to alight* CHINA

2 *It is not enough for people to know how to ride; they*
  must know how to fall MEXICO

3 *A fall into a ditch makes you wiser* CHINA

4 *Even monkeys fall from trees* KOREA

5 *The apple does not fall far from the apple-tree* ALBANIA

6   *If we knew where we would fall, we would spread straw there first*   FINLAND

7   *No stone ever falls alone*   BELGIUM

8   *'Tis the one who runs that falls*   IRELAND

9   *Those who place their ladder too steeply will easily fall backwards*   CZECH REPUBLIC

10   *That which falls in the snow comes to light in the thaw*   DENMARK

11   *Do not lift the club too high, it may fall on your head*   FINLAND

12   *It's not so bad to fall in the gutter, but it's worse to lay there*   USA

13   *One never falls but on the side towards which one leans*   FRANCE

14   *Those who tremble to hear a leaf fall should keep out of the wood*   FRANCE

15   *No more leaves can fall in autumn than were grown in spring*   GERMANY

16   *Those who lie on the ground have no place from which to fall*   LATIN

17   *Falling hurts least those who fly low*   CHINA

18   *To fall is no shame, but to remain fallen is*   SWEDEN

19   *What falls into salt becomes salt*   INDIA

20   *Don't look where you fell, but where you slipped*
        LIBERIA

21   *The twig that falls in the water will never become a fish*
        CÔTE D'IVOIRE

22   *The bigger they come, the harder they fall*   USA

23   *Fall down seven times, get up eight*   JAPAN

24   *If the sky fell down, all sparrows would be dead*
        NETHERLANDS

25   *A worm is about the only thing that doesn't fall down*
        USA

26   *Kick an attorney downstairs and he'll stick to you for life*
        SCOTLAND

27   *Everyone pushes a falling fence*   CHINA

28   *Don't get off the merry-go-round before it stops*   USA

29   *If you are worried by the rain you can always plunge into
        the sea*   CHINA

30   *Those who jump over a big stone often stumble over a
        pebble*   NETHERLANDS

31   *Those who stumble twice over the same stone are fools*
        LATIN

32   *They cannot climb up who cannot climb down*   NORWAY

33   *One loose pebble can start a landslide*   USA

34   *If you climb up a tree, you must climb down the same
        tree*   SIERRA LEONE

35   *What goes up must come down*   ENGLAND

36   *You cannot climb a ladder by pushing others down*
ENGLAND

37   *The stairs are swept downwards, not upwards*
ROMANIA

38   *The careful person has also tumbled downstairs*
SWITZERLAND

159 LIFTING – RISING

1   *Do not lift the club too high, it may fall on your head*
FINLAND

2   *It is no use lifting your leg until you come to the stile*
ENGLAND

3   *The eye does not rise above the eyebrow*   SYRIA

4   *Fortune lifts up art, but not art fortune*   GREECE

5   *Fall down seven times, get up eight*   JAPAN

6   *When you pick up a stick at one end, you also pick up the other end*   USA

7   *You won't help shoots grow by pulling them up higher*
CHINA

8   *The one who is not strong enough to lift the stone must roll it*   ESTONIA

9   *Those who sleep with dogs must rise with fleas*
SCOTLAND

10   *Those who simultaneously eat and sing rise up fools*
PHILIPPINES

11   *If your neighbour is an early riser, you will become one*
ALBANIA

12   *The more you stroke a cat, the more it lifts its tail*
ESTONIA

13   *No one will lift the cat's tail unless the cat itself does*
FINLAND

14   *One foot is better than two stilts*   FRANCE

160   LOWERING – DROPPING

1   *They will see their nose who lower their eyes*   NIGERIA

2   *Lower your head modestly while passing, and you will harvest bananas*   REPUBLIC OF CONGO

3   *Those who do not know how to squander their money – buy some porcelain and drop it*   NETHERLANDS

4   *Too many affairs are like pumpkins in water; one pops up while you try to hold down the other*   CHINA

5   *Where should we pour the gravy if not on the rice?*
MALAYSIA

6   *Love your neighbour, yet pull not down your hedge*
ENGLAND

7   *If you try to sit on two chairs, you'll sit on the floor*   USA

8   *God knows on which knee the camel will squat down*
     AFGHANISTAN

9   *They must stoop who have a low door*   SCOTLAND

10   *The junk capsizes and the shark has its bellyful*
     MALAYSIA

11   *When a canoe capsizes, everyone gets wet*   MADAGASCAR

12   *The lot of the coconut shell is to float and the lot of the
     stone is to sink*   INDONESIA

161 JUMPING

1   *By trying often, the monkey learns to jump from the tree*
     CAMEROON

2   *Those who plant a hedge round their garden invite it to
     be jumped*   RUSSIA

3   *Do not jump high under a low ceiling*   CZECH REPUBLIC

4   *Those who jump over a big stone often stumble over a
     pebble*   NETHERLANDS

5   *Empty gossip jumps with one leg*   ESTONIA

6   *Ambition and fleas jump high*   GERMANY

7   *You cannot jump over two ditches at the same time*
     NETHERLANDS

8   *When the cat's not home, the mice jump on the table*
NETHERLANDS

9   *Never say 'whoopee' before you jump*   CANADA

10 *A dog in desperation will leap over a wall*   CHINA

11 *Everyone leaps the dyke where it's lowest*   SCOTLAND

12 *One must draw back in order to leap further*   FRANCE

13 *Look before you leap*   ENGLAND

14 *When one sheep is over the dam, the rest will follow*
NETHERLANDS

162 REVOLVING

1   *Grief and joy are a revolving wheel*   INDIA

2   *Strong people can spin their top in the sand*   JAPAN ·

3   *A good driver turns in a small space*   FRANCE

4   *Those who have the frying-pan in their hand turn it at
will*   NETHERLANDS

5   *The steam that blows the whistle never turns the wheel*
USA

6   *It is the turning of the mill that makes the flour heap*
INDIA

7   *The one who is not strong enough to lift the stone must
roll it*   ESTONIA

8   The roughest stone becomes smooth when it is much
     rolled   SWITZERLAND

9   The energy of the dung-beetle is put into rolling its ball
     of dung   CHINA

10   A rolling stone gathers no moss   ENGLAND

11   You never know your luck till the wheel stops   USA

163 SHAKING

1   A tree with ripe fruit needs little shaking   SWITZERLAND

2   If you don't like my apples, don't shake my tree   USA

3   Turn your tongue seven times before speaking   FRANCE

4   Words shake but examples attract   SERBIA

5   The saddest dog sometimes wags its tail   ENGLAND

6   If you get into the pack you need not bark, but wag your
     tail you must   RUSSIA

7   The tail wags the dog   ENGLAND

164 THINGS

1   Those who do not wish little things do not deserve big
     things   BELGIUM

2   You can't find a thing except in the place it is   IRELAND

3 *God, what things we see when we go out without a gun!*
   SOUTH AFRICA

4 *An indispensable thing never has much value*   GEORGIA

5 *In darkness all things are black*   SLOVENIA

6 *When you give a child a nut, give it also something to
   break it with*   GEORGIA

7 *Even the bottom of a basket finds something to hold*
   MADAGASCAR

8 *If you look in a chief's bag you will always find
   something*   UGANDA

9 *If you wish to be angry, pay for something in advance*
   MONTENEGRO

165 MATERIALS

1 *The final lead weights are the heaviest*   NETHERLANDS

2 *Empty barns need no thatch*   ENGLAND

3 *You may know a carpenter by his chips*   ENGLAND

4 *It takes a long time to sharpen a hammer made of wood*
   NETHERLANDS

5 *Rotten wood cannot be carved*   CHINA

6 *Not every sort of wood is fit to make an arrow*   FRANCE

7 *A little wood will heat a little oven*   ENGLAND

8   *It isn't every kind of wood that can make a whistle*
LATVIA

9   *Any wood will do to make a signpost*   GREECE

10   *Wood half-burnt is easily kindled*   ENGLAND

11   *In crooked wood one recognizes the artist*   TOGO

12   *Golden bishop, wooden crozier; wooden bishop, golden crozier*   FRANCE

13   *Don't spoil the ship for a ha'porth of tar*   ENGLAND

14   *A cloth is not woven from a single thread*   CHINA

15   *If you pound palm-nuts, some will stain your cloth*
CÔTE D'IVOIRE

16   *A white cloth and a stain never agree*   NIGERIA

17   *Cut your coat according to your cloth*   ENGLAND

18   *The wife of the amber-turner wears pearls of glass*   IRAN

19   *One must not shoot a glass arrow into a painted deer*
EGYPT

20   *People who live in glass houses shouldn't throw stones*
ENGLAND

21   *Where paper speaks, beards are silent*   FRANCE

22   *Paper can't wrap up a fire*   CHINA

23   *If it is your own lantern, do not poke holes in the paper*
CHINA

24   *Paper does not blush*   ITALY

166 WORLD

1   *It's a small world*   ENGLAND

2   *All the wealth of the world is in the weather*   SCOTLAND

3   *To be in the habit of no habit is the worst habit in the world*   WALES

4   *The world is dark an inch ahead*   JAPAN

5   *A frog beneath a coconut shell believes there is no other world*   MALAYSIA

6   *Every head is a world*   CUBA

7   *No matter how much the world changes, cats will never lay eggs*   MALI

8   *Money makes the world go round*   USA

167 SUN – MOON – STARS

1   *When the sun shines the moon has nothing to do*
    FRANCE

2   *Even in the sun there are spots*   HUNGARY

3   *The sun shines on both sides of the hedge*   ENGLAND

4   *A shadow is a feeble thing but no sun can drive it away*
    SWEDEN

5   *The sun cannot shine into an inverted bowl*   CHINA

* * * * * * * * * * * * * * * * * * *

14 FIRST PERSON PROVERBS

Proverbs, being generalizations, are usually expressed in the third person. But occasionally we find some in the first person. They make up less than twenty of the 2,000 or so proverbs in this book.

> *I gave an order to a cat, and the cat gave it to its tail.*
> *If I keep a green bough in my heart, a singing-bird will come.*
> *'If I rest, I rust', says the key.*
> *God does not shave – why should I?*
> *I can tell by my own pot how the others are boiling.*
> *The fish said, 'I have much to say, but my mouth is full*
> *of water.'*
> *Ideas start with 'I'.*
> *Who teaches me for a day is my father for a lifetime.*
> *Those who cheat me once, shame fall them; those who cheat me*
> *twice, shame fall me.*
> *Their mosquito won't bite me.*
> *The friends of my friends are my friends.*
> *The enemies of my enemies are my friends.*
> *My banjo has no bells on it.*
> *If my aunt had wheels, she might be an omnibus.*
> *If you don't like my apples, don't shake my tree.*
> *Your liberty ends where my nose begins.*

* * * * * * * * * * * * * * * * * * *

6   *We can never see the sun rise by looking into the west*
JAPAN

7   *Make hay while the sun shines*   ENGLAND

8   *An old moon's mist never died of thirst*   IRELAND

9   *God saves the moon from the wolves*   POLAND

10   *Even the moon does not shine before it rises*   FINLAND

11   *When you show the moon to a child, it sees only your finger*   ZAMBIA

12   *A blind dog won't bark at the moon*   IRELAND

13   *If you love, love the moon; if you steal, steal a camel*
EGYPT

14   *The moon moves slowly, but it gets across the town*
CÔTE D'IVOIRE

15   *If it were not for the night, we could never know the stars*
GERMANY

16   *Even a small star shines in the darkness*   FINLAND

168 SKY – CLOUDS – WEATHER

1   *If it weren't for the wind the spiders would web the sky*
SERBIA

2   *Stars shine always in a clear sky*   ESTONIA

3   *If the sky fell down, all sparrows would be dead*
NETHERLANDS

4   *The highest hill is usually covered with clouds*
SCOTLAND

5   *Every cloud has a silver lining*   ENGLAND

6   *Thunder-clouds do not always give rain*   ARMENIA

7   *All the wealth of the world is in the weather*   SCOTLAND

8   *Never rely on love or the weather*   GERMANY

9   *Everybody talks about the weather, but nobody does anything about it*   USA

10   *A misty morning may have a fine day*   ENGLAND

11   *An old moon's mist never died of thirst*   IRELAND

12   *Rain doesn't remain in the sky*   ESTONIA

13   *Rain which does not fall remains in the sky*   ITALY

14   *When it rains, the roof always drips the same way*
LIBERIA

15   *To the ant, a few drops of rain is a flood*   JAPAN

16   *Who has been almost drowned fears not the rain*
ALBANIA

17   *Rain does not fall only on one roof*   CAMEROON

18   *A scalded cock runs away from the rain*   BULGARIA

19   *Raindrops can't tell broadcloth from jeans*   USA

20   *Remember the rain that made your corn grow*   HAITI

21   *If you are worried by the rain you can always plunge into the sea*   CHINA

22 *Rain falls where it has rained before*   INDIA

23 *When it rains on one it only drips on another*
      NETHERLANDS

24 *Under trees it rains twice*   SWITZERLAND

25 *While it rains, fill the jar*   TURKEY

26 *Don't be so much in love that you can't tell when it's
      raining*   MADAGASCAR

27 *It never rains but it pours*   ENGLAND

28 *Save your bottles; it may rain whiskey*   USA

29 *No one thinks of the snow that fell last year*   SWEDEN

30 *A bee was never caught in a shower*   ENGLAND

31 *It is the first shower that wets*   ITALY

32 *A hat is not made for one shower*   ENGLAND

169   WIND

1 *The copse does not rustle if the wind does not blow*
      HUNGARY

2 *After a typhoon there are pears to gather up*   CHINA

3 *The one who enters as a whirlwind will depart as an ant*
      INDONESIA

4 *There is no fence that does not let the wind through*
      CHINA

5   *A stone is never uprooted by the wind*
REPUBLIC OF CONGO

6   *Each bay has its own wind*   FIJI

7   *The dog barks, the wind carries*   ESTONIA

8   *If there is a wave, there must be a wind*   CHINA

9   *We cannot direct the wind, but we can adjust the sails*
GERMANY

10   *Words and feathers are taken by the wind*
SPAIN: BASQUE

11   *If it weren't for the wind the spiders would web the sky*
SERBIA

12   *A north-easterly wind is heaven's broom*   ESTONIA

13   *It is folly to put flour into a bag facing the wind*
GERMANY

14   *Upon what tree does the wind not strike?*   INDIA

15   *Tomorrow blows the wind of tomorrow*   JAPAN

16   *It's an ill wind that blows nobody good*   ENGLAND

170   WEIGHT

1   *A blanket becomes heavier as it becomes wetter*   INDIA

2   *The final lead weights are the heaviest*   NETHERLANDS

3   *Not the load, but the overload kills*   SPAIN

4   *A buffalo does not feel the weight of his own horns*
    INDIA

5   *Words and feathers are taken by the wind*
    SPAIN: BASQUE

6   *A feather does not stick without gum*   AFGHANISTAN

7   *There is no light burden on a long road*   CHINA

8   *In rivers and bad government, the lightest things swim at
    the top*   USA

9   *An ounce of luck is better than a pound of knowledge*
    BELGIUM

10 *Fame is a gull floating on water*   CHINA

11 *The lot of the coconut shell is to float and the lot of the
    stone is to sink*   INDONESIA

12 *The fruit on a creeper is no burden to it*   SRI LANKA

13 *No elephant is burdened by its own trunk*
    SOUTH AFRICA

171 HARD – BRITTLE – SOFT

1   *Endurance pierces marble*   MOROCCO

2   *The empty nut is the hardest*   WALES

3   *The older the buck, the harder his horn*   SCOTLAND

4   *Where the finger-nail will enter, there is no need of iron*
    INDIA

5   *If you had teeth of steel, you could eat iron coconuts*
SENEGAL

6   *Knock before crossing even a stone bridge*   KOREA

7   *The tighter the string, the sooner it will break*   WALES

8   *Fortune is glass; just when it is bright it is broken*
LATIN

9   *Those who do not know how to squander their money –*
buy some porcelain and drop it   NETHERLANDS

10   *When the beans get too thick, the pot burns*   USA

11   *Blood is thicker than water*   ENGLAND

12   *Sticks in a bundle are unbreakable*   KENYA

13   *Ashes will always blow back into the face of the thrower*
NIGERIA

14   *If you laugh at your mother-in-law, you'll get dirt in*
your eye   KENYA

15   *The dust raised by the sheep does not choke the wolf*
ENGLAND

16   *There is no dust so blinding as gold dust*   USA

17   *It is folly to put flour into a bag facing the wind*
GERMANY

18   *Laws have wax noses*   FRANCE

19   *Many have bees and buy wax*   GERMANY

20   *Have a mouth as sharp as a dagger, but a heart as soft*
as tofu   CHINA

21   *One cannot ski so softly that the traces cannot be seen*
         FINLAND

22   *It is the softness of the lime that is fatal to the bird*
         MADAGASCAR

23   *Carve good deeds in stone, bad ones in sand*   ESTONIA

24   *Strong people can spin their top in the sand*   JAPAN

25   *A blow on the purse of another is like a blow on a sand-
      hill*   EGYPT

172 FLOUR

1   *Enter the mill and you come out floury*   SERBIA

2   *The way of the wheat is through the mill*   AFGHANISTAN

3   *No mill will grind wet corn*   ESTONIA

4   *The mills of God grind slowly*   ENGLAND

5   *It is the turning of the mill that makes the flour heap*
         INDIA

6   *Those who will have a cake out of the wheat must tarry
      the grinding*   ENGLAND

7   *That miller is honest who has hair on his teeth*
         GERMANY

173 RUBBING – LUBRICATING

1   *A gem cannot be polished without friction, nor a person perfected without trials*   CHINA

2   *One does not rub buttocks with a porcupine*   GHANA

3   *The world will not conquer him who is always rubbing his beard*   INDIA

4   *Be like the mouth and hand: when the hand is hurt the mouth blows on it; when the mouth is hurt the hand rubs it*   MADAGASCAR

5   *The wheel that does the squeaking is the one that gets the grease*   USA

6   *A greased cartwheel does not squeak*   ESTONIA

7   *That which creaks must be oiled*   LATVIA

8   *Oil and water will not mix*   ENGLAND

9   *With patience and saliva, the elephant swallows an ant*   COLOMBIA

174 WATER

1   *Where water has once flowed it will flow again*   MONTENEGRO

2   *Community is as strong as water, and as stupid as a pig*   RUSSIA

3   *Blood is thicker than water*   ENGLAND

4   *Dogs do not know how to swim until the water reaches their ears*   UKRAINE

5   *Cabbage is the best invalid, it needs only a little water*
    SERBIA

6   *It is easy to drive a frog into the water*   SERBIA

7   *Any water puts out fire*   FRANCE

8   *A little drop of water silences a boiling pot*   GERMANY

9   *The fish said, 'I have much to say, but my mouth is full of water.'*   GEORGIA

10 *Those who have been scalded with hot soup blow on cold water*   UKRAINE

11 *Do not fear a stain that disappears with water*   SPAIN

12 *If water is noisy, there are no fish in it*   MYANMAR

13 *The dragon in shallow water becomes the butt of shrimps*
    CHINA

14 *Where would the gravy be but for the water?*   ZANZIBAR

15 *If you put your nose into water you will also wet your cheeks*   GEORGIA

16 *Oil and water will not mix*   ENGLAND

17 *The water is shallowest where it babbles*   WALES

18 *A coconut shell full of water is a sea to an ant*
    ZANZIBAR

19 *No matter how hard you throw a dead fish in the water, it still won't swim*   REPUBLIC OF CONGO

20 *Even if water flows in all directions, the sand will remain at the bottom* GEORGIA

21 *Don't stand by the water and long for fish; go home and weave a net* CHINA

22 *Far waters cannot quench near fires* CHINA

23 *The water is the same on both sides of the boat* FINLAND

24 *Cast no dirt into the well that has given you water* ENGLAND

25 *It is no use throwing water on a drowned rat* IRELAND

26 *Water will run where it ran before* BULGARIA

27 *A clean face needs no water* BOHEMIA

28 *Too many affairs are like pumpkins in water; one pops up while you try to hold down the other* CHINA

29 *It is hard to swim between two stretches of bad water* NETHERLANDS

30 *If the bucket has been long in the well, it ought to come out with water* NIGERIA

31 *If familiarity were useful, water wouldn't cook fish* CAMEROON

32 *Still waters run deep* ENGLAND

33 *Only a fool tests the depth of the water with both feet* NAMIBIA

34 *A lobster loves water, but not when he's being cooked in it* SENEGAL

35 *Warm water never forgets that it was once cold* NIGERIA

36 *The twig that falls in the water will never become a fish* CÔTE D'IVOIRE

37 *Fame is a gull floating on water* CHINA

38 *The lazy ox drinks dirty water* COLOMBIA

39 *Dirty water cannot be washed* TOGO

40 *Those who live in the attic know where the roof leaks* NIGERIA

175 SEMI-LIQUIDS – SEMI-SOLIDS

1 *On a slimy shore it is easy to push a canoe* CAMEROON

2 *That which falls in the snow comes to light in the thaw* DENMARK

3 *Froth is no beer* NETHERLANDS

4 *It's a poor crust that can't grease its own plate* USA

5 *Precious ointments are put in small boxes* FRANCE

176 WET – DRY

1   *No mill will grind wet corn*   ESTONIA

2   *When a canoe capsizes, everyone gets wet*   MADAGASCAR

3   *You cannot cross a river without getting wet*
       SOUTH AFRICA

4   *The damp burns with the dry*   TURKEY

5   *Every blade of grass gets its own drop of dew*
       SCOTLAND

6   *Painting the pump will not clean out the well*   ENGLAND

7   *A blanket becomes heavier as it becomes wetter*   INDIA

8   *Cats love fish but fear to wet their paws*   CHINA

9   *If you put your nose into water you will also wet your
cheeks*   GEORGIA

10   *A dry spoon scratches the mouth*   RUSSIA

11   *Even deep water-holes may get dry*   SOUTH AFRICA

12   *A dry bone is never licked*   ALBANIA

13   *The damp burns with the dry*   TURKEY

14   *Go fishing for three days and dry the nets for two*
       CHINA

15   *Those who have been in the oven know how pears are
dried*   BELGIUM

16   *You can't catch trout with dry trousers*   USA

177 SEAS

1 *A coconut shell full of water is a sea to an ant*
ZANZIBAR

2 *Bacchus has drowned more people than Neptune*
GERMANY

3 *Better a neighbour over the wall than a brother over the sea* ALBANIA

4 *Follow the river and you will reach the sea* FRANCE

5 *In a calm sea everyone is a pilot* ENGLAND

6 *Do a good deed and throw it into the sea* BULGARIA

7 *Those who go to sea without biscuits return without teeth*
FRANCE: CORSICA

8 *Before going to war say one prayer; before going to sea, two; before getting married, three* POLAND

9 *Those who wish to learn to pray must go to sea*
ENGLAND

10 *If you are worried by the rain you can always plunge into the sea* CHINA

11 *The sea is made bigger even by one drop* RUSSIA

12 *The existence of the sea means the existence of pirates*
MALAYSIA

13 *All rivers do what they can for the sea* ENGLAND

14 *Don't plant a seed in the sea* KENYA

15   *Time and tide wait for no one*   ENGLAND

16   *If there is a wave, there must be a wind*   CHINA

17   *Each bay has its own wind*   FIJI

178 RIVERS – STREAMS

1   *The brook would lose its song if you removed the rocks*
USA

2   *The shrimp that sleeps is carried away by the current*
CHILE

3   *Even if water flows in all directions, the sand will remain
at the bottom*   GEORGIA

4   *Where water has once flowed it will flow again*
MONTENEGRO

5   *Slowly, slowly makes the slug arrive at the fountain*
RWANDA

6   *Those who have no thirst have no business at the
fountain*   NETHERLANDS

7   *Well water does not invade river water*   CHINA

8   *No matter how full the river, it still wants to grow*
REPUBLIC OF CONGO

9   *Follow the river and you will reach the sea*   FRANCE

10   *All rivers do what they can for the sea*   ENGLAND

11 *Although the river is broad there are times when boats collide* CHINA

12 *A river is filled by its tributaries* ZIMBABWE

13 *In the middle of the river do not change horses* PERU

14 *No matter how long a log floats on the river it will never be a crocodile* MALI

15 *You cannot cross a river without getting wet*
    SOUTH AFRICA

16 *In rivers and bad government, the lightest things swim at the top* USA

17 *Those who are carried down the stream need not row*
    ENGLAND

18 *Water will run where it ran before* BULGARIA

19 *Still waters run deep* ENGLAND

20 *When you want to test the depth of a stream, don't use both feet* CHINA

21 *Dead fish go always with the stream* ENGLAND

22 *Slander by the stream will be heard by the frogs*
    MOZAMBIQUE

179 INLAND WATER

1   *An ant may well destroy a whole dam*   CHINA

2   *When one sheep is over the dam, the rest will follow*
    NETHERLANDS

3   *Two crocodiles don't live in one pond*   GAMBIA

4   *The rhinoceros which has no calf takes itself to the muddy
pool*   SOUTH AFRICA

5   *There's a puddle at every door, and before some doors
there are two*   SCOTLAND

6   *Many drops make a puddle*   NETHERLANDS

7   *Even deep water-holes may get dry*   SOUTH AFRICA

8   *If there is a marsh there will be frogs*   UKRAINE

9   *Oats pull the cart out of the mud*   SERBIA

10   *Those who mix themselves with the mud will be eaten by
the swine*   NETHERLANDS

180 CONDUITS

1   *A fall into a ditch makes you wiser*   CHINA

2   *To fill a ditch a mound must come down*   ARMENIA

3   *You cannot jump over two ditches at the same time*
    NETHERLANDS

4   *There's nothing like being bespattered for making someone defy the gutter*   FRANCE

5   *It's not so bad to fall in the gutter, but it's worse to lay there*   USA

181   LAND – GROUND

1   *Everyone is foolish until they buy land*   IRELAND

2   *Those who cannot build the dyke should hand over the land*   NETHERLANDS

3   *A house is not built on earth, but on a woman*   SERBIA

4   *Sweetest the grass next to the ground*   WALES

5   *One is usually at a loss to know how to sweep the ground in a market-place*   NIGERIA

6   *If you don't scale the mountain, you can't see the plain*   CHINA

7   *Even if water flows in all directions, the sand will remain at the bottom*   GEORGIA

8   *On a slimy shore it is easy to push a canoe*   CAMEROON

9   *It is not a fish until it is on the bank*   IRELAND

10   *Wherever there is a field, there are grasshoppers*   MALAYSIA

11   *Out of old fields come new grain*   USA

12   *When in love, a cliff becomes a meadow*   ETHIOPIA

182 ROCKS – STONES

1   *A boulder is the father of the rocks*   NIGERIA

2   *The brook would lose its song if you removed the rocks*
    USA

3   *No stone ever falls alone*   BELGIUM

4   *A word and a stone let go cannot be called back*
    ENGLAND

5   *The lot of the coconut shell is to float and the lot of the
    stone is to sink*   INDONESIA

6   *Boil a stone in butter and its juice will be drunk*
    IRELAND

7   *A stationary stone gathers moss*   RUSSIA

8   *A rolling stone gathers no moss*   ENGLAND

9   *Those who jump over a big stone often stumble over a
    pebble*   NETHERLANDS

10   *No land without stones, or meat without bones*
    ENGLAND

11   *Carve good deeds in stone, bad ones in sand*   ESTONIA

12   *The one who is not strong enough to lift the stone must
    roll it*   ESTONIA

13   *On a level road a small stone upsets the cartload*
    ESTONIA

14   *Those who stumble twice over the same stone are fools*
    LATIN

15   *The roughest stone becomes smooth when it is much rolled*   SWITZERLAND

16   *It is easy to hurt yourself on a stone that has sharp corners*   KOREA

17   *You can't get blood out of a stone*   ENGLAND

18   *A stone is never uprooted by the wind*
     REPUBLIC OF CONGO

19   *The throwers of stones fling away the strength of their own arms*   NIGERIA

20   *If you believe, it is a deity; otherwise, a stone*   INDIA

21   *Abundance will make cotton pull a stone*   NIGERIA

22   *A stone from the hand of a friend is an apple*
     MAURITANIA

23   *Whether the stone bumps the jug, or the jug bumps the stone, it is bad for the jug*   USA

24   *People who live in glass houses shouldn't throw stones*
     ENGLAND

25   *You can get used to anything except a rock in your shoe*
     USA

26   *Better a diamond with a flaw than a pebble without one*
     CHINA

27   *One pebble doesn't make a floor*   NIGERIA

28   *One loose pebble can start a landslide*   USA

29   *A fallen lighthouse is more dangerous than a reef*
CHINA

183 BREATHING – BLOWING

1   *The tortoise breathes; it is only its shell that prevents our noticing it* NIGERIA

2   *What is inflated too much will burst into fragments*
ETHIOPIA

3   *What reliance can be placed on a sneeze?* INDIA

4   *Do not blow into a bear's ear* CZECH REPUBLIC

5   *Those who blow in the fire will get sparks in their eyes*
GERMANY

6   *Those who have been scalded with hot soup blow on cold water* UKRAINE

7   *Those who have burnt their mouth with milk blow on ice-cream* TURKEY

8   *Be like the mouth and hand: when the hand is hurt the mouth blows on it; when the mouth is hurt the hand rubs it* MADAGASCAR

9   *The steam that blows the whistle never turns the wheel*
USA

10   *The dust raised by the sheep does not choke the wolf*
ENGLAND

11 *Ashes will always blow back into the face of the thrower*
NIGERIA

184 BIRTH

1 *No one is a blacksmith at birth* NAMIBIA

2 *At birth we cry – at death we see why* BULGARIA

3 *Where one was born, every blade of grass pleases* ITALY

4 *There's one born every minute* USA

5 *A crab does not beget a bird* CÔTE D'IVOIRE

6 *The shell is needed till the bird is hatched* RUSSIA

7 *Don't count your chickens before they're hatched*
ENGLAND

185 LIFE

1 *A smile will gain you ten more years of life* CHINA

2 *Bread is the staff of life, but the pudding makes a good crutch* SCOTLAND

3 *As long as life lasts, the cow never stops moving its tail*
NIGERIA

4 *Kick an attorney downstairs and he'll stick to you for life*
SCOTLAND

* * * * * * * * * * * * * * * * * *

15 A CHARACTER CALLED PROVERBS

The Elizabethan scholar Henry Porter is known from one surviving play, *The pleasant history of the two angry women of Abington* [that is, Abingdon in Oxfordshire], published in 1599. Its title page continues: 'With the humorous mirth of Dicke Coomes and Nicholas Prouerbes, two seruingmen'. As we might expect from his name, Nicholas is full of proverbs – a trait which does not always go down well with his companions.

* * * * * * * * * * * * * * * * * *

5   *The best things in life are free*   USA

6   *Seven days is the length of a guest's life*   MYANMAR

7   *Variety is the spice of life*   ENGLAND

8   *Before marrying live wildly for three years*   POLAND

9   *It's a great life if you don't weaken*   USA

10   *The more one sleeps the less one lives*   PORTUGAL

11   *It is the prudent hyena that lives long*   ZAMBIA

12   *Life is just one damned thing after another*   USA

186 DEATH

1   *The miser and the pig are useless unless they are dead*
FRANCE

2   *No matter how hard you throw a dead fish in the water,
it still won't swim*   REPUBLIC OF CONGO

3   *Dead fish go always with the stream*   ENGLAND

4   *What good is the hay if the horse is dead?*   PHILIPPINES

5   *An empty sack can't stand, nor a dead cat walk*
IRELAND

6   *It is in sugar that you see the dead ant*   MALAYSIA

7   *Those who wait for a dead person's shoes are in danger
of going barefoot*   FRANCE

8   *A bad thing never dies*   ENGLAND

9   *If the sky fell down, all sparrows would be dead*
NETHERLANDS

10   *What's the use of consulting a dead person's horoscope?*
SENEGAL

11   *On a dead tree there are no monkeys*   MOZAMBIQUE

12   *Dead men tell no tales*   ENGLAND

13   *Habit is a shirt that we wear till death*   RUSSIA

14   *Death and proverbs love brevity*   GERMANY

15   *Poets and pigs are appreciated only after their death*
ITALY

16 *Who knows when death or a customer will come?*
INDIA

17 *There dies a poet in everyone* ENGLAND

18 *Those who must die must die in the dark, even though they sell candles* COLOMBIA

19 *An old moon's mist never died of thirst* IRELAND

20 *If you drink you die, if you don't drink you die, so it is better to drink* RUSSIA

21 *An elephant does not die from one broken rib* KENYA

22 *Generals die in bed* USA

23 *Old soldiers never die* ENGLAND

24 *No one wages war with ghosts*
DEMOCRATIC REPUBLIC OF CONGO

25 *When an ant gets wings it perishes* SERBIA

26 *To part is to die a little* FRANCE

187 LIFE v DEATH

1 *Life without literature is death* LATIN

2 *What is said over the dead lion's body could not be said to him alive* REPUBLIC OF CONGO

3 *Those who live with hope die with desire* BELGIUM

4 *It is a fine thing to die for one's fatherland, but a still finer thing to live for it* HUNGARY

5   *Better one living word than a hundred dead ones*
     GERMANY

6   *At birth we cry – at death we see why*   BULGARIA

7   *Teachers die, but books live on*   NETHERLANDS

188 KILLING

1   *We each have our own way of killing fleas*   SPAIN

2   *There are more ways than one to kill a cat*   ENGLAND

3   *Curiosity killed the cat*   ENGLAND

4   *If you kill, kill an elephant; if you rob, rob a treasury*
     INDIA

5   *A roaring lion kills no game*   UGANDA

6   *Kill a chicken before a monkey*   CHINA

7   *Why use poison when you can kill with honey?*
     BELGIUM

8   *Nothing kills like doing nothing*   DENMARK

9   *To kill with words is also murder*   GERMANY

10   *Not the load, but the overload kills*   SPAIN

11   *You need not take someone else's hand to crush a sand-
     fly*   NIGERIA

12   *The mouth is the healer and executioner of the body*
     DENMARK

13 *It is the softness of the lime that is fatal to the bird*
MADAGASCAR

189 DROWNING

1 *Bacchus has drowned more people than Neptune*
GERMANY

2 *Coupled sheep drown each other* NETHERLANDS

3 *It is no use throwing water on a drowned rat* IRELAND

4 *A drowning man will clutch at a straw* ENGLAND

5 *Who has been almost drowned fears not the rain*
ALBANIA

190 CORPSES – BURIALS

1 *What is said over the dead lion's body could not be said to him alive* REPUBLIC OF CONGO

2 *Where a carcass is, there will vultures be* MALAYSIA

3 *If you follow a crow long enough you light on carrion*
ALBANIA

4 *Will the crocodile reject the carcass?* MALAYSIA

5 *Those who seek a constant friend go to the cemetery*
RUSSIA

6   *Those who read many epitaphs, lose their memory*
     LATIN

7   *There is no marriage where there is no weeping, and no
     funeral where there is no laughing*   ITALY

8   *The one who seeks revenge should remember to dig two
     graves*   CHINA

9   *There is time enough to yawn in the grave*   ESTONIA

10   *A young doctor makes a full graveyard*   CHINA

11   *A shroud has no pockets*   SCOTLAND

12   *Shed no tears until seeing the coffin*   CHINA

13   *Every time we laugh a nail is removed from our coffin*
     ITALY

191   BEARS

1   *Do not blow into a bear's ear*   CZECH REPUBLIC

2   *Sell not your bearskin until you have the bear*   USA

3   *Everyone knows the bear, but the bear knows no one*
     FINLAND

4   *The one who has taken the bear into the boat must cross
     over with him*   SWEDEN

5   *Time to catch bears is when they're out*   USA

192 CAMELS

1   *God knows on which knee the camel will squat down*
AFGHANISTAN

2   *The dog barks, but the camel passes on*   SUDAN

3   *One camel does not make fun of another camel's hump*
GUINEA

4   *If you love, love the moon; if you steal, steal a camel*
EGYPT

193 CATS

1   *Beware of people who dislike cats*   IRELAND

2   *Wake not a sleeping cat*   FRANCE

3   *You come with a cat and call it a rabbit*   CAMEROON

4   *Cats love fish but fear to wet their paws*   CHINA

5   *The dog may be wonderful prose, but only the cat is poetry*   FRANCE

6   *It is a cunning mouse which nests in the cat's ear*
ENGLAND

7   *What should you expect from a cat but a kitten?*
IRELAND

8   *In a cat's eye, all things belong to cats*   ENGLAND

9   *An old cat will not learn how to dance*   MOROCCO

10   *Happy owner, happy cat; indifferent owner, reclusive cat*
      CHINA

11   *A cat may look at a king*   ENGLAND

12   *A cat with mittens won't catch mice*   SCOTLAND

13   *The cat who frightens the mice away is as good as the cat who eats them*   GERMANY

14   *A cat may go to a monastery, but she still remains a cat*
      ETHIOPIA

15   *When rats infest the palace a lame cat is better than the swiftest horse*   CHINA

16   *A good cat deserves a good rat*   ENGLAND

17   *An empty sack can't stand, nor a dead cat walk*
      IRELAND

18   *Politeness pleases even a cat*   CZECH REPUBLIC

19   *The more you stroke a cat, the more it lifts its tail*
      ESTONIA

20   *In the dark all cats are grey*   ENGLAND

21   *No one will lift the cat's tail unless the cat itself does*
      FINLAND

22   *When you have trodden on the cat, what help is it to stroke her back?*   SWITZERLAND

23   *The cat does not catch mice for God*   INDIA

24   *Curiosity killed the cat*   ENGLAND

25 When the mouse laughs at the cat, there is a hole
GAMBIA

26 When the cat's not home, the mice jump on the table
NETHERLANDS

27 There are more ways than one to kill a cat   ENGLAND

28 No matter how much the world changes, cats will never
lay eggs   MALI

29 While the cat's away, the mice will play   ENGLAND

30 The idle person will put the cat in the fire   SCOTLAND

31 I gave an order to a cat, and the cat gave it to its tail
CHINA

194 CATTLE – OXEN

1 Men hold the buffalo by its rope, a ruler by his word
INDONESIA

2 The one who carries the bludgeon owns the buffalo
INDIA

3 One buffalo brings mud and all the herd are smeared
with it   MALAYSIA

4 A buffalo does not feel the weight of his own horns
INDIA

5 A bull does not enjoy fame in two herds   ZAMBIA

6 Why feed a bullock after it is sold?   INDIA

7 *New-born calves don't fear tigers* CHINA

8 *It is possible to talk to cattle if you have common sense*
SWITZERLAND

9 *Black cows give white milk* GERMANY

10 *Milk the cow that stands still* ENGLAND

11 *The cow which has the loudest bellowing has the
slenderest tail* IRELAND

12 *Why should the cow trouble to think if she has plenty of
hay?* SLOVAKIA

13 *If you want to keep your milk sweet, leave it in the cow*
LIBERIA

14 *As long as life lasts, the cow never stops moving its tail*
NIGERIA

15 *You never know how a cow catches a rabbit*
NETHERLANDS

16 *A cow that has no tail should not try to chase away flies*
GUINEA

17 *Cows can't catch no rabbits* USA

18 *Those who steal a pin will steal an ox* KOREA

19 *The hindermost ox also reaches the kraal*
SOUTH AFRICA

20 *An ox is bound with ropes and a person with words*
ITALY

21 *Beauty draws more than oxen* ENGLAND

22   *The lazy ox drinks dirty water*   COLOMBIA

23   *The end of an ox is beef, and the end of a lie is grief*
     MADAGASCAR

24   *Those who have lost their oxen are always hearing bells*
     SPAIN

195 DOGS

1   *If you get to thinking you're someone of influence, try
    ordering around someone else's dog*   USA

2   *A dog in desperation will leap over a wall*   CHINA

3   *Eat with the dogs, howl with the wolves*   ALBANIA

4   *A dog may look at a bishop*   FRANCE

5   *Do not dwell in a city where a horse does not neigh nor a
    dog bark*   ENGLAND

6   *The saddest dog sometimes wags its tail*   ENGLAND

7   *One dog can't fight*   IRELAND

8   *Those who sleep with dogs must rise with fleas*
    SCOTLAND

9   *A little dog is really brave in front of his master's house*
    HAITI

10 *The greatest love is mother-love; after that comes a dog's
    love; and after that the love of a sweetheart*   POLAND

11 *Let sleeping dogs lie*   ENGLAND

12   *Dogs do not know how to swim until the water reaches their ears*   UKRAINE

13   *A dog last year is a dog this year*   SERBIA

14   *Don't snap your fingers at the dogs before you are outside the village*   FRANCE

15   *The dog barks, the wind carries*   ESTONIA

16   *A dog's mouth yields no ivory*   CHINA

17   *A blind dog won't bark at the moon*   IRELAND

18   *Before you beat a dog, find out who its master is*   CHINA

19   *Pelt a dog with a bone and you will not offend him*   ITALY

20   *Every dog has its day*   ENGLAND

21   *Never feed a dog with corn, nor attempt to pick your teeth with a pair of scissors*   CHINA

22   *Numerous calls confuse the dog*   TANZANIA

23   *The dog barks, but the camel passes on*   SUDAN

24   *You can't teach an old dog new tricks*   ENGLAND

25   *The dog on three legs ain't always lame*   USA

26   *Only thin dogs become wild*   MADAGASCAR

27   *A reasonable amount of fleas is good for a dog; they keep him from broodin' on being a dog*   USA

28   *The dogs will go into the corner that's open*   SCOTLAND

29   *There's no use in having a dog and barking yourself*
ENGLAND

30   *The dog may be wonderful prose, but only the cat is
poetry*   FRANCE

31   *The tail wags the dog*   ENGLAND

32   *Those who have not bread to spare should not keep a dog*
CHINA

33   *Who goes around the village long enough will get either a
dog-bite or a dinner*   SERBIA

34   *A greyhound finds its food in its feet*   IRELAND

35   *Dog does not eat dog*   ENGLAND

36   *A howlin' coyote ain't stealin' no chickens*   USA

37   *The more naked the jackal the larger the tail*
SOUTH AFRICA

38   *Wash a dog, comb a dog: still a dog*   USA

39   *A dog with money is addressed 'Mr Dog'*   USA

196   ELEPHANTS

1   *No elephant is burdened by its own trunk*
SOUTH AFRICA

2   *A fly before one's own eye is bigger than an elephant in
the next field*   CHINA

3   *If you kill, kill an elephant; if you rob, rob a treasury*
    INDIA

4   *When two elephants struggle, it is the grass that suffers*
    ZANZIBAR

5   *An elephant does not die from one broken rib*   KENYA

6   *People carrying elephant's flesh on their head should not look for crickets underground*   NIGERIA

7   *The bird can drink much, but the elephant drinks more*
    SENEGAL

8   *When an elephant chases you, you climb a prickly tree*
    KENYA

9   *An elephant never forgets*   ENGLAND

10   *With patience and saliva, the elephant swallows an ant*
    COLOMBIA

197 FOXES

1   *When the fox starts preaching, look to the hens*
    SPAIN: BASQUE

2   *Foxes are caught with foxes*   FINLAND

3   *A fox knows much; a hedgehog one great thing*   GREECE

4   *The fox believes that everyone eats hens like himself*
    FRANCE

198 GOATS

1   *It don't need a genius to spot a goat in a flock of sheep*
     USA

2   *By candle-light a goat looks like a lady*   FRANCE

3   *The lame goat has no siesta*   SPAIN

4   *The cry of the hyena and the loss of the goat are one*
     NIGERIA

5   *Goats cannot live in a herd of leopards*   MALI

6   *Truth is greater than ten goats*   NIGERIA

199 HORSES – DONKEYS

1   *Be on a horse when you're searching for a better one*
     CHINA

2   *What good is the hay if the horse is dead?*   PHILIPPINES

3   *The horse must graze where it is tethered*   BELGIUM

4   *Do not dwell in a city where a horse does not neigh nor a dog bark*   ENGLAND

5   *Donkey's lips do not fit onto a horse's mouth*   CHINA

6   *If you want to catch a wild horse, find a tight corral*
     HAITI

7   *One cannot shoe a running horse*   NETHERLANDS

8   *In buying horses and in taking a wife, shut your eyes tight and commend yourself to God*   ITALY

9   *When rats infest the palace a lame cat is better than the swiftest horse*   CHINA

10   *An old horse doesn't fear the whip*   SWITZERLAND

11   *When two ride on one horse one must sit behind*   ENGLAND

12   *In the middle of the river do not change horses*   PERU

13   *Four horses cannot overtake the tongue*   CHINA

14   *A horse never goes straight up a hill*   USA

15   *There's no such thing as a horse that can't be rode or a cowboy that can't be throwed*   USA

16   *Don't put the cart before the horse*   ENGLAND

17   *It's no good locking the stable door after the horse is stolen*   ENGLAND

18   *Judge not the horse by his saddle*   CHINA

19   *A blind horse is no judge of colours*   SCOTLAND

20   *A blind mule ain't afraid of darkness*   USA

21   *A nod's as good as a wink to a blind horse*   ENGLAND

22   *Sickness comes riding on horseback and goes away on foot*   BELGIUM

23   *The toughest broncs is always them you've rode some other place*   USA

24 *In one stable there may be a steed and an ass* BELGIUM

25 *Rein in the horse at the edge of the cliff* CHINA

26 *Many donkeys need much straw* SPAIN: BASQUE

27 *When a donkey is well off he goes dancing on ice*
CZECH REPUBLIC

200 HYENAS

1 *The hyena of your own country does not break your bones*
KENYA

2 *The cry of the hyena and the loss of the goat are one*
NIGERIA

3 *It is the prudent hyena that lives long* ZAMBIA

4 *It is the hyenas of the same den that hate one another*
KENYA

5 *Don't show a hyena how well you can bite* KENYA

201 LIONS – TIGERS – LEOPARDS

1 *What is said over the dead lion's body could not be said
to him alive* REPUBLIC OF CONGO

2 *A roaring lion kills no game* UGANDA

3 *Assistance conquers a lion* MOROCCO

4 *If the panther knew how much it is feared, it would do much more harm* CAMEROON

5 *Once on a tiger's back, it is hard to alight* CHINA

6 *You cannot catch a tiger cub unless you enter the tiger's den* JAPAN

7 *One can paint the fur of a tiger but not his joints* KOREA

8 *New-born calves don't fear tigers* CHINA

9 *Do not blame God for having created the tiger, but thank Him for not having given it wings* ETHIOPIA

10 *Goats cannot live in a herd of leopards* MALI

11 *The leopard cannot change its spots* ENGLAND

12 *When the leopard moves away, it takes its tail with it* NIGERIA

202 MICE − RATS

1 *Little houses have fat mice* TANZANIA

2 *When the mouse laughs at the cat, there is a hole* GAMBIA

3 *When the cat's not home, the mice jump on the table* NETHERLANDS

4 *While the cat's away, the mice will play* ENGLAND

5 *A cat with mittens won't catch mice* SCOTLAND

6 *The mouse is not crushed under the haystack*
SCOTLAND

7 *A good cat deserves a good rat*   ENGLAND

8 *An old rat is a brave rat*   FRANCE

9 *It is no use throwing water on a drowned rat*   IRELAND

10 *It is a cunning mouse which nests in the cat's ear*
ENGLAND

11 *The cat who frightens the mice away is as good as the cat who eats them*   GERMANY

12 *The cat does not catch mice for God*   INDIA

13 *It's a poor mouse that has but one hole*   NETHERLANDS

14 *Birds hear talk in daytime, rats hear talk at night*
KOREA

15 *When rats infest the palace a lame cat is better than the swiftest horse*   CHINA

16 *The rat has a double stomach*   NEW ZEALAND

17 *The one who hunts two rats will catch neither*   UGANDA

203 MONKEYS – GORILLAS

1 *Even monkeys fall from trees*   KOREA

2 *By trying often, the monkey learns to jump from the tree*
CAMEROON

3   *It is a hard job to make old monkeys pull faces*
     BELGIUM

4   *What monkey forgets its tail?*   CAMEROON

5   *Kill a chicken before a monkey*   CHINA

6   *Do not sow groundnuts when the monkey is watching*
     NIGERIA

7   *Only a monkey understands a monkey*   SIERRA LEONE

8   *On a dead tree there are no monkeys*   MOZAMBIQUE

9   *You do not teach the paths of the forest to an old gorilla*
     REPUBLIC OF CONGO

204   PIGS

1   *The pig dreams of his trough*   FINLAND

2   *Pigs might fly*   ENGLAND

3   *A pig won't spare even the most beautiful fruit*   ALBANIA

4   *Scholars talk books; butchers talk pigs*   CHINA

5   *What can you expect from a pig but a grunt?*   IRELAND

6   *Community is as strong as water, and as stupid as a pig*
     RUSSIA

7   *The miser and the pig are useless unless they are dead*
     FRANCE

8   *To the pig a carrot is a present*   GERMANY

* * * * * * * * * * * * * * * * * *

16 COUNTRY VARIATIONS – ANIMALS

Animals provide one of the most distinctive ways in which a proverbial theme achieves culturally specific expression.

Truth is greater than ten goats (NIGERIA)

Don't call the alligator a big-mouth till you have crossed the river (BELIZE)

By trying often, the monkey learns to jump from the tree (CAMEROON)

What is said over the dead lion's body could not be said to him alive (REPUBLIC OF CONGO)

Because we concentrated on the snake, we missed the scorpion (EGYPT)

The hindermost ox also reaches the kraal (SOUTH AFRICA)

Everyone knows the bear, but the bear knows no one (FINLAND)

The dragon in shallow water becomes the butt of shrimps (CHINA)

A skunk smells its own hole first (USA)

Even monkeys fall from trees (KOREA)

You cannot catch a tiger cub unless you enter the tiger's den (JAPAN)

On a green tree there are many parrots (INDIA)

Will the crocodile reject the carcass? (MALAYSIA)

The one who carries the bludgeon owns the buffalo (INDIA)

The junk capsizes and the shark has its bellyful (MALAYSIA)

The rhinoceros which has no calf takes itself to the muddy pool (SOUTH AFRICA)

What monkey forgets its tail? (CAMEROON)

The hyena of your own country does not break your bones
   (KENYA)
A roaring lion kills no game (UGANDA)
There never was a persimmon except there was a possum to eat it
   (USA)
If you cross in a crowd, the crocodile won't eat you
   (MADAGASCAR)
The dog barks, but the camel passes on (SUDAN)
When two elephants struggle, it is the grass that suffers
   (ZANZIBAR)
A debt is like a hippo's footprints (NIGERIA)
When the leopard moves away, it takes its tail with it
   (NIGERIA)
There is nothing so eloquent as a rattlesnake's tail (USA)
One camel does not make fun of another camel's hump
   (GUINEA)
The cobra knows its length (NAMIBIA)
No matter how long a log floats on the river it will never be a
   crocodile (MALI)
When an elephant chases you, you climb a prickly tree (KENYA)
Goats cannot live in a herd of leopards (MALI)
Only a monkey understands a monkey (SIERRA LEONE)
You do not teach the paths of the forest to an old gorilla
   (REPUBLIC OF CONGO)
If the panther knew how much it is feared, it would do much
   more harm (CAMEROON)

SEE ALSO Country variations – climate (p. 90); artefacts
(p. 151); plants (p. 323); beliefs and behaviour (p. 562)

* * * * * * * * * * * * * * * * * *

9   *Poets and pigs are appreciated only after their death*
ITALY

10   *You can't take the grunt out of a pig* USA

11   *No sow so dirty but finds a boar to kiss her* GERMANY

12   *A barren sow was never good to pigs* ENGLAND

13   *Those who mix themselves with the mud will be eaten by the swine* NETHERLANDS

14   *Don't shuck your corn till the hogs come home* USA

15   *When you are chased by a wolf you call the boar your uncle* SLOVENIA

205 RABBITS – HARES

1   *A sly rabbit will have three openings to its den* CHINA

2   *You come with a cat and call it a rabbit* CAMEROON

3   *When God made the rabbit He made bushes too*
HUNGARY

4   *You never know how a cow catches a rabbit*
NETHERLANDS

5   *Cows can't catch no rabbits* USA

6   *Those who have not seen a hare run, must not speak of fear* ITALY

7   *The one who hunts two hares will catch neither*
FRANCE

206 SHEEP

1 *When one sheep is over the dam, the rest will follow*
NETHERLANDS

2 *While the sheep bleats it loses its mouthful* BELGIUM

3 *The dust raised by the sheep does not choke the wolf*
ENGLAND

4 *Coupled sheep drown each other* NETHERLANDS

5 *Black sheep hide mighty easy in the dark* USA

6 *It don't need a genius to spot a goat in a flock of sheep*
USA

7 *It is a silly sheep that makes the wolf her confessor*
FRANCE

8 *It is hard to catch wolves with sheep* NETHERLANDS

9 *Might as well be hanged for a sheep as a lamb*
ENGLAND

207 WOLVES

1 *The wolf changes his hair, but not his skin* ALBANIA

2 *It is a silly sheep that makes the wolf her confessor*
FRANCE

3 *The dust raised by the sheep does not choke the wolf*
ENGLAND

AS THEY SAY IN ZANZIBAR

4   *Those who see the wolf shout; those who see it not, shout twice*   BULGARIA

5   *God saves the moon from the wolves*   POLAND

6   *When you are chased by a wolf you call the boar your uncle*   SLOVENIA

7   *Eat with the dogs, howl with the wolves*   ALBANIA

8   *A wolf does not step on the tail of a wolf*   ESTONIA

9   *It is hard to catch wolves with sheep*   NETHERLANDS

208   OTHER WILD ANIMALS

1   *The hippo blocked up the ford, and no one could cross*
    NIGERIA

2   *Darkness conceals the hippopotamus*   SOUTH AFRICA

3   *A debt is like a hippo's footprints*   NIGERIA

4   *The rhinoceros which has no calf takes itself to the muddy pool*   SOUTH AFRICA

5   *Don't value a badger skin before catching the badger*
    JAPAN

6   *A fox knows much; a hedgehog one great thing*   GREECE

7   *Even a mole may instruct a philosopher on the art of digging*   CHINA

8   *It is in vain to look for yesterday's fish in the house of the otter*   INDIA

9   *One does not rub buttocks with a porcupine*   GHANA

10   *There never was a persimmon except there was a possum to eat it*   USA

11   *You can never get all the possums up the same tree*   USA

12   *Slowly, slowly makes the slug arrive at the fountain*   RWANDA

13   *The squirrel is not heard in the forest*   ZANZIBAR

14   *Everyone must skin their own skunk*   USA

15   *A skunk smells its own hole first*   USA

16   *It is the sick duck that is worried by the weasel*   CHINA

17   *A weasel comes to say Happy New Year to the chickens*   CHINA

18   *The older the buck, the harder his horn*   SCOTLAND

19   *The dragon in shallow water becomes the butt of shrimps*   CHINA

20   *Never follow a beast into its lair*   SOUTH AFRICA

209   BIRDS

1   *A chattering bird builds no nest*   CAMEROON

2   *A beautiful bird is the only kind we cage*   CHINA

3   *A bird does not sing because it has an answer; it sings because it has a song*   CHINA

4   *Clumsy birds need early flight*   CHINA

5   *One bird in the dish is better than a hundred in the air*
GERMANY

6   *A bird in the hand is worth two in the bush*   ENGLAND

7   *Birds hear talk in daytime, rats hear talk at night*
KOREA

8   *The shell is needed till the bird is hatched*   RUSSIA

9   *God gives birds their food, but they must fly for it*
NETHERLANDS

10 *You cannot prevent the birds of sadness from flying over
your head, but you can prevent them from nesting in your
hair*   CHINA

11 *A crab does not beget a bird*   CÔTE D'IVOIRE

12 *A bat is not a bird*   NAMIBIA

13 *A bird with a beautiful plumage doesn't sit in the corner*
CAMEROON

14 *A clever bird builds its nest with other birds' feathers*
ZIMBABWE

15 *Every little bird has a long beak*   NAMIBIA

16 *When the figs are ripe, all the birds want to eat*   KENYA

17 *It is the softness of the lime that is fatal to the bird*
MADAGASCAR

18 *The bird can drink much, but the elephant drinks more*
SENEGAL

19 *Birds of a feather flock together*   ENGLAND

20 *The early bird catches the worm*   ENGLAND

210 TYPES OF BIRD

1 *Buzzards do not sing in bleak regions*   PERU

2 *A sparrow in the hand is better than a crane on the wing*
   FRANCE

3 *Those who fear wild cranes should not sow beans*
   MALTA

4 *A word flies away like a sparrow and returns to the house
   like a crow*   GERMANY

5 *Crows everywhere are equally black*   CHINA

6 *If you follow a crow long enough you light on carrion*
   ALBANIA

7 *Little crows have the largest beaks*   BELGIUM

8 *If you had not been among the crows, you would not
   have been shot*   SCOTLAND

9 *A whitewashed crow soon shows black again*   CHINA

10 *A crow in a cage won't talk like a parrot*   USA

11 *Eagles do not catch flies*   HUNGARY

12 *Puttin' feathers on a buzzard won't make it no eagle*
    USA

13   *Fame is a gull floating on water*   CHINA

14   *Only a nightingale understands a rose*   INDIA

15   *Only an owl knows the worth of an owl*   INDIA

16   *Every owl has its olive-tree*   CUBA

17   *On a green tree there are many parrots*   INDIA

18   *It is still a parrot, whether roasted or raw*
      NEW ZEALAND

19   *Sparrows who aspire to be peacocks are likely to break a
      thigh*   MYANMAR

20   *The worm don't see nothing pretty in the robin's song*
      USA

21   *The seagull sees furthest who flies highest*   FRANCE

22   *If I keep a green bough in my heart, a singing-bird will
      come*   CHINA

23   *Sparrows clean their beaks against the branch on which
      they sit*   ESTONIA

24   *If the sky fell down, all sparrows would be dead*
      NETHERLANDS

25   *Only heaven can see the back of a sparrow*
      SOUTH AFRICA

26   *Where there are frogs, there are also storks*
      NETHERLANDS

27   *One swallow does not make a summer*   ENGLAND

28   *Where a carcass is, there will vultures be*   MALAYSIA

29   *Vultures eat with their blood relations*   SOUTH AFRICA

30   *The vulture's foot spoils the soup*   NIGERIA

211 POULTRY

1   *Those who spend a night with a chicken will cackle in the morning*   TUNISIA

2   *Keep your chickens in your own backyard*   USA

3   *One needn't devour the whole chicken to know the flavour of the bird*   CHINA

4   *Although he chirps, he is no chick*   UKRAINE

5   *Kill a chicken before a monkey*   CHINA

6   *Even though chickens don't wash, their eggs are still white*   SIERRA LEONE

7   *If you get mixed with bran, you'll soon be pecked by chickens*   LIBYA

8   *A weasel comes to say Happy New Year to the chickens*   CHINA

9   *A howlin' coyote ain't stealin' no chickens*   USA

10   *Chickens come home to roost*   ENGLAND

11   *Don't count your chickens before they're hatched*   ENGLAND

12   *From fried eggs come no chickens*   USA

13 *A scalded cock runs away from the rain* BULGARIA

14 *It is the sick duck that is worried by the weasel* CHINA

15 *The quiet duck puts his foot on the unobservant worm*
CHINA

16 *Those who wait for roast duck to fly into their mouth
must wait a very, very long time* CHINA

17 *Words are good, but fowls lay eggs* GERMANY

18 *You cannot take one part of a fowl for cooking and leave
the other part to lay eggs* INDIA

19 *The feathers make the fowl big* CÔTE D'IVOIRE

20 *A wild goose never lays a tame egg* ENGLAND

21 *Sauce for the goose is sauce for the gander* ENGLAND

22 *A blind hen can sometimes find her corn* FRANCE

23 *When the fox starts preaching, look to the hens*
SPAIN: BASQUE

24 *A black hen can lay a white egg* SCOTLAND

25 *Those who steal the egg will also steal the hen* MALTA

26 *The fox believes that everyone eats hens like himself*
FRANCE

27 *Even a hen, when it drinks, looks towards heaven*
TURKEY

28 *Every cackling hen was an egg at first*
RWANDA AND BURUNDI

29 *Better an egg today than a hen tomorrow* USA

30 *It is not common for hens to have pillows* SCOTLAND

212 FISH – FISHING

1 *No matter how hard you throw a dead fish in the water, it still won't swim* REPUBLIC OF CONGO

2 *Dead fish go always with the stream* ENGLAND

3 *Cats love fish but fear to wet their paws* CHINA

4 *A guest and a fish after three days are poison* FRANCE

5 *It is not a fish until it is on the bank* IRELAND

6 *The fish does not go after the hook, but after the bait* CZECH REPUBLIC

7 *The fish said, 'I have much to say, but my mouth is full of water.'* GEORGIA

8 *Go fishing for three days and dry the nets for two* CHINA

9 *Don't stand by the water and long for fish; go home and weave a net* CHINA

10 *All is fish that goes into the net* SCOTLAND

11 *Fish begin to stink from the head* ALBANIA

12 *If water is noisy, there are no fish in it* MYANMAR

13 *It is in vain to look for yesterday's fish in the house of the otter* INDIA

14　*Different holes have different fish*　MALAYSIA

15　*Looking for fish? Don't climb a tree*　CHINA

16　*If familiarity were useful, water wouldn't cook fish*
　　CAMEROON

17　*A big fish is caught with big bait*　SIERRA LEONE

18　*The twig that falls in the water will never become a fish*
　　CÔTE D'IVOIRE

19　*If you catch fish you're a fisherman*　USA

213　TYPES OF FISH – CRUSTACEANS

1　*It's no wonder that the herring vessel smells of herring*
　　SCOTLAND

2　*A lobster loves water, but not when he's being cooked in it*　SENEGAL

3　*The junk capsizes and the shark has its bellyful*
　　MALAYSIA

4　*A crab does not beget a bird*　CÔTE D'IVOIRE

5　*The dragon in shallow water becomes the butt of shrimps*
　　CHINA

6　*The shrimp that sleeps is carried away by the current*
　　CHILE

7　*You can't catch trout with dry trousers*　USA

214 FROGS – TOADS

1   Never try to catch two frogs with one hand   CHINA

2   A frog's baby is a frog   JAPAN

3   If there is a marsh there will be frogs   UKRAINE

4   It is easy to drive a frog into the water   SERBIA

5   A frog beneath a coconut shell believes there is no other world   MALAYSIA

6   Where there are frogs, there are also storks
    NETHERLANDS

7   Slander by the stream will be heard by the frogs
    MOZAMBIQUE

8   It is because the toad is too tenderhearted that he has no intelligence   HAITI

9   The toad doesn't know that its skin is rough
    CAMEROON

215 REPTILES

1   Don't call the alligator a big-mouth till you have crossed the river   BELIZE

2   Will the crocodile reject the carcass?   MALAYSIA

3   If you cross in a crowd, the crocodile won't eat you
    MADAGASCAR

4 *Two crocodiles don't live in one pond* GAMBIA

5 *No matter how long a log floats on the river it will never be a crocodile* MALI

6 *A starving crocodile is never pleasant* MADAGASCAR

7 *The smaller the lizard, the greater its hope of becoming a crocodile* ETHIOPIA

8 *However much the beetle is afraid, it will not stop the lizard swallowing it* CAMEROON

9 *The one who was surprised by a turtle is surprised by a pot cover* KOREA

10 *It's the tortoise that discounts the value of a pair of fast legs* JAPAN

11 *The tortoise breathes; it is only its shell that prevents our noticing it* NIGERIA

12 *There is nothing so eloquent as a rattlesnake's tail* USA

13 *The cobra knows its length* NAMIBIA

14 *Warm a frozen serpent, and it will sting you first*
ARMENIA

15 *Add legs to the snake after you have finished drawing it*
CHINA

16 *Because we concentrated on the snake, we missed the scorpion* EGYPT

17 *Draw the snake from its hole by someone else's hand*
SPAIN

18   *Poke a bamboo thicket, drive out a snake*   JAPAN

19   *A viper is a viper, whether big or small*   SLOVENIA

216   WORMS

1   *Silent worms bore holes in the wall*   JAPAN

2   *The worm don't see nothing pretty in the robin's song*
     USA

3   *The quiet duck puts his foot on the unobservant worm*
     CHINA

4   *A worm is about the only thing that doesn't fall down*
     USA

5   *The early bird catches the worm*   ENGLAND

217   ANTS

1   *Ants can attack with a grain of rice*   MADAGASCAR

2   *An ant may well destroy a whole dam*   CHINA

3   *A coconut shell full of water is a sea to an ant*
     ZANZIBAR

4   *To the ant, a few drops of rain is a flood*   JAPAN

5   *The one who enters as a whirlwind will depart as an ant*
     INDONESIA

6   *When an ant gets wings it perishes* SERBIA

7   *It is in sugar that you see the dead ant* MALAYSIA

8   *With patience and saliva, the elephant swallows an ant*
   COLOMBIA

9   *Any spoke will lead the ant to the hub* USA

218 BEES

1   *A bee was never caught in a shower* ENGLAND

2   *Beware of a person's shadow and a bee's sting*
   MYANMAR

3   *When the bee comes to your house, let her have beer; you may want to visit the bee's house some day*
   REPUBLIC OF CONGO

4   *Bees that have honey in their mouths have stings in their tails* FRANCE

5   *Many have bees and buy wax* GERMANY

6   *Better a handful of bees than a basketful of flies*
   MOROCCO

7   *Where there are bees there is honey* ENGLAND

219 FLEAS

1 *Nothing should be done in a hurry except catching fleas*
GERMANY

2 *Those who sleep with dogs must rise with fleas*
SCOTLAND

3 *We each have our own way of killing fleas* SPAIN

4 *Ambition and fleas jump high* GERMANY

5 *A reasonable amount of fleas is good for a dog; they keep him from broodin' on being a dog* USA

6 *Have patience, fleas, the night is long* NICARAGUA

220 FLIES

1 *Flies have ears* KENYA

2 *Flies never visit an egg that has no crack* CHINA

3 *A closed mouth catches no flies* ENGLAND

4 *A fly before one's own eye is bigger than an elephant in the next field* CHINA

5 *Law is a spider's web; big flies break through but the little ones are caught* HUNGARY

6 *Laws catch flies but let hornets go free* ENGLAND

7 *Flies never alight on boiling pots* UKRAINE

8 *The spider does not weave its web for one fly* SLOVENIA

9   *Eagles do not catch flies*   HUNGARY

10   *Even a fly has a cough*   ITALY

11   *Do not remove a fly from your friend's forehead with a hatchet*   CHINA

12   *The fly will never leave the confectioner's shop*   INDIA

13   *Two pieces of meat confuse the mind of the fly*   NIGERIA

14   *The fly flutters about the candle until at last it gets burnt*
NETHERLANDS

15   *Better a handful of bees than a basketful of flies*
MOROCCO

16   *A cow that has no tail should not try to chase away flies*
GUINEA

17   *The sweeter the perfume, the uglier the flies which gather round the bottle*   CHINA

18   *If you are looking for a fly in your food, it means you are full*   SOUTH AFRICA

221   OTHER INSECTS

1   *One beetle knows another*   IRELAND

2   *However much the beetle is afraid, it will not stop the lizard swallowing it*   CAMEROON

3   *Proverbs are like butterflies; some are caught and some fly away*   GERMANY

4   People carrying elephant's flesh on their head should not
    look for crickets underground   NIGERIA

5   The energy of the dung-beetle is put into rolling its ball of
    dung   CHINA

6   Wherever there is a field, there are grasshoppers
    MALAYSIA

7   The grub eats round the edges of the leaves
    NEW ZEALAND

8   Laws catch flies but let hornets go free   ENGLAND

9   The hornet also comes to the sugar-pot   CHINA

10 Insects do not nest in a busy door-hinge   CHINA

11 A louse in the cabbage is better than no meat at all
    NETHERLANDS

12 New clothes have no lice   NAMIBIA

13 A hungry louse bites hard   USA

14 If you run away from a mosquito the sharper will its
    sting be   SLOVENIA

15 Every cabin has its mosquito   JAMAICA

16 Their mosquito won't bite me   CÔTE D'IVOIRE

17 They dread a moth, who have been stung by a wasp
    ALBANIA

18 Much treasure, many moths   ESTONIA

19 The candle is put into the lantern and the moth is left
    outside fluttering   IRAN

20 *You need not take someone else's hand to crush a sand-fly* NIGERIA

21 *Because we concentrated on the snake, we missed the scorpion* EGYPT

22 *The spider does not weave its web for one fly* SLOVENIA

23 *Law is a spider's web; big flies break through but the little ones are caught* HUNGARY

24 *If it weren't for the wind the spiders would web the sky* SERBIA

25 *In every house there are always cobwebs* SERBIA

26 *Small termites collapse the roof* ETHIOPIA

222 FORESTS – WOODS

1 *You can only go halfway into the darkest forest; then you are coming out the other side* CHINA

2 *How can there be a forest without a crooked tree?* BULGARIA

3 *The forest is the poor person's fur-coat* ESTONIA

4 *The squirrel is not heard in the forest* ZANZIBAR

5 *You do not teach the paths of the forest to an old gorilla* REPUBLIC OF CONGO

6 *Those who tremble to hear a leaf fall should keep out of the wood* FRANCE

* * * * * * * * * * * * * * * * * * *

17 COUNTRY VARIATIONS – PLANTS

The crops and agricultural practices of a country readily
transfer into proverbial expression.

When the date-crop is over, everyone mocks at the palm-tree
(ETHIOPIA)
If you pound palm-nuts, some will stain your cloth (CÔTE
D'IVOIRE)
The smartest housewife cannot cook a meal without rice (CHINA)
The laden almond-tree by the wayside is sure to be bitter (JAPAN)
Every pumpkin is known by its stem (USA)
A coconut shell full of water is a sea to an ant (ZANZIBAR)
You cannot hold two water-melons in one hand (IRAN)
Make hay while the sun shines (ENGLAND)
When eating bamboo sprouts, remember the one who planted
them (CHINA)
Little by little grow the bananas (REPUBLIC OF CONGO)
When walking through your neighbour's melon-patch, don't tie
your shoe (CHINA)
If you have two loaves of bread, sell one and buy a lily (CHINA)
Gin caresses lungs and liver (NETHERLANDS)
Ploughing, we learn to plough; mowing, we learn to mow
(LITHUANIA)

SEE ALSO Country variations – climate (p. 90); artefacts
(p. 151); animals (p. 302); beliefs and behaviour (p. 562)

* * * * * * * * * * * * * * * * * *

7 *As one calls in the wood, so comes the echo back again*
ESTONIA

8 *A handleless axe does not scare the forest* BULGARIA

9 *From the midst of the wood the hatchet gets its handle*
GERMANY

10 *Strawberries ripen sooner in a low wood than in a high one* ESTONIA

11 *Other trees, other woodcutters* LITHUANIA

12 *The copse does not rustle if the wind does not blow*
HUNGARY

223 TREES

1 *Poke a bamboo thicket, drive out a snake* JAPAN

2 *Blossoms are not fruits* NETHERLANDS

3 *What matter what blossom it is if there is no fruit?*
SERBIA

4 *If I keep a green bough in my heart, a singing-bird will come* CHINA

5 *Those who love the tree love the branch* ENGLAND

6 *Sparrows clean their beaks against the branch on which they sit* ESTONIA

7 *Every owl has its olive-tree* CUBA

8 *On a green tree there are many parrots* INDIA

9   *No more leaves can fall in autumn than were grown in spring*   GERMANY

10   *To the timorous all leaves seem to rustle*   SWITZERLAND

11   *The axe forgets, but the cut log does not*   ZIMBABWE

12   *No matter how long a log floats on the river it will never be a crocodile*   MALI

13   *Big oaks from little acorns grow*   ENGLAND

14   *Better a free meal of acorns than a honey feast on trust*   WALES

15   *When the date-crop is over, everyone mocks at the palm-tree*   ETHIOPIA

16   *When you see the palm-tree, the palm-tree has seen you*   SENEGAL

17   *Who sits under a pear-tree will eat pears*   BULGARIA

18   *One only goes to look at the prickly pear-tree when it is bearing fruit*   MEXICO

19   *One generation plants the trees; another gets the shade*   CHINA

20   *How can there be a forest without a crooked tree?*   BULGARIA

21   *Other trees, other woodcutters*   LITHUANIA

22   *There is always something to be cut off young trees if they are to grow well*   GERMANY

23   *A tree with ripe fruit needs little shaking*   SWITZERLAND

24 *Upon what tree does the wind not strike?* INDIA

25 *If you don't like my apples, don't shake my tree* USA

26 *An axe with a loose head is the bane of a man up a tree*
NIGERIA

27 *When an elephant chases you, you climb a prickly tree*
KENYA

28 *Looking for fish? Don't climb a tree* CHINA

29 *If you climb up a tree, you must climb down the same
tree* SIERRA LEONE

30 *Even monkeys fall from trees* KOREA

31 *On a dead tree there are no monkeys* MOZAMBIQUE

32 *You can never get all the possums up the same tree* USA

33 *The twig that falls in the water will never become a fish*
CÔTE D'IVOIRE

34 *Under trees it rains twice* SWITZERLAND

35 *Big tree but no shade* PHILIPPINES

36 *If you want one year of prosperity, grow grain. If you
want ten years of prosperity, grow trees. If you want a
hundred years of prosperity, grow people* CHINA

37 *By trying often, the monkey learns to jump from the tree*
CAMEROON

38 *The best time to plant a tree was twenty years ago; the
second-best time is now* CHINA

224 GRASS – HAY

1 *Every blade of grass gets its own drop of dew*
SCOTLAND

2 *Where one was born, every blade of grass pleases* ITALY

3 *Where everyone goes, the grass never grows* GERMANY

4 *Sweetest the grass next to the ground* WALES

5 *If the grass is mown it is not uprooted* BULGARIA

6 *Grass must turn to hay* LATIN

7 *Make hay while the sun shines* ENGLAND

8 *When two elephants struggle, it is the grass that suffers*
ZANZIBAR

9 *The grass always looks greener on the other side of the
fence* ENGLAND

10 *A drowning man will clutch at a straw* ENGLAND

11 *Many donkeys need much straw* SPAIN: BASQUE

12 *If we knew where we would fall, we would spread straw
there first* FINLAND

13 *By the stubble you may guess the grain* USA

225 BUSHES – HEDGES

1 *A bird in the hand is worth two in the bush*   ENGLAND

2 *When God made the rabbit He made bushes too*
HUNGARY

3 *The grub eats round the edges of the leaves*
NEW ZEALAND

4 *Better keep under an old hedge than creep under a new furze-bush*   ENGLAND

5 *Though honey is sweet, do not lick it off a briar*
IRELAND

6 *It is easy to make pipes sitting amongst bulrushes*
CZECH REPUBLIC

7 *The one who will fight will find a cudgel in every hedge*
ENGLAND

226 FLOWERS – GARDENS

1 *Daisies won't tell*   USA

2 *If you have two loaves of bread, sell one and buy a lily*
CHINA

3 *Those who want the rose must also take the thorns*
GERMANY

4 *A bit of fragrance always clings to the hand that gives you roses*   CHINA

5 *Better be stung by a nettle than pricked by a rose*
ENGLAND

6 *The rose that is smelt by many loses its fragrance*
SPAIN

7 *Only a nightingale understands a rose* INDIA

8 *The fruit on a creeper is no burden to it* SRI LANKA

9 *If the brain sows not corn, it plants thistles* ENGLAND

10 *A stationary stone gathers moss* RUSSIA

11 *A rolling stone gathers no moss* ENGLAND

12 *Weeds never perish* NETHERLANDS

13 *People have enough to do weeding their own garden*
BELGIUM

14 *Those who plant a hedge round their garden invite it to be jumped* RUSSIA

15 *A gardener's flirtations take place outside the garden*
AFGHANISTAN

227 AGRICULTURE

1 *A big crop is best, but a little crop will do* SCOTLAND

2 *Remember the rain that made your corn grow* HAITI

3 *If you want one year of prosperity, grow grain. If you want ten years of prosperity, grow trees. If you want a hundred years of prosperity, grow people* CHINA

4   *You won't help shoots grow by pulling them up higher*
CHINA

5   *Little by little grow the bananas*   REPUBLIC OF CONGO

6   *Where everyone goes, the grass never grows*   GERMANY

7   *The rod that will hang him is still growing*   IRELAND

8   *We must take the crop as it grows*   SCOTLAND

9   *There is always something to be cut off young trees if they are to grow well*   GERMANY

10   *A fruit-tree that grows on a dunghill is sure to flourish*
NEW ZEALAND

11   *The fruit must have a stem before it grows*   LIBERIA

12   *Crooked furrows grow straight grain*   CANADA

13   *Big oaks from little acorns grow*   ENGLAND

14   *Lower your head modestly while passing, and you will harvest bananas*   REPUBLIC OF CONGO

15   *The mouse is not crushed under the haystack*
SCOTLAND

16   *Making money selling manure is better than losing money selling musk*   EGYPT

17   *If the grass is mown it is not uprooted*   BULGARIA

18   *Ploughing, we learn to plough; mowing, we learn to mow*
LITHUANIA

19   *God preserve us from pitch-forks, for they make three holes*   SWITZERLAND

20 *One generation plants the trees; another gets the shade*
CHINA

21 *Don't plant a seed in the sea* KENYA

22 *When eating bamboo sprouts, remember the one who planted them* CHINA

23 *Do not sow groundnuts when the monkey is watching*
NIGERIA

24 *If the brain sows not corn, it plants thistles* ENGLAND

25 *The best time to plant a tree was twenty years ago; the second-best time is now* CHINA

26 *Those who fear wild cranes should not sow beans*
MALTA

27 *A vineyard does not require prayers, but a hoe* TURKEY

228 PEOPLE – PEOPLES

1 *Three sorts of people are always to be found, soldiers, professors, and women* GERMANY

2 *Scholars are the treasure of a nation* CHINA

3 *If you want one year of prosperity, grow grain. If you want ten years of prosperity, grow trees. If you want a hundred years of prosperity, grow people* CHINA

4 *Those who cannot cut the bread evenly cannot get on well with people* CZECH REPUBLIC

5   *Mountains cannot meet, people can*   BULGARIA

6   *Proverbs are the coins of the people*   RUSSIA

7   *Mad folks and proverbs reveal many truths*   USA

8   *A proverb characterizes nations, but must first dwell among them*   SWITZERLAND

9   *Many people are like clocks, they show one hour and strike another*   DENMARK

10   *If two people tell you you are blind, shut one eye*   GEORGIA

11   *You are as many a person as languages you know*   ARMENIA

12   *When it rains on one it only drips on another*   NETHERLANDS

13   *It takes one to know one*   ENGLAND

14   *There's one born every minute*   USA

15   *An ox is bound with ropes and a person with words*   ITALY

16   *The world will not conquer him who is always rubbing his beard*   INDIA

17   *Adam must have an Eve, to blame for his own faults*   GERMANY

18   *Public money is like holy water, one helps oneself to it*   ITALY

19   *Some guys got it, and some guys ain't got it*   USA

20 *Good nature is stronger than tomahawks* USA

21 *It is easier to rule a nation than a son* CHINA

22 *Happy nations have no history* BELGIUM

23 *A nation's health is a nation's wealth* USA

24 *A nation without a language is a nation without a heart*
     WALES

229 MEN

1 *When a man eats, his own beard moves and not
   another's* TOGO

2 *A bald-headed man cannot grow hair by getting excited
   about it* REPUBLIC OF CONGO

3 *Never trust a fellow that wears a suit* USA

4 *A blind man's wife needs no painting* SCOTLAND

5 *Honest men marry soon; wise men never* ENGLAND

6 *The game's not over until the last man strikes out* USA

7 *A coward's fear makes a brave man braver* SCOTLAND

8 *A red-nosed man may not be a drinker, but he will find
   nobody to believe it* CHINA

9 *A man's hat in his hand never did him any harm*
   SCOTLAND

10 *Beware the man with only one gun* USA

11   *One cannot grab a bald man by the hair*   NETHERLANDS

12   *You cannot shave a man's head in his absence*   NIGERIA

13   *Take away the wife of a strong man only when he is out*
       UGANDA

14   *Revolutions are not made by men in spectacles*   USA

230 WOMEN

1   *Girls will be girls*   USA

2   *The smartest housewife cannot cook a meal without rice*
       CHINA

3   *By candle-light a goat looks like a lady*   FRANCE

4   *Look the other way when the girl in the tea-house smiles*
       JAPAN

5   *It ain't over till the fat lady sings*   USA

6   *Faint heart never won fair lady*   ENGLAND

7   *A beautiful maiden is a devil's pocket*   PHILIPPINES

8   *Priests and women never forget*   GERMANY

9   *A house is not built on earth, but on a woman*   SERBIA

10   *She is a foolish woman who blames her own cabbage*
       DENMARK

11   *Three sorts of people are always to be found, soldiers,
professors, and women*   GERMANY

12   *Leave women alone, and go and study mathematics*
     ITALY

13   *The woman who sells fans often shades her eyes with her hands* CHINA

14   *Never marry a woman who has bigger feet than you*
     MOZAMBIQUE

231 MEN v WOMEN

1   *Three kinds of men fail to understand women – young men, old men, and middle-aged men* IRELAND

2   *If you would understand men, study women* FRANCE

3   *Women in mischief are wiser than men* ENGLAND

4   *A hundred men may make an encampment, but it needs a woman to make a home* CHINA

232 HEART – BLOOD

1   *A fire in the heart makes smoke in the head* GERMANY

2   *Have a mouth as sharp as a dagger, but a heart as soft as tofu* CHINA

3   *Absence makes the heart grow fonder* ENGLAND

4   *Rather once cry your heart out than always sigh* CHINA

5   *What comes from the heart goes to the heart* ENGLAND

6 *The heart's letter is read in the eyes* ENGLAND

7 *A nation without a language is a nation without a heart*
WALES

8 *A satisfied heart will often sigh* FRANCE

9 *Faint heart never won fair lady* ENGLAND

10 *One thread for the needle, one love for the heart* SUDAN

11 *What the eye cannot see, the heart cannot grieve about*
ENGLAND

12 *If I keep a green bough in my heart, a singing-bird will
come* CHINA

13 *Home is where the heart is* ENGLAND

14 *Blood is thicker than water* ENGLAND

15 *You can't get blood out of a stone* ENGLAND

16 *You cannot tie up another's wound while your own is
still bleeding* ESTONIA

17 *If one finger is gashed, all the fingers are covered with
blood* REPUBLIC OF CONGO

233 BONES – JOINTS

1 *An elephant does not die from one broken rib* KENYA

2 *Sparrows who aspire to be peacocks are likely to break a
thigh* MYANMAR

3 *One can paint the fur of a tiger but not his joints*
KOREA

4 *The tongue has no bones, yet breaks its own skull*
ALBANIA

5 *No land without stones, or meat without bones*
ENGLAND

6 *A dry bone is never licked* ALBANIA

7 *Pelt a dog with a bone and you will not offend him*
ITALY

8 *The nearer the bone, the sweeter the meat* ENGLAND

9 *The hyena of your own country does not break your bones*
KENYA

234 BACK – BUTTOCKS

1 *Swimmers do not see their own back* TOGO

2 *You cannot push yourself forward by patting yourself on the back* CHINA

3 *Never trust your back to a slap* SCOTLAND

4 *When you have trodden on the cat, what help is it to stroke her back?* SWITZERLAND

5 *Once on a tiger's back, it is hard to alight* CHINA

6 *Only heaven can see the back of a sparrow*
SOUTH AFRICA

7   A good buttock finds a bench for itself   ESTONIA

8   One does not rub buttocks with a porcupine   GHANA

235   STOMACH – LIVER

1   An army marches on its stomach   FRANCE

2   The stomach never becomes full with licking   ESTONIA

3   The rat has a double stomach   NEW ZEALAND

4   To an empty stomach white bread tastes like brown
    ESTONIA

5   You cannot fill your belly by painting pictures of bread
    CHINA

6   Hungry bellies have no ears   ENGLAND

7   A blessing does not fill the belly   IRELAND

8   The belly teaches all arts   ENGLAND

9   Gin caresses lungs and liver   NETHERLANDS

236   SKIN – FUR – SHELL – FEATHERS

1   Don't value a badger skin before catching the badger
    JAPAN

2   The skin creaks according to the country   ETHIOPIA

3   *The toad doesn't know that its skin is rough*
CAMEROON

4   *The wolf changes his hair, but not his skin*   ALBANIA

5   *Straps come from the same leather*   ARGENTINE

6   *One can paint the fur of a tiger but not his joints*
KOREA

7   *The tortoise breathes; it is only its shell that prevents our noticing it*   NIGERIA

8   *A clever bird builds its nest with other birds' feathers*
ZIMBABWE

9   *The feathers make the fowl big*   CÔTE D'IVOIRE

10   *Puttin' feathers on a buzzard won't make it no eagle*
USA

11   *Birds of a feather flock together*   ENGLAND

12   *A bird with a beautiful plumage doesn't sit in the corner*
CAMEROON

237   HEAD

1   *Do not lift the club too high, it may fall on your head*
FINLAND

2   *Be not a baker if your head be butter*   FRANCE

3   *A head without a brain has no need of a hat*   SPAIN

4   *Why should someone without a head want a hat?*
     CHILE

5   *Who has no head has legs*   ALBANIA

6   *You cannot prevent the birds of sadness from flying over
     your head, but you can prevent them from nesting in your
     hair*   CHINA

7   *Pull the ear, the head follows*   BANGLADESH

8   *Justice becomes injustice when it makes two wounds on a
     head which only deserves one*   REPUBLIC OF CONGO

9   *The one on whose head we would break a coconut never
     stands still*   NIGERIA

10   *Every head is a world*   CUBA

11   *Fish begin to stink from the head*   ALBANIA

12   *Lower your head modestly while passing, and you will
     harvest bananas*   REPUBLIC OF CONGO

13   *A bald head is soon shaved*   SCOTLAND

14   *The head is older than the book*   BELGIUM

15   *The tongue talks at the head's cost*   ENGLAND

16   *People carrying elephant's flesh on their head should not
     look for crickets underground*   NIGERIA

17   *Give your tongue more holidays than your head*
     SCOTLAND

18   *A big head, a big headache*   BULGARIA

19 *An axe with a loose head is the bane of a man up a tree*
NIGERIA

20 *When a single hair has fallen from your head, you are
not yet bald* SIERRA LEONE

21 *You cannot shave a man's head in his absence* NIGERIA

22 *Two heads are better than one* ENGLAND

23 *A fire in the heart makes smoke in the head* GERMANY

24 *A buffalo does not feel the weight of his own horns*
INDIA

25 *The older the buck, the harder his horn* SCOTLAND

26 *Move your neck according to the music* ETHIOPIA

27 *The tongue has no bones, yet breaks its own skull*
ALBANIA

238 HAIR (OR NOT)

1 *Short hair is soon brushed* GERMANY

2 *Long hair – short brains* MONTENEGRO

3 *Beware of those who squint or have red hair* SERBIA

4 *You cannot prevent the birds of sadness from flying over
your head, but you can prevent them from nesting in your
hair* CHINA

5 *A bald-headed man cannot grow hair by getting excited
about it* REPUBLIC OF CONGO

6   *Tangled hair needs a wide comb*   SERBIA

7   *That miller is honest who has hair on his teeth*
GERMANY

8   *One cannot grab a bald man by the hair*   NETHERLANDS

9   *When a single hair has fallen from your head, you are
not yet bald*   SIERRA LEONE

10   *A bald head is soon shaved*   SCOTLAND

11   *The bald need no comb*   POLAND

12   *He who has a beard has also a comb*   ALBANIA

13   *The world will not conquer him who is always rubbing
his beard*   INDIA

14   *When a man eats, his own beard moves and not
another's*   TOGO

15   *A long beard does not prevent a house going to bed
hungry*   CAMEROON

16   *A kiss without a beard is like an egg without salt*
NETHERLANDS

239 FACE

1   *When the face is washed, you finish at the chin*
NIGERIA

2   *The face came before the photograph*   USA

3   *One hand washes the other; both hands wash the face*
ALBANIA

4   *A big nose never spoiled a handsome face*   FRANCE

5   *A clean face needs no water*   BOHEMIA

6   *Joy and courage make a handsome face*   FRANCE

7   *Ashes will always blow back into the face of the thrower*
NIGERIA

8   *Do not remove a fly from your friend's forehead with a
hatchet*   CHINA

9   *Who is able to wipe off what is written on the forehead?*
INDIA

10 *Those who have a great nose think everyone speaks of it*
SCOTLAND

11 *They must have clean fingers who would blow another's
nose*   DENMARK

12 *Those who want the last drop out of the can get the lid
on their nose*   NETHERLANDS

13 *If you put your nose into water you will also wet your
cheeks*   GEORGIA

14 *Strange bread makes the cheeks red*   SWITZERLAND

15 *They will see their nose who lower their eyes*   NIGERIA

16 *Laws have wax noses*   FRANCE

17 *Everything is possible, except to bite your own nose*
NETHERLANDS

18   *Your liberty ends where my nose begins*   USA

19   *No elephant is burdened by its own trunk*
      SOUTH AFRICA

20   *Don't lead with your chin*   USA

240   MOUTH

1   *Never scald your lips with someone else's porridge*
     IRELAND

2   *There's many a slip between cup and lip*   ENGLAND

3   *Donkey's lips do not fit onto a horse's mouth*   CHINA

4   *A closed mouth catches no flies*   ENGLAND

5   *A dog's mouth yields no ivory*   CHINA

6   *Have a mouth as sharp as a dagger, but a heart as soft
     as tofu*   CHINA

7   *Bees that have honey in their mouths have stings in their
     tails*   FRANCE

8   *God gives the wideness of the mouth according to the
     bigness of the spoon*   POLAND

9   *A dry spoon scratches the mouth*   RUSSIA

10   *The mouth is the healer and executioner of the body*
     DENMARK

11   *The fish said, 'I have much to say, but my mouth is full
     of water.'*   GEORGIA

12   *Those who wait for roast duck to fly into their mouth must wait a very, very long time*   CHINA

13   *It is no use standing with an open mouth in front of an oven*   DENMARK

14   *A proverb places the words in one's mouth*   SWITZERLAND

15   *Those who have burnt their mouth with milk blow on ice-cream*   TURKEY

16   *Be like the mouth and hand: when the hand is hurt the mouth blows on it; when the mouth is hurt the hand rubs it*   MADAGASCAR

17   *Open your mouth before you eat*   MAURITANIA

241   TONGUE

1   *The tongue has no bones, yet breaks its own skull*   ALBANIA

2   *Four horses cannot overtake the tongue*   CHINA

3   *Turn your tongue seven times before speaking*   FRANCE

4   *The tongue talks at the head's cost*   ENGLAND

5   *Give your tongue more holidays than your head*   SCOTLAND

6   *The tongue always goes to the aching tooth*   BULGARIA

242 TEETH

1   *Aching teeth are ill tenants*   ENGLAND

2   *When the hands and the feet are bound, the tongue runs faster*   GERMANY

3   *That miller is honest who has hair on his teeth*
     GERMANY

4   *One must chew according to one's teeth*   NORWAY

5   *A good word never broke a tooth*   IRELAND

6   *Never show your teeth unless you can bite*   IRELAND

7   *Those who go to sea without biscuits return without teeth*
     FRANCE: CORSICA

8   *Without practice one cannot even clean one's teeth*
     SRI LANKA

9   *Feigned laughter ruins the teeth*   INDIA

10   *Eating pears always cleans one's teeth*   KOREA

11   *If you had teeth of steel, you could eat iron coconuts*
     SENEGAL

243 EARS

1   *Steal a bell with your ears covered*   CHINA

2   *When you buy, use your eyes not your ears*
     CZECH REPUBLIC

* * * * * * * * * * * * * * * * * * *

18 CONTRASTS

About half the proverbs in this collection express a two-part contrast, almost always reinforcing the contrast through parallelism in the grammatical construction:

> *The lot of the coconut shell is to float and the lot of the stone is to sink.*
>
> *Speak of the miracle, but don't mention the saint.*
>
> *A gem cannot be polished without friction, nor a person perfected without trials.*
>
> *Priests return to the temple; merchants to the shop.*

The 'better' construction is a succinct means of highlighting a two-part contrast:

> *Better to light a candle than to curse the darkness.*
>
> *Better a diamond with a flaw than a pebble without one.*
>
> *Better do a good deed near at home than go far away to burn incense.*
>
> *Better an egg today than a hen tomorrow.*

Three-part contrasts are much less common. A Chinese example is:

> *If you want one year of prosperity, grow grain. If you want ten years of prosperity, grow trees. If you want a hundred years of prosperity, grow people.*

SEE ALSO Belonging together (p. 120)

* * * * * * * * * * * * * * * * * *

3   *Hungry bellies have no ears*   ENGLAND

4   *The big toe never does the ear any harm*   NIGERIA

5   *Dogs do not know how to swim until the water reaches their ears*   UKRAINE

6   *Pull the ear, the head follows*   BANGLADESH

7   *Do not blow into a bear's ear*   CZECH REPUBLIC

8   *Flies have ears*   KENYA

9   *The hollow of the ear is never full*   SENEGAL

10   *An old story does not open the ear as a new one does*
      NIGERIA

11   *It is a cunning mouse which nests in the cat's ear*
      ENGLAND

244 EYES

1   *The eye does not rise above the eyebrow*   SYRIA

2   *You should never touch your eye but with your elbow*
      ENGLAND

3   *Those who can read and write have four eyes*   ALBANIA

4   *When you buy, use your eyes not your ears*
      CZECH REPUBLIC

5   *A fly before one's own eye is bigger than an elephant in the next field*   CHINA

6   *All are not asleep who have their eyes shut*   GERMANY

7   *Don't hold the dime so near your eye that you can't see the dollar*   USA

8   *The eyes have one language everywhere*   ENGLAND

9   *Eyes see everything except themselves*   BULGARIA

10   *One missing button strikes the eye more than one missing day*   ESTONIA

11   *If two people tell you you are blind, shut one eye*   GEORGIA

12   *If you don't light fires, smoke won't get in your eyes*   GERMANY

13   *In buying horses and in taking a wife, shut your eyes tight and commend yourself to God*   ITALY

14   *In a cat's eye, all things belong to cats*   ENGLAND

15   *Present to the eye, present to the mind*   CHINA

16   *The heart's letter is read in the eyes*   ENGLAND

17   *The eyes close in sleep, but the pillow remains awake*   MALAYSIA

18   *The spear of kinship soon pierces the eye*   CAMEROON

19   *You can't look into a bottle with both eyes*   TOGO

20   *They will see their nose who lower their eyes*   NIGERIA

21   *If you laugh at your mother-in-law, you'll get dirt in your eye*   KENYA

22   *What the eye cannot see, the heart cannot grieve about*
ENGLAND

23   *The woman who sells fans often shades her eyes with her hands* CHINA

24   *Those who blow in the fire will get sparks in their eyes*
GERMANY

25   *Every deceiver's eyes are full of tears* BELGIUM

26   *Beware of those who squint or have red hair* SERBIA

27   *It is no use applying eye-medicine from a two-storey window* JAPAN

245 ARMS

1   *Keep your broken arm inside your sleeve* CHINA

2   *If you don't hear the story clearly, don't carry it off with you under your arm* THAILAND

3   *The throwers of stones fling away the strength of their own arms* NIGERIA

4   *You should never touch your eye but with your elbow*
ENGLAND

246 HANDS

1 *Hand washes hand* LATIN

2 *A smith has tongs to save his hands* SERBIA

3 *Those who have the frying-pan in their hand turn it at will* NETHERLANDS

4 *If you have fire-tongs, why use your hands?* ESTONIA

5 *Draw the snake from its hole by someone else's hand* SPAIN

6 *The woman who sells fans often shades her eyes with her hands* CHINA

7 *It takes two hands to clap* INDIA

8 *You cannot hold two water-melons in one hand* IRAN

9 *Never try to catch two frogs with one hand* CHINA

10 *One hand can't tie a bundle* LIBERIA

11 *Nothing wipes your tears away but your own hand* EGYPT

12 *You need not take someone else's hand to crush a sand-fly* NIGERIA

13 *One hand washes the other; both hands wash the face* ALBANIA

14 *Someone without a friend is like the right hand without the left* BELGIUM

15 *When the hands and the feet are bound, the tongue runs faster*   GERMANY

16 *Lazy people think their hands and feet were lent them*   GEORGIA

17 *A bird in the hand is worth two in the bush*   ENGLAND

18 *A bit of fragrance always clings to the hand that gives you roses*   CHINA

19 *A sparrow in the hand is better than a crane on the wing*   FRANCE

20 *Nothing enters into a closed hand*   SCOTLAND

21 *A man's hat in his hand never did him any harm*   SCOTLAND

22 *Adversity comes with instruction in its hand*   WALES

23 *Where hands are needed words and letters are useless*   GERMANY

24 *A stone from the hand of a friend is an apple*   MAURITANIA

25 *Practice with the left hand while the right hand is still there*   LIBERIA

26 *Be like the mouth and hand: when the hand is hurt the mouth blows on it; when the mouth is hurt the hand rubs it*   MADAGASCAR

27 *A dollar in the bank is worth two in the hand*   USA

28 *The devil finds work for idle hands*   ENGLAND

29 *A cake on the palm won't toast or burn*   SCOTLAND

30 *Keep your hurry in your fist*   IRELAND

31 *Cats love fish but fear to wet their paws*   CHINA

247 FINGERS – THUMBS

1 *Your fingers can't be of the same length*   CHINA

2 *Whichever finger you bite, every one hurts*   RUSSIA

3 *Those who have the tongs do not burn their fingers*
ALBANIA

4 *Don't snap your fingers at the dogs before you are outside the village*   FRANCE

5 *There is no grace in a benefit that sticks to the fingers*
ENGLAND

6 *Don't snuff the light too close, or you will burn your fingers*   DENMARK

7 *When luck offers a finger one must take the whole hand*
SWEDEN

8 *Among the ten fingers there are long and short*   CHINA

9 *If one finger is gashed, all the fingers are covered with blood*   REPUBLIC OF CONGO

10 *When you show the moon to a child, it sees only your finger*   ZAMBIA

11 *They must have clean fingers who would blow another's nose* DENMARK

12 *Without fingers the hand would be a spoon* SENEGAL

13 *Fingers were made before forks* ENGLAND

14 *Where the finger-nail will enter, there is no need of iron* INDIA

15 *Even the best smith sometimes hits his thumb* NETHERLANDS

248 LEGS

1 *A lie has no legs, but a scandal has wings* ENGLAND

2 *Who has no head has legs* ALBANIA

3 *Add legs to the snake after you have finished drawing it* CHINA

4 *Both legs in the stocks or only one is all the same* GERMANY

5 *It is no use lifting your leg until you come to the stile* ENGLAND

6 *It's the tortoise that discounts the value of a pair of fast legs* JAPAN

7 *A lie stands upon one leg, but truth upon two* ENGLAND

8 *Empty gossip jumps with one leg* ESTONIA

9 *The dog on three legs ain't always lame* USA

10   *Stretch your legs according to the length of your bedspread*   LIBYA

11   *Don't be breaking your shin on a stool that's not in your way*   IRELAND

12   *Consult anyone, even your knees*   JAPAN

13   *God knows on which knee the camel will squat down*   AFGHANISTAN

249   FEET – TOES

1   *Do not put each foot on a different boat*   CHINA

2   *A handsome shoe often pinches the feet*   FRANCE

3   *Sickness comes riding on horseback and goes away on foot*   BELGIUM

4   *A greyhound finds its food in its feet*   IRELAND

5   *Even a young foot finds ease in an old slipper*   SCOTLAND

6   *Habit hardens the feet*   NETHERLANDS

7   *When you want to test the depth of a stream, don't use both feet*   CHINA

8   *A smooth way makes the foot slip*   ESTONIA

9   *Parents who are afraid to put their foot down will have children who step on their toes*   CHINA

10 *When the hands and the feet are bound, the tongue runs faster* GERMANY

11 *Lazy people think their hands and feet were lent them* GEORGIA

12 *One foot is better than two stilts* FRANCE

13 *The vulture's foot spoils the soup* NIGERIA

14 *The quiet duck puts his foot on the unobservant worm* CHINA

15 *Only a fool tests the depth of the water with both feet* NAMIBIA

16 *Never marry a woman who has bigger feet than you* MOZAMBIQUE

17 *You can't dance at two weddings with one pair of feet* USA

18 *On an unknown path every foot is slow* IRELAND

19 *Better a crease in the shoe than a blister on the toe* ESTONIA

20 *The big toe never does the ear any harm* NIGERIA

250 TAIL

1   *When the leopard moves away, it takes its tail with it*
    NIGERIA

2   *I gave an order to a cat, and the cat gave it to its tail*
    CHINA

3   *Bees that have honey in their mouths have stings in their tails* FRANCE

4   *The saddest dog sometimes wags its tail* ENGLAND

5   *The cow which has the loudest bellowing has the slenderest tail* IRELAND

6   *If you get into the pack you need not bark, but wag your tail you must* RUSSIA

7   *The more naked the jackal the larger the tail*
    SOUTH AFRICA

8   *No one will lift the cat's tail unless the cat itself does*
    FINLAND

9   *The more you stroke a cat, the more it lifts its tail*
    ESTONIA

10 *What monkey forgets its tail?* CAMEROON

11 *As long as life lasts, the cow never stops moving its tail*
    NIGERIA

12 *There is nothing so eloquent as a rattlesnake's tail* USA

13 *A wolf does not step on the tail of a wolf* ESTONIA

14 *A cow that has no tail should not try to chase away flies*
GUINEA

15 *The tail wags the dog* ENGLAND

251 WASHING

1 *When the face is washed, you finish at the chin*
NIGERIA

2 *One hand washes the other; both hands wash the face*
ALBANIA

3 *Hand washes hand* LATIN

4 *Wash a dog, comb a dog: still a dog* USA

5 *The night washes what the day has soaped*
SWITZERLAND

6 *Even though chickens don't wash, their eggs are still white* SIERRA LEONE

7 *Dirty water cannot be washed* TOGO

8 *Some hang out more than they wash* USA

252 FEELING

1 *Pride feels no pain* EGYPT

2 *The autumn chill is the first thing felt by a thin person*
CHINA

3   *A buffalo does not feel the weight of his own horns*
     INDIA

4   *Longest at the fire soonest finds cold*   SCOTLAND

5   *Poverty is the sixth sense*   GERMANY

253   TOUCH

1   *Dirt will not stain unless you touch it*   POLAND

2   *An untouched drum does not speak*   LIBERIA

3   *You should never touch your eye but with your elbow*
     ENGLAND

4   *Nothing wipes your tears away but your own hand*
     EGYPT

5   *The stomach never becomes full with licking*   ESTONIA

6   *A dry bone is never licked*   ALBANIA

7   *Though honey is sweet, do not lick it off a briar*
     IRELAND

8   *Poke a bamboo thicket, drive out a snake*   JAPAN

9   *In eating and scratching, everything is in the beginning*
     COLOMBIA

10   *People scratch where they can reach*   KENYA

11   *Conscience is like tickling, some fear it and some don't*
     ITALY

12 *Those who tickle themselves laugh when they like*
GERMANY

254 HEAT – WARMTH

1 *A little nest is warmer than a big nest*   IRELAND

2 *The borrowed cloak never warms*   SYRIA

3 *Warm a frozen serpent, and it will sting you first*
ARMENIA

4 *A kind word warms for three winters*   CHINA

5 *Labour warms, sloth harms*   NETHERLANDS

6 *Warm water never forgets that it was once cold*
NIGERIA

7 *Those who have been scalded with hot soup blow on cold water*   UKRAINE

8 *Those who have burnt their mouth with milk blow on ice-cream*   TURKEY

9 *The soup is never swallowed as hot as it is cooked*
GERMANY

10 *A hot needle burns the thread*   CÔTE D'IVOIRE

11 *Genius is one percent inspiration, ninety-nine percent perspiration*   USA

12 *To be a smith you must work at the forge*   LATIN

13 *Little kettles soon boil over*   ESTONIA

14 *Those who have been in the oven know how pears are dried* BELGIUM

15 *A little wood will heat a little oven* ENGLAND

16 *It is no use standing with an open mouth in front of an oven* DENMARK

255 FIRE

1 *A burnt bairn dreads the fire* SCOTLAND

2 *Paper can't wrap up a fire* CHINA

3 *Fire is a good slave, but a bad master* ALBANIA

4 *If you don't light fires, smoke won't get in your eyes* GERMANY

5 *Strike a flint and you get fire* USA

6 *There's no smoke without fire* ENGLAND

7 *Those who blow in the fire will get sparks in their eyes* GERMANY

8 *Those who cut their own firewood have it warm them twice* USA

9 *Those who have the tongs do not burn their fingers* ALBANIA

10 *Wood half-burnt is easily kindled* ENGLAND

11 *Better do a good deed near at home than go far away to burn incense* CHINA

12   *One sprinkles the most sugar where the tart is burnt*
NETHERLANDS

13   *Don't snuff the light too close, or you will burn your
fingers*   DENMARK

14   *The damp burns with the dry*   TURKEY

15   *A hot needle burns the thread*   CÔTE D'IVOIRE

16   *Don't burn your candle at both ends*   ENGLAND

17   *The fly flutters about the candle until at last it gets burnt*
NETHERLANDS

18   *Don't keep all your tongs in one fire*   CANADA

19   *When the beans get too thick, the pot burns*   USA

20   *The idle person will put the cat in the fire*   SCOTLAND

21   *A little wood will heat a little oven*   ENGLAND

22   *One should not light a fire unless one wants to cook*
DENMARK

23   *A cake on the palm won't toast or burn*   SCOTLAND

24   *Only when all contribute their firewood can they build up
a good fire*   CHINA

25   *A crooked log makes a good fire*   FRANCE

26   *Longest at the fire soonest finds cold*   SCOTLAND

27   *The only insurance against fire is to have two houses*
NIGERIA

256 EXTINGUISHING

1   *Fire is not put out by fire*   GREECE

2   *Any water puts out fire*   FRANCE

3   *When an old barn begins to burn, it is hard to put out*
    NETHERLANDS

4   *Far waters cannot quench near fires*   CHINA

257 FUEL – SMOKE

1   *A crooked log makes a good fire*   FRANCE

2   *Only when all contribute their firewood can they build up
    a good fire*   CHINA

3   *Those who cut their own firewood have it warm them
    twice*   USA

4   *Wood half-burnt is easily kindled*   ENGLAND

5   *If you don't light fires, smoke won't get in your eyes*
    GERMANY

6   *Strike a flint and you get fire*   USA

7   *Every chimney makes its own smoke*   ITALY

8   *Every ember has its smoke*   MALTA

9   *A fire in the heart makes smoke in the head*   GERMANY

10 *There's no smoke without fire*   ENGLAND

258 COLD – COOL

1 *The autumn chill is the first thing felt by a thin person*
CHINA

2 *Longest at the fire soonest finds cold*   SCOTLAND

3 *Those who have been scalded with hot soup blow on cold water*   UKRAINE

4 *A good day is that in which to lay by cold porridge*
MALAWI

5 *Hunger doesn't say, 'Stale bread,' and cold doesn't say 'Old coat.'*   GEORGIA

6 *Warm water never forgets that it was once cold*
NIGERIA

7 *Gaming money won't get cold*   SCOTLAND

8 *The broth from a distance grows cool on the road*
KENYA

9 *Warm a frozen serpent, and it will sting you first*
ARMENIA

10 *When a donkey is well off he goes dancing on ice*
CZECH REPUBLIC

11 *You do not know who is your friend or who is your enemy until the ice breaks*   ICELAND

12 *Thin ice and thick ice look the same from a distance*
USA

13 *That which falls in the snow comes to light in the thaw*
DENMARK

14 *A good deed is written on snow*   ESTONIA

15 *No one thinks of the snow that fell last year*   SWEDEN

16 *The woman who sells fans often shades her eyes with her hands*   CHINA

259   TASTE

1 *One needn't devour the whole chicken to know the flavour of the bird*   CHINA

2 *Beauty is in the oleander and the oleander is bitter*
MOROCCO

3 *Cheap soup has no taste*   TURKESTAN

4 *Good medicine is bitter to the taste*   KOREA

5 *Those who have not tasted bitter know not what sweet is*
GERMANY

6 *Food tastes best when one eats it with one's own spoon*
DENMARK

7 *To an empty stomach white bread tastes like brown*
ESTONIA

8 *An onion shared with a friend tastes like roast lamb*
EGYPT

9 *More than one mother can make tasty soup*   NIGERIA

* * * * * * * * * * * * * * * * * * *

19 PROVERB GRAMMAR

To express a point as succinctly as possible, many proverbs have been reduced to a grammatical minimum – the essential meaning-carrying words and nothing else. *Sooner begun, sooner done* carries much more impact than some such alternative as 'The sooner you have begun, the sooner you will have done'. This kind of elliptical phrasing can be seen in many languages, and is a special feature of logographic languages such as Chinese, where any translation into English is invariably wordier than the original. Other English examples include:

> *Once bitten, twice shy.*
> *Easy come, easy go.*
> *The better the day, the better the deed.*
> *Waste not, want not.*

The omission of a grammatical word (such as *a, the, is*) can be seen here:

> *Faint heart never won fair lady.*
> *Dog does not eat dog.*
> *Sweetest the grass next to the ground.*

Unusual word order is common, sometimes reflecting a preferred rhythm, sometimes the need to make a particular word prominent at the beginning of a sentence:

If the brain sows not corn, it plants thistles (ENGLAND)
Love your neighbour, yet pull not down your hedge (ENGLAND)
Sell not your bearskin until you have the bear (USA)
Wider will the cow-dung be for trampling on it (WALES)

Sometimes the grammatical character of a local way of speaking is reflected in the proverb, as in these examples from Ireland:

Don't be breaking your shin on a stool that's not in your way.
It is not the one way everyone goes mad.
What should you expect from a cat but a kitten?
What can you expect from a pig but a grunt?
'Tis the one who runs that falls.

Or this pidginized translation from China:

Man who waits for roast duck to fly into mouth must wait very, very long time.

*   *   *   *   *   *   *   *   *   *   *   *   *   *   *   *   *   *

10   *After three days without reading, talk becomes flavourless*
         CHINA

11   *The soup would be none the worse for more meat*
         SUDAN

12   *Overdone is worse than underdone*   CANADA

13   *Crab apples make good jelly too*   USA

14 *A good cat deserves a good rat* ENGLAND

15 *Even beech leaves are good when they are fried in butter*
SERBIA

16 *Too many cooks oversalt the porridge* NETHERLANDS

17 *Don't chew your tobacco twice* USA

260 SWEET

1 *One sprinkles the most sugar where the tart is burnt*
NETHERLANDS

2 *The hornet also comes to the sugar-pot* CHINA

3 *If you want to keep your milk sweet, leave it in the cow*
LIBERIA

4 *Those who have not tasted bitter know not what sweet is*
GERMANY

5 *Sweetest the grass next to the ground* WALES

6 *You can't expect both ends of a sugar cane to be as sweet*
CHINA

7 *Though honey is sweet, do not lick it off a briar*
IRELAND

8 *The nearer the bone, the sweeter the meat* ENGLAND

9 *The sweetest wine makes the sharpest vinegar*
GERMANY

10 *The sweeter the perfume, the uglier the flies which gather round the bottle* CHINA

261 SOUR

1 *Is it necessary to add acid to the lemon?* INDIA

2 *The laden almond-tree by the wayside is sure to be bitter* JAPAN

3 *Good medicine is bitter to the taste* KOREA

4 *No melon-seller cries: Bitter melons!* CHINA

5 *Those who have not tasted bitter know not what sweet is* GERMANY

6 *Beauty is in the oleander and the oleander is bitter* MOROCCO

7 *The sweetest wine makes the sharpest vinegar* GERMANY

8 *In vinegar, sharpness is a virtue* RUSSIA

9 *If there is falsity in a proverb, then milk can be sour* INDIA

262 SMELL

1 *A rich person's sickness and a poor person's pancake are smelt a long way off* BELGIUM

2   *Those who deal in onions no longer smell them*
GERMANY

3   *The rose that is smelt by many loses its fragrance*
SPAIN

4   *The sweeter the perfume, the uglier the flies which gather round the bottle*   CHINA

5   *A skunk smells its own hole first*   USA

6   *It's no wonder that the herring vessel smells of herring*
SCOTLAND

7   *A bit of fragrance always clings to the hand that gives you roses*   CHINA

8   *Making money selling manure is better than losing money selling musk*   EGYPT

9   *Fish begin to stink from the head*   ALBANIA

10 *Old droppings don't stink*   KENYA

263   SOUND

1   *Don't cough in a hiding place*   SUDAN

2   *When one starts the song too high it isn't finished*
GERMANY

3   *If water is noisy, there are no fish in it*   MYANMAR

4   *Who hears but one bell hears but one sound*   FRANCE

5   *The fuller the cask, the duller its sound*   GERMANY

6   *Those who ring the bell hear the sound*   ESTONIA

7   *If they do not open after three knocks, do not wait*
     POLAND

8   *Those who bring good news knock hard*   ENGLAND

9   *Knock before crossing even a stone bridge*   KOREA

10   *A clear conscience never fears midnight knocking*   CHINA

264   SILENCE

1   *Small cares make many words, great ones are mute*
     GERMANY

2   *The quiet duck puts his foot on the unobservant worm*
     CHINA

3   *A little drop of water silences a boiling pot*   GERMANY

4   *Silent worms bore holes in the wall*   JAPAN

5   *With silence we irritate the devil*   BULGARIA

6   *Good silence is called saintliness*   PORTUGAL

7   *'Tis a good word that can better a good silence*
     NETHERLANDS

8   *Silence is a fence round wisdom*   GERMANY

9   *Wise silence has never been written down*   ITALY

10   *They are truly superior who can look upon a game of chess in silence*   CHINA

11 *Speech is silver; silence is golden* ENGLAND

12 *A child learns quicker to talk than to be silent* NORWAY

13 *Good words make us laugh; good deeds make us silent*
FRANCE

14 *Those who are silent do not say nothing* SPAIN

15 *One may say what one has kept silent, but not keep silent what one has said* SWITZERLAND

16 *Where paper speaks, beards are silent* FRANCE

265 FAINT NOISE

1 *The water is shallowest where it babbles* WALES

2 *The fuller the cask, the duller its sound* GERMANY

3 *To the timorous all leaves seem to rustle* SWITZERLAND

4 *The copse does not rustle if the wind does not blow*
HUNGARY

5 *The sigh goes further than the shout* SCOTLAND

6 *A soft answer turns away wrath* ENGLAND

7 *The clock ticks nowhere as it ticks at home*
NETHERLANDS

8 *A bad word whispered will echo a hundred miles*
CHINA

266 LOUDNESS

1   *Actions speak louder than words*   ENGLAND

2   *The cow which has the loudest bellowing has the slenderest tail*   IRELAND

3   *None sigh deeper than those who have no troubles*
     NORWAY

4   *The bell is loud because it is empty*   POLAND

5   *Those who laugh last laugh loudest*   ENGLAND

6   *A roaring lion kills no game*   UGANDA

267 OBJECT NOISES

1   *A single bracelet doesn't jingle*   GUINEA

2   *Hit one ring and the whole chain will resound*
     SOUTH AFRICA

3   *If you don't toot your own horn, nobody else will*   USA

4   *Not even a bell always rings the same way*   SERBIA

5   *Those who ring the bell are quite safe*   SPAIN

6   *Those who ring the bell hear the sound*   ESTONIA

7   *The brook would lose its song if you removed the rocks*
     USA

8   *That which creaks must be oiled*   LATVIA

9   *The skin creaks according to the country*   ETHIOPIA

10   *Creaking wagons are long in passing*   NETHERLANDS

11   *A greased cartwheel does not squeak*   ESTONIA

12   *The wheel that does the squeaking is the one that gets the grease*   USA

268   ANIMAL NOISES

1   *Do not dwell in a city where a horse does not neigh nor a dog bark*   ENGLAND

2   *A blind dog won't bark at the moon*   IRELAND

3   *The dog barks, but the camel passes on*   SUDAN

4   *The dog barks, the wind carries*   ESTONIA

5   *If you get into the pack you need not bark, but wag your tail you must*   RUSSIA

6   *There's no use in having a dog and barking yourself*   ENGLAND

7   *The cow which has the loudest bellowing has the slenderest tail*   IRELAND

8   *While the sheep bleats it loses its mouthful*   BELGIUM

9   *First lay the egg, then cackle*   ESTONIA

10   *Those who spend a night with a chicken will cackle in the morning*   TUNISIA

11   *Every cackling hen was an egg at first*
RWANDA AND BURUNDI

12   *A chattering bird builds no nest*   CAMEROON

13   *What can you expect from a pig but a grunt?*   IRELAND

14   *You can't take the grunt out of a pig*   USA

15   *Eat with the dogs, howl with the wolves*   ALBANIA

16   *The cry of the hyena and the loss of the goat are one*
NIGERIA

17   *A howlin' coyote ain't stealin' no chickens*   USA

269 HUMAN NOISES

1   *Numerous calls confuse the dog*   TANZANIA

2   *As one calls in the wood, so comes the echo back again*
ESTONIA

3   *Call out a name in a crowd and somebody is sure to
answer*   CHINA

4   *Although he chirps, he is no chick*   UKRAINE

5   *No melon-seller cries: Bitter melons!*   CHINA

6   *The sigh goes further than the shout*   SCOTLAND

7   *Those who see the wolf shout; those who see it not, shout
twice*   BULGARIA

8   *Don't shout before the birch-rod falls*   LATVIA

9   *Rather once cry your heart out than always sigh*   CHINA

10   *None sigh deeper than those who have no troubles*
NORWAY

11   *A satisfied heart will often sigh*   FRANCE

12   *A bad word whispered will echo a hundred miles*
CHINA

13   *The echo knows all languages*   FINLAND

270 MUSIC

1   *We get the note by striking the string*   INDIA

2   *A borrowed fiddle does not finish a tune*   ZIMBABWE

3   *They heard the music, but understood not the tune*
SCOTLAND

4   *You cannot have harmony without noise*   ALBANIA

5   *Who hears music feels his solitude*   FRANCE

6   *Everything will perish save love and music*   SCOTLAND

7   *Music unheard has no value*   GREECE

8   *Where there is music, there can be no harm*   SPAIN

9   *Move your neck according to the music*   ETHIOPIA

10   *Those who hear not the music think the dancers mad*
CHINA

11   *When the music changes, so does the dance*   NIGERIA

271 SONG

1   A bird does not sing because it has an answer; it sings
    because it has a song   CHINA

2   Buzzards do not sing in bleak regions   PERU

3   Every song has its end   SLOVENIA

4   A good song can be sung twice   ESTONIA

5   When one starts the song too high it isn't finished
    GERMANY

6   Angels gave the gift of song, and while one sings one
    thinks no wrong   ITALY

7   The worm don't see nothing pretty in the robin's song
    USA

8   The longest chant has an end   SCOTLAND

9   Those who simultaneously eat and sing rise up fools
    PHILIPPINES

10 It ain't over till the fat lady sings   USA

11 Loving and singing are not to be forced   GERMANY

12 Those who sing worst, let them begin first   ENGLAND

13 Bed is the poor person's opera   EGYPT

272 MUSICAL INSTRUMENTS

1   *My banjo has no bells on it*   NIGERIA

2   *Steal a bell with your ears covered*   CHINA

3   *Who hears but one bell hears but one sound*   FRANCE

4   *The bell is loud because it is empty*   POLAND

5   *Not even a bell always rings the same way*   SERBIA

6   *Those who ring the bell hear the sound*   ESTONIA

7   *Those who have lost their oxen are always hearing bells*
    SPAIN

8   *A good question is like one beating a bell*   CHINA

9   *An untouched drum does not speak*   LIBERIA

10 *A borrowed drum never makes good dancing*   HAITI

11 *Where the drum is burst is the place to mend it*
    REPUBLIC OF CONGO

12 *It is very difficult to beat a drum with a sickle*   NIGERIA

13 *Those who have no authority will not have ceremonial
    drums*   CAMEROON

14 *Those who have only one bow should be content with one
    fiddle*   GERMANY

15 *A borrowed fiddle does not finish a tune*   ZIMBABWE

16 *'Thank you' won't pay the fiddler*   SCOTLAND

17 *One bad pipe ruins the entire organ*   NETHERLANDS

18   *All are not hunters who blow the horn*   FRANCE

19   *It is easy to make pipes sitting amongst bulrushes*
CZECH REPUBLIC

20   *We get the note by striking the string*   INDIA

21   *It isn't every kind of wood that can make a whistle*
LATVIA

273 HEARING

1   *Those who hear not the music think the dancers mad*
CHINA

2   *Who hears but one bell hears but one sound*   FRANCE

3   *Go abroad and you'll hear news of home*   ENGLAND

4   *Walls hear without warnings*   ENGLAND

5   *When everyone speaks, no one hears*   SCOTLAND

6   *Say kind words to hear kind words*   KOREA

7   *Ask no questions and you'll hear no lies*   ENGLAND

8   *Those who ring the bell hear the sound*   ESTONIA

9   *Those who tremble to hear a leaf fall should keep out of
the wood*   FRANCE

10   *Those who have lost their oxen are always hearing bells*
SPAIN

11   *If you don't hear the story clearly, don't carry it off with
you under your arm*   THAILAND

* * * * * * * * * * * * * * * * * *

20 A CATCH-PHRASE BECOMING A PROVERB

In the 1970s, in the US television comedy show *Rowan and Martin's Laugh-In,* Flip Wilson appeared as a cross-dressing character called Geraldine. His catch-phrase was 'What you see is what you get'. A decade later it appeared in the computing world, especially in desk-top publishing, referring to software which allows you to see in the output (such as a print-out) exactly what appears on the screen.

It has since come to be applied to a diverse range of social situations – one of the preconditions of an emerging proverb. I have seen it used as part of a restaurant advertisement, referring to the relationship between the photographs of dishes outside and the food on your plate inside. It has also graced more than one tourist brochure, referring to the beautiful scenery which awaits you if you visit a certain country. And it received an accolade when pop singer Britney Spears used it in one of her songs: 'Cus I can promise you baby, what U see is what U get'.

* * * * * * * * * * * * * * * * * *

12   *The squirrel is not heard in the forest*   ZANZIBAR

13   *Who hears music feels his solitude*   FRANCE

14   *Slander by the stream will be heard by the frogs*
MOZAMBIQUE

15   *They heard the music, but understood not the tune*
SCOTLAND

16   *There are none so deaf as those who will not hear*
ENGLAND

17   *To tell the truth is dangerous, to listen to it is annoying*
DENMARK

18   *Music unheard has no value*   GREECE

19   *Birds hear talk in daytime, rats hear talk at night*
KOREA

274   LIGHT

1   *The used key is always bright*   ENGLAND

2   *Fortune is glass; just when it is bright it is broken*
LATIN

3   *Stars shine always in a clear sky*   ESTONIA

4   *All that glitters is not gold*   ENGLAND

5   *A gem cannot be polished without friction, nor a person perfected without trials*   CHINA

6   *A little spark shines in the dark*   FRANCE

7   *The sun shines on both sides of the hedge*   ENGLAND

8   *Even a small star shines in the darkness*   FINLAND

9   *When the sun shines the moon has nothing to do*
FRANCE

10   *Make hay while the sun shines*   ENGLAND

275 CANDLES – LANTERNS

1   *Better to light a candle than to curse the darkness*
    CHINA

2   *Those who must die must die in the dark, even though they sell candles* COLOMBIA

3   *A candle lights others and consumes itself* ENGLAND

4   *You may light another's candle at your own without loss*
    DENMARK

5   *The candle is put into the lantern and the moth is left outside fluttering* IRAN

6   *The fly flutters about the candle until at last it gets burnt*
    NETHERLANDS

7   *Don't burn your candle at both ends* ENGLAND

8   *Don't snuff the light too close, or you will burn your fingers* DENMARK

9   *It is not economical to go to bed early to save the candles if the result is twins* CHINA

10 *By candle-light a goat looks like a lady* FRANCE

11 *The game is not worth the candle* ENGLAND

12 *Every day cannot be a feast of lanterns* CHINA

13 *If it is your own lantern, do not poke holes in the paper*
    CHINA

14 *Look at the light, not at the lantern* ENGLAND

15 *At the foot of the lighthouse it is dark*   JAPAN

16 *A fallen lighthouse is more dangerous than a reef*
        CHINA

276 DARK

1 *The world is dark an inch ahead*   JAPAN

2 *Black sheep hide mighty easy in the dark*   USA

3 *In the dark all cats are grey*   ENGLAND

4 *You can only go halfway into the darkest forest; then you
   are coming out the other side*   CHINA

5 *Those who must die must die in the dark, even though
   they sell candles*   COLOMBIA

6 *Who suffers from diarrhoea is not afraid of the dark*
        SOUTH AFRICA

7 *The darkest hour is just before the dawn*   ENGLAND

8 *Better to light a candle than to curse the darkness*
        CHINA

9 *Even a small star shines in the darkness*   FINLAND

10 *In darkness all things are black*   SLOVENIA

11 *At the foot of the lighthouse it is dark*   JAPAN

12 *A blind mule ain't afraid of darkness*   USA

13 *A little spark shines in the dark*   FRANCE

14 *Darkness conceals the hippopotamus* SOUTH AFRICA

15 *Where there is love there is no darkness* BURUNDI

16 *If it were not for the night, we could never know the stars*
GERMANY

17 *Don't snuff the light too close, or you will burn your*
fingers DENMARK

18 *The sun cannot shine into an inverted bowl* CHINA

19 *Even the moon does not shine before it rises* FINLAND

277 LOOKING – SEEING

1 *Those who look fixedly at gold lose their sight*
NETHERLANDS

2 *We can never see the sun rise by looking into the west*
JAPAN

3 *One only goes to look at the prickly pear-tree when it is*
bearing fruit MEXICO

4 *Take a second look; it costs you nothing* CHINA

5 *Look at the light, not at the lantern* ENGLAND

6 *There is a time to squint, and a time to look straight*
SCOTLAND

7 *Look the other way when the girl in the tea-house smiles*
JAPAN

8 *There is no limit to looking upward* JAPAN

9   *Even a hen, when it drinks, looks towards heaven*
    TURKEY

10 *Don't look where you fell, but where you slipped*
    LIBERIA

11 *Never look an auto bargain under the hood*   USA

12 *Look before you leap*   ENGLAND

13 *A dog may look at a bishop*   FRANCE

14 *A cat may look at a king*   ENGLAND

15 *If you don't scale the mountain, you can't see the plain*
    CHINA

16 *The village that can be seen needs no signpost*   ALBANIA

17 *The more one walks the more hills one sees*   FINLAND

18 *The seagull sees furthest who flies highest*   FRANCE

19 *Eyes see everything except themselves*   BULGARIA

20 *Shed no tears until seeing the coffin*   CHINA

21 *Those who haven't seen a church bow before a fireplace*
    POLAND

22 *God, what things we see when we go out without a gun!*
    SOUTH AFRICA

23 *Those who see the wolf shout; those who see it not, shout
    twice*   BULGARIA

24 *One cannot ski so softly that the traces cannot be seen*
    FINLAND

25 *Love is not blind, it merely doesn't see* GERMANY

26 *Those who have not seen a hare run, must not speak of fear* ITALY

27 *It is in sugar that you see the dead ant* MALAYSIA

28 *Swimmers do not see their own back* TOGO

29 *What the eye cannot see, the heart cannot grieve about* ENGLAND

30 *When you see the palm-tree, the palm-tree has seen you* SENEGAL

31 *They will see their nose who lower their eyes* NIGERIA

32 *The worm don't see nothing pretty in the robin's song* USA

33 *When you show the moon to a child, it sees only your finger* ZAMBIA

34 *Someone who stands behind a wall can see nothing else* JAPAN

35 *Only heaven can see the back of a sparrow* SOUTH AFRICA

36 *Don't hold the dime so near your eye that you can't see the dollar* USA

37 *There are none so blind as those who will not see* ENGLAND

38 *Seeing is believing* ENGLAND

39 *One missing button strikes the eye more than one missing day* ESTONIA

40 *Love takes away the sight and matrimony restores it* GERMANY

41 *A village in sight does not require a guide* TURKEY

42 *It don't need a genius to spot a goat in a flock of sheep* USA

43 *Advice should be viewed from behind and not from in front* SWEDEN

44 *There is no better looking-glass than an old friend* ENGLAND

45 *That which falls in the snow comes to light in the thaw* DENMARK

278 BLINDNESS

1 *A blind dog won't bark at the moon* IRELAND

2 *A blind hen can sometimes find her corn* FRANCE

3 *A blind horse is no judge of colours* SCOTLAND

4 *A blind mule ain't afraid of darkness* USA

5 *A nod's as good as a wink to a blind horse* ENGLAND

6 *Love and blindness are twin sisters* UKRAINE

7 *Love is not blind, it merely doesn't see* GERMANY

8   *A blind man's wife needs no painting*   SCOTLAND

9   *A blind person needs no looking-glass*   SCOTLAND

10   *If two people tell you you are blind, shut one eye*
       GEORGIA

11   *When a blind person carries the banner, woe to those who
follow*   FRANCE

12   *There are none so blind as those who will not see*
       ENGLAND

13   *There is no dust so blinding as gold dust*   USA

279   COLOURS

1   *A blind horse is no judge of colours*   SCOTLAND

2   *Grapes get their colour from grapes*   IRAN

3   *In the dark all cats are grey*   ENGLAND

4   *To an empty stomach white bread tastes like brown*
       ESTONIA

5   *Cheese and bread make the cheeks red*   GERMANY

6   *Beware of those who squint or have red hair*   SERBIA

7   *Strange bread makes the cheeks red*   SWITZERLAND

8   *A red-nosed man may not be a drinker, but he will find
nobody to believe it*   CHINA

9   *To the jaundiced all things seem yellow*   FRANCE

10 *If I keep a green bough in my heart, a singing-bird will come* CHINA

11 *On a green tree there are many parrots* INDIA

12 *The grass always looks greener on the other side of the fence* ENGLAND

280 BLACK – WHITE

1 *Crows everywhere are equally black* CHINA

2 *In darkness all things are black* SLOVENIA

3 *Beyond black there is no colour* IRAN

4 *Black sheep hide mighty easy in the dark* USA

5 *In every family's cooking-pot is one black spot* CHINA

6 *It isn't in a coal-sack that one finds white flour* BELGIUM

7 *Black cows give white milk* GERMANY

8 *A black hen can lay a white egg* SCOTLAND

9 *A whitewashed crow soon shows black again* CHINA

10 *To an empty stomach white bread tastes like brown* ESTONIA

11 *Even though chickens don't wash, their eggs are still white* SIERRA LEONE

12 *A white cloth and a stain never agree* NIGERIA

281 WATCHING

1 *Do not sow groundnuts when the monkey is watching*
   NIGERIA

2 *It takes little effort to watch someone carry a load*
   CHINA

3 *A watched pot never boils*   ENGLAND

4 *A careless watch bids the thief come in*   SCOTLAND

5 *If you want an audience, start a fight*   CHINA

6 *The spectator is a great hero*   AFGHANISTAN

7 *They are truly superior who can look upon a game of chess in silence*   CHINA

282 APPEARING – DISAPPEARING

1 *The circumstances of people will appear from the condition of their hat*   SRI LANKA

2 *To the jaundiced all things seem yellow*   FRANCE

3 *An ulcer and a boil do not choose where to appear*
   JAPAN

4 *It is a hard job to make old monkeys pull faces*
   BELGIUM

5 *You may read Pompeii in some people's faces*   ITALY

6 *The other side of the road always looks cleanest*
   ENGLAND

7   *By candle-light a goat looks like a lady*   FRANCE

8   *Thin ice and thick ice look the same from a distance*
     USA

9   *The grass always looks greener on the other side of the
fence*   ENGLAND

10   *When the only thing you have is a hammer, everything
looks like a nail*   FRANCE

11   *A whitewashed crow soon shows black again*   CHINA

12   *Revolutions are not made by men in spectacles*   USA

13   *There are many paths to the top of the mountain – but
the view is always the same*   CHINA

14   *Talk of the devil and he will appear*   ENGLAND

15   *Never show your teeth unless you can bite*   IRELAND

16   *Many people are like clocks, they show one hour and
strike another*   DENMARK

17   *Too many affairs are like pumpkins in water; one pops up
while you try to hold down the other*   CHINA

18   *Do not fear a stain that disappears with water*   SPAIN

19   *Old countries don't disappear overnight; they stay for
breakfast*   EGYPT

20   *Good scribes are not those who write well, but who erase
well*   RUSSIA

21   *Here today and gone tomorrow*   ENGLAND

283 MIND

1 Where there is most mind there is least money LATIN

2 A contented mind is a continual feast ENGLAND

3 The mind does not grow old WALES

4 Present to the eye, present to the mind CHINA

5 Two pieces of meat confuse the mind of the fly NIGERIA

6 A needle cannot hold two threads or a mind two thoughts
ETHIOPIA

7 Great minds think alike ENGLAND

8 The broad-minded see the truth in different religions; the
narrow-minded see only the differences CHINA

284 THINKING

1 Think much, say little, write less FRANCE

2 Nobody is hanged for thinking HUNGARY

3 Angels gave the gift of song, and while one sings one
thinks no wrong ITALY

4 They that think no ill are soonest beguiled ENGLAND

5 Why should the cow trouble to think if she has plenty of
hay? SLOVAKIA

6 The morning is the mother of trades and the evening the
mother of thoughts ITALY

7   *Great minds think alike*   ENGLAND

8   *Many books do not use up words; many words do not use up thoughts*   CHINA

9   *A needle cannot hold two threads or a mind two thoughts*   ETHIOPIA

10   *Idle curiosity sometimes fills the mousetrap*   NETHERLANDS

11   *Curiosity killed the cat*   ENGLAND

12   *Ideas start with 'I'*   USA

13   *Necessity is the mother of invention*   ENGLAND

14   *It is not healthy to swallow books without chewing*   GERMANY

15   *If rivals are annoying you by playing well, consider adopting their strategy*   CHINA

16   *The first stage of folly is to consider oneself wise*   BELGIUM

17   *Who refuses, muses*   FRANCE

18   *Even a mole may instruct a philosopher on the art of digging*   CHINA

19   *Genius is one percent inspiration, ninety-nine percent perspiration*   USA

20   *Those who think they are building a mound may only in reality be digging a pit*   CHINA

21 *Those who have a great nose think everyone speaks of it*
SCOTLAND

22 *Drinking and thinking don't mix* USA

285 ATTENTION – INATTENTION

1 *Because we concentrated on the snake, we missed the scorpion* EGYPT

2 *God listens to short prayers* ITALY

3 *When the fox starts preaching, look to the hens*
SPAIN: BASQUE

4 *Speak of the miracle, but don't mention the saint*
PHILIPPINES

5 *The tortoise breathes; it is only its shell that prevents our noticing it* NIGERIA

6 *Before you go, think of your return* BELGIUM

7 *Those who seek the entrance should also think of the exit*
GERMANY

8 *A careless watch bids the thief come in* SCOTLAND

9 *The quiet duck puts his foot on the unobservant worm*
CHINA

10 *No one thinks of the snow that fell last year* SWEDEN

11 *Not even a schoolteacher notices bad grammar in a compliment* USA

12   *I can tell by my own pot how the others are boiling*
FRANCE

13   *Don't be so much in love that you can't tell when it's raining* MADAGASCAR

286 CAREFUL – CARELESS

1   *The careful person has also tumbled downstairs*
SWITZERLAND

2   *Keep your chickens in your own backyard* USA

3   *Those who have not bread to spare should not keep a dog*
CHINA

4   *It is the prudent hyena that lives long* ZAMBIA

5   *It's the tortoise that discounts the value of a pair of fast legs* JAPAN

6   *Never put off till tomorrow what can be done today*
ENGLAND

287 QUESTIONS

1   *To know the road ahead, ask those coming back* CHINA

2   *Never ask a barber if you need a haircut* USA

3   *Better ask twice than go wrong once* GERMANY

* * * * * * * * * * * * * * * * * *

21 NONSTANDARD LANGUAGE

The universal application of proverbs makes them ideal candidates for expression in the standard language of a country, as that will be the dialect most widely understood. It is fairly unusual to find proverbs containing nonstandard grammar or spelling; but the present collection has some instances, especially from the USA, where creoles and other varieties of English have left their mark. The following examples illustrate nonstandard use of two negatives (as in *can't catch no*), agreement between subject and verb (as in *broncs is*), past participle forms (*rode, throwed*), pronoun forms (*them, what*), adverbs (*mighty easy*), and the use of *ain't*.

> *The toughest broncs is always them you've rode some other place.*
> *Cows can't catch no rabbits.*
> *The worm don't see nothing pretty in the robin's song.*
> *The dog on three legs ain't always lame.*
> *Advice that ain't paid for ain't no good.*
> *If you aren't what you ain't, then you ain't what you are.*
> *It ain't half so bad if you can afford it.*
> *It ain't over till the fat lady sings.*
> *Pretty near ain't quite.*
> *Some guys got it, and some guys ain't got it.*
> *A blind mule ain't afraid of darkness.*
> *A howlin' coyote ain't stealin' no chickens.*
> *It don't need a genius to spot a goat in a flock of sheep.*
> *Black sheep hide mighty easy in the dark.*
> *Education don't come by bumping against the school-house.*

Folks is mighty generous with money what they ain't got.

There's no such thing as a horse that can't be rode or a cowboy that can't be throwed.

SEE ALSO Proverb grammar (p. 366)

* * * * * * * * * * * * * * * * * *

4 *The one who asks a question is a fool for five minutes; the one who does not ask a question is a fool forever*
    CHINA

5 *One should not ask the time of a rusty clock*
    NETHERLANDS

6 *It's a poor thing that's not worth asking*   SCOTLAND

7 *Ask a silly question, get a silly answer*   ENGLAND

8 *One does not lose by asking the way*   CHINA

9 *Courteous asking breaks even city walls*   UKRAINE

10 *Ask no questions and you'll hear no lies*   ENGLAND

11 *No one is informed but those who enquire*   WALES

12 *A good question is like one beating a bell*   CHINA

13 *Hasty questions require slow answers*   NETHERLANDS

288 ANSWERS

1 *No answer is also an answer* DENMARK

2 *A bird does not sing because it has an answer; it sings because it has a song* CHINA

3 *A soft answer turns away wrath* ENGLAND

4 *Hasty questions require slow answers* NETHERLANDS

5 *Ask a silly question, get a silly answer* ENGLAND

6 *Call out a name in a crowd and somebody is sure to answer* CHINA

7 *As one calls in the wood, so comes the echo back again* ESTONIA

289 SEEKING

1 *It is in vain to look for yesterday's fish in the house of the otter* INDIA

2 *If you look in a chief's bag you will always find something* UGANDA

3 *Looking for fish? Don't climb a tree* CHINA

4 *If you are looking for a fly in your food, it means you are full* SOUTH AFRICA

5 *Be on a horse when you're searching for a better one* CHINA

6 *People carrying elephant's flesh on their head should not look for crickets underground* NIGERIA

7 *Those who seek a constant friend go to the cemetery* RUSSIA

8 *Those who seek the entrance should also think of the exit* GERMANY

9 *Why seek the key of an open door?* INDIA

290 COUNTING – TESTING – MEASURING

1 *Count not what is lost but what is left* CHINA

2 *Don't count your chickens before they're hatched* ENGLAND

3 *When you want to test the depth of a stream, don't use both feet* CHINA

4 *Only a fool tests the depth of the water with both feet* NAMIBIA

5 *Measure twice, cut once* SLOVAKIA

6 *One must measure to know which is longer* KOREA

7 *The proof of the pudding is in the eating* ENGLAND

8 *Don't show a hyena how well you can bite* KENYA

291 POSSIBLE – PROBABLE – IMPOSSIBLE

1 *It is possible to talk to cattle if you have common sense*
SWITZERLAND

2 *Everything is possible, except to bite your own nose*
NETHERLANDS

3 *Sparrows who aspire to be peacocks are likely to break a thigh* MYANMAR

4 *Those whose mother is naked are not likely to clothe their aunt* SUDAN

5 *The impossible requires no excuse* NETHERLANDS

292 CERTAIN – UNCERTAIN

1 *There is bound to be a knot in a very long string* KENYA

2 *The laden almond-tree by the wayside is sure to be bitter* JAPAN

3 *Someone with a watch knows what time it is; someone with two watches is never sure* FRANCE

4 *Call out a name in a crowd and somebody is sure to answer* CHINA

5 *Slowly but surely the excrement of foreign poets will come to your village* MALI

6 *Two pieces of meat confuse the mind of the fly* NIGERIA

7 *Numerous calls confuse the dog* TANZANIA

8 *Never confuse asthma with passion* USA

9 *The crossroads always confuse the stranger* NIGERIA

10 *When in doubt, do nothing* ENGLAND

11 *When in doubt, gallop* FRENCH FOREIGN LEGION

12 *Those who hesitate are lost* ENGLAND

293 JUDGING

1 *Judge not the horse by his saddle* CHINA

2 *A blind horse is no judge of colours* SCOTLAND

3 *You can't judge a book by its cover* USA

4 *Those who have once had luck cannot always call themselves unlucky* BELGIUM

5 *Give with discretion, accept with memory*
    CZECH REPUBLIC

6 *Discretion is the better part of valour* ENGLAND

7 *By the stubble you may guess the grain* USA

8 *Only with a new ruler do you appreciate the value of the old* MYANMAR

9 *The broad-minded see the truth in different religions; the narrow-minded see only the differences* CHINA

294 DISCOVERING

1 *An hour of play discovers more than a year of conversation* PORTUGAL

2 *Sadness is a valuable treasure, only discovered in people you love* MADAGASCAR

3 *It isn't in a coal-sack that one finds white flour* BELGIUM

4 *The one who will fight will find a cudgel in every hedge* ENGLAND

5 *At the bottom of the bag one finds the bill* NETHERLANDS

6 *If you look in a chief's bag you will always find something* UGANDA

7 *Before you beat a dog, find out who its master is* CHINA

8 *Those who come too late find the platter turned over* NETHERLANDS

9 *Those who wake up and find themselves famous haven't been asleep* CHINA

295 BELIEF – UNBELIEF

1 *A red-nosed man may not be a drinker, but he will find nobody to believe it* CHINA

2   *When people praise, few believe it, but when they blame, all believe it* BELGIUM

3   *Don't believe those who come from afar, but those who return from it* SPAIN

4   *The fox believes that everyone eats hens like himself* FRANCE

5   *It is better to be entirely without a book than to believe it entirely* CHINA

6   *A lie becomes true when one believes it* GERMANY

7   *If you believe, it is a deity; otherwise, a stone* INDIA

8   *A frog beneath a coconut shell believes there is no other world* MALAYSIA

9   *Seeing is believing* ENGLAND

10   *Miracles come to those who believe in them* FRANCE

11   *Those who have to go ten miles must regard nine as only halfway* GERMANY

12   *Children regard their father's guest as a slave* REPUBLIC OF CONGO

13   *The afternoon knows what the morning never suspected* SWEDEN

14   *Gossips always suspect that others are talking about them* NIGERIA

15   *Think not because the cane is bent the sugar is crooked too* MALAYSIA

16 *If you get to thinking you're someone of influence, try ordering around someone else's dog* USA

17 *Those who hear not the music think the dancers mad* CHINA

18 *Some have been thought brave because they were afraid to run away* ENGLAND

19 *Lazy people think their hands and feet were lent them* GEORGIA

20 *Never trust a fellow that wears a suit* USA

21 *To wish to know is to wish to doubt* FRANCE

22 *If you suspect people, don't employ them; if you employ them, don't suspect them* CHINA

23 *Doubt, and you'll not be deceived* FRANCE

24 *To always win brings suspicion, to always lose brings contempt* GERMANY

25 *Don't rely on the label of the bag* FRANCE

296 KNOWLEDGE

1 *You are as many a person as languages you know* ARMENIA

2 *Who knows the language is at home everywhere* NETHERLANDS

3   *Let those who do not know what war is go to war*
     CHINA

4   *The meaning is best known to the speaker*   FRANCE

5   *Those who have been in the oven know how pears are
     dried*   BELGIUM

6   *One beetle knows another*   IRELAND

7   *Better the devil you know than the devil you don't*
     ENGLAND

8   *A new broom sweeps clean, but the old brush knows the
     corners*   IRELAND

9   *Those who do not know how to squander their money –
     buy some porcelain and drop it*   NETHERLANDS

10   *Everyone knows the bear, but the bear knows no one*
     FINLAND

11   *Necessity knows no law*   ENGLAND

12   *Only an owl knows the worth of an owl*   INDIA

13   *Those who speak much must either know a lot or lie a lot*
     GERMANY

14   *A fox knows much; a hedgehog one great thing*   GREECE

15   *You do not know who is your friend or who is your
     enemy until the ice breaks*   ICELAND

16   *Only the sweep knows what is up the chimney*   ITALY

17   *The echo knows all languages*   FINLAND

18   *The afternoon knows what the morning never suspected*
     SWEDEN

19   *Who knows much, mistakes much*   ARMENIA

20   *Who knows when death or a customer will come?*
     INDIA

21   *God knows on which knee the camel will squat down*
     AFGHANISTAN

22   *It takes one to know one*   ENGLAND

23   *The bazaar knows neither father nor mother*   TURKEY

24   *If you know what hurts yourself, you know what hurts
     others*   MADAGASCAR

25   *If you know the beginning well, the end will not trouble
     you*   SENEGAL

26   *The cobra knows its length*   NAMIBIA

27   *If the panther knew how much it is feared, it would do
     much more harm*   CAMEROON

28   *You never know your luck till the wheel stops*   USA

29   *It's a wise child that knows its own father*   ENGLAND

30   *An ounce of luck is better than a pound of knowledge*
     BELGIUM

31   *Familiarity breeds contempt*   ENGLAND

32   *To understand your parents' love, bear your own children*
     CHINA

33   *If you would understand men, study women*   FRANCE

34 *Only a nightingale understands a rose* INDIA

35 *To grow is to see* SOUTH AFRICA

    See also: **311 INFORMATION**

297 IGNORANCE

1 *Admiration is the daughter of ignorance* SPAIN

2 *Ignorance is a medicine* KOREA

3 *If ignorance is bliss, why be otherwise?* USA

4 *On an unknown path every foot is slow* IRELAND

5 *Those who have not tasted bitter know not what sweet is*
   GERMANY

6 *The toad doesn't know that its skin is rough*
   CAMEROON

7 *You never know how a cow catches a rabbit*
   NETHERLANDS

8 *Those who have no children do not understand love*
   ITALY

298 SCHOLARSHIP

1 *If pride were an art, how many graduates we should
   have* ITALY

2   *Three sorts of people are always to be found, soldiers, professors, and women*   GERMANY

3   *Scholars are the treasure of a nation*   CHINA

4   *Scholars talk books; butchers talk pigs*   CHINA

5   *Leave women alone, and go and study mathematics*
    ITALY

299 TRUTH

1   *A true word is not beautiful and a beautiful word is not true*   JAPAN

2   *It may be true what some say; it must be true what all say*   SCOTLAND

3   *A lie becomes true when one believes it*   GERMANY

4   *If love be timid, it is not true*   SPAIN

5   *Many a true word is spoken in jest*   ENGLAND

6   *The broad-minded see the truth in different religions; the narrow-minded see only the differences*   CHINA

7   *A lie stands upon one leg, but truth upon two*   ENGLAND

8   *Wine and children speak the truth*   ROMANIA

9   *A true jest is no jest*   SCOTLAND

10   *To tell the truth is dangerous, to listen to it is annoying*
    DENMARK

11   *Truth is the daughter of time*   GERMANY

12   *Truth is greater than ten goats*   NIGERIA

13   *Mad folks and proverbs reveal many truths*   USA

14   *Proverbs are so called because they are proved*   ITALY

15   *The exception proves the rule*   ENGLAND

16   *What is the use of running when we are not on the right road?*   GERMANY

17   *The beginning of wisdom is to call things by their right names*   CHINA

18   *Right church but wrong pew*   USA

300   ERROR

1   *Error is always in a hurry*   ENGLAND

2   *Who knows much, mistakes much*   ARMENIA

3   *They wouldn't make erasers if we didn't make mistakes*   USA

4   *There's many a slip between cup and lip*   ENGLAND

5   *Better ask twice than go wrong once*   GERMANY

6   *Right church but wrong pew*   USA

7   *Not even a schoolteacher notices bad grammar in a compliment*   USA

8   *Two wrongs do not make a right*   ENGLAND

* * * * * * * * * * * * * * * * * *

22 PAREMIOGRAPHERS

Paroemiography, or *paremiography,* is the technical term for the writing of proverbs or a collection of proverbs. The word is from Greek, where *paroimia* meant 'proverb' or 'by-word' – something uttered 'by the way' or 'along the road'. It arrived in English in the 1580s – a period when many Latin and Greek words were entering the language. The scholar George Puttenham, for example, says this in his *English Poesie* (1589):

> Parimia, or Prouerb, or, as we vse to call them, old said sawes, as thus: As the olde cocke crowes so doeth the chick: A bad Cooke that cannot his owne fingers lick.

Paremia is the name of a Spanish journal devoted to the study of proverbs.

There is no record of the term *paroemiographer* until the end of the eighteenth century. And soon after, we find the associated term for the study of proverbs, *paroemiology.* I am, it would appear, the latest in a long line of *paroemiologists.*

* * * * * * * * * * * * * * * * * *

301 PROVERBS – SAYINGS

1   *Proverbs are like butterflies; some are caught and some fly away*   GERMANY

2   *Proverbs are the children of experience*   ENGLAND

3   *Proverbs are the coins of the people*   RUSSIA

4   *A proverb never lies, it is only its meaning which deceives*
   GERMANY

5   *Proverbs are so called because they are proved*   ITALY

6   *Proverbs are little gospels*   SPAIN

7   *A proverb characterizes nations, but must first dwell among them*   SWITZERLAND

8   *The wise make proverbs but fools repeat them*
   ENGLAND

9   *A proverb places the words in one's mouth*
   SWITZERLAND

10   *If there is falsity in a proverb, then milk can be sour*
   INDIA

11   *When the occasion comes, the proverb comes*   GHANA

12   *Mad folks and proverbs reveal many truths*   USA

13   *Death and proverbs love brevity*   GERMANY

14   *Don't quote your proverb until you bring your ship to port*   SCOTLAND

15   *It's a poor rule that doesn't work both ways*
   ENGLAND

16   *Proverbs are constantly warring against each other*
   SWITZERLAND

17   *Old sayings contain no lies*   SPAIN: BASQUE

18   *Great consolation may grow out of the smallest saying*
SWITZERLAND

19   *There is no saying without a double meaning* KENYA

302 INTELLIGENCE

1   *A clever bird builds its nest with other birds' feathers*
ZIMBABWE

2   *It is not clever to play but to stop playing* USA

3   *Cleverness eats its owner* SOUTH AFRICA

4   *It is possible to talk to cattle if you have common sense*
SWITZERLAND

5   *Genius is one percent inspiration, ninety-nine percent
perspiration* USA

6   *Genius means patience* FRANCE

7   *The broad-minded see the truth in different religions; the
narrow-minded see only the differences* CHINA

8   *It don't need a genius to spot a goat in a flock of sheep*
USA

9   *If bravery is ten, nine is strategy* TURKEY

10   *The smartest housewife cannot cook a meal without rice*
CHINA

303 WISDOM

1   *The beginning of wisdom is to call things by their right names*   CHINA

2   *Silence is a fence round wisdom*   GERMANY

3   *You have no wisdom if you go to sleep before you make your bed*   UGANDA

4   *Honest men marry soon; wise men never*   ENGLAND

5   *A fall into a ditch makes you wiser*   CHINA

6   *The first stage of folly is to consider oneself wise*
    BELGIUM

7   *The wise make proverbs but fools repeat them*   ENGLAND

8   *The wise person is cheated only once*   FINLAND

9   *Who does not understand half a word will not be wiser for a whole word*   FINLAND

10   *Women in mischief are wiser than men*   ENGLAND

11   *Wise silence has never been written down*   ITALY

12   *The wise read a letter backwards*   GERMANY

13   *It's a wise child that knows its own father*   ENGLAND

304 STUPIDITY

1 *Good luck is the guardian of the stupid* SWEDEN

2 *Community is as strong as water, and as stupid as a pig*
RUSSIA

3 *The first stage of folly is to consider oneself wise*
BELGIUM

4 *It is folly to put flour into a bag facing the wind*
GERMANY

5 *Those who physic themselves poison a fool* ENGLAND

6 *Everyone is foolish until they buy land* IRELAND

7 *She is a foolish woman who blames her own cabbage*
DENMARK

8 *The wise make proverbs but fools repeat them* ENGLAND

9 *In chess the fools are nearest the kings* FRANCE

10 *Those who stumble twice over the same stone are fools*
LATIN

11 *A fool and his money are soon parted* ENGLAND

12 *It is difficult to recognize a fool who is also a proprietor*
SOUTH AFRICA

13 *Those who simultaneously eat and sing rise up fools*
PHILIPPINES

14 *The one who asks a question is a fool for five minutes;
the one who does not ask a question is a fool forever*
CHINA

15 *They are fools who make their doctor their heir* FRANCE

16 *Experience is the mistress of fools* ENGLAND

17 *Fools need no passport* DENMARK

18 *Fools seldom differ* ENGLAND

19 *Someone may learn and learn and yet remain a fool*
GREECE

20 *Only a fool tests the depth of the water with both feet*
NAMIBIA

21 *Fools rush in where angels fear to tread* ENGLAND

22 *It is a silly sheep that makes the wolf her confessor*
FRANCE

23 *Ask a silly question, get a silly answer* ENGLAND

24 *It is because the toad is too tenderhearted that he has no
intelligence* HAITI

25 *If the brain sows not corn, it plants thistles* ENGLAND

26 *A head without a brain has no need of a hat* SPAIN

27 *Long hair – short brains* MONTENEGRO

28 *Love teaches asses to dance* FRANCE

305 MADNESS

1 *Those who hear not the music think the dancers mad*
CHINA

2   *It is not the one way everyone goes mad*   IRELAND

3   *Those who do not eat cheese will go mad*   FRANCE

4   *Mad folks and proverbs reveal many truths*   USA

5   *Lovers, lunatics*   LATIN

306   REMEMBERING

1   *Happy nations have no history*   BELGIUM

2   *Teachers die, but books live on*   NETHERLANDS

3   *The best memory is not so firm as faded ink*   CHINA

4   *Give with discretion, accept with memory*
    CZECH REPUBLIC

5   *Those who read many epitaphs, lose their memory*
    LATIN

6   *When eating bamboo sprouts, remember the one who
    planted them*   CHINA

7   *To want to forget something is to remember it*   FRANCE

8   *The one who seeks revenge should remember to dig two
    graves*   CHINA

9   *Remember the rain that made your corn grow*   HAITI

307 FORGETTING

1   *To want to forget something is to remember it*   FRANCE

2   *Priests and women never forget*   GERMANY

3   *Those who are not in the habit of riding forget the spurs*
    IRELAND

4   *Learn, so that you may have something to forget*
    GERMANY

5   *When the house is built the carpenter is forgotten*   INDIA

6   *What monkey forgets its tail?*   CAMEROON

7   *The axe forgets, but the cut log does not*   ZIMBABWE

8   *Warm water never forgets that it was once cold*
    NIGERIA

9   *An elephant never forgets*   ENGLAND

10 *To learn costs you one effort, to unlearn, two*   BULGARIA

308 EXPECTATION

1   *What should you expect from a cat but a kitten?*
    IRELAND

2   *What can you expect from a pig but a grunt?*   IRELAND

3   *Who plays at bowls must expect the ball returned*
    NETHERLANDS

4   *What reliance can be placed on a sneeze?*   INDIA

5   *Never rely on love or the weather*   GERMANY

6   *Those who will have a cake out of the wheat must tarry the grinding*   ENGLAND

7   *Those who wait for roast duck to fly into their mouth must wait a very, very long time*   CHINA

8   *Those who wait for a dead person's shoes are in danger of going barefoot*   FRANCE

9   *Everything comes to those who wait*   ENGLAND

10   *A waiting appetite kindles many a spite*   ENGLAND

11   *The one who was surprised by a turtle is surprised by a pot cover*   KOREA

12   *What's the use of consulting a dead person's horoscope?*   SENEGAL

309 DESTINY

1   *Hanging and wiving go by destiny*   ENGLAND

2   *The lot of the coconut shell is to float and the lot of the stone is to sink*   INDONESIA

3   *Fortune is glass; just when it is bright it is broken*   LATIN

310 MEANING

1   *The meaning is best known to the speaker*   FRANCE

2   *A proverb never lies, it is only its meaning which deceives*
    GERMANY

3   *There is no saying without a double meaning*   KENYA

4   *Every word has three explanations and three
interpretations*   IRELAND

5   *Empty gossip jumps with one leg*   ESTONIA

6   *If you don't hear the story clearly, don't carry it off with
you under your arm*   THAILAND

7   *Who does not understand half a word will not be wiser
for a whole word*   FINLAND

8   *Only a monkey understands a monkey*   SIERRA LEONE

9   *Every definition is dangerous*   LATIN

10   *You may read Pompeii in some people's faces*   ITALY

11   *Three kinds of men fail to understand women – young
men, old men, and middle-aged men*   IRELAND

12   *They heard the music, but understood not the tune*
    SCOTLAND

13   *The heart's letter is read in the eyes*   ENGLAND

14   *Genius means patience*   FRANCE

15   *The existence of the sea means the existence of pirates*
    MALAYSIA

16 *If he calls it a silly and childish game, that means his wife can beat him at it* USA

17 *There's no accounting for tastes* ENGLAND

18 *Translators, traitors* ITALY

311 INFORMATION

1 *No one is informed but those who enquire* WALES

2 *If you want to be acquainted with the past and the present, you must read five cartloads of books* CHINA

3 *A village in sight does not require a guide* TURKEY

4 *To know the road ahead, ask those coming back* CHINA

5 *If we knew where we would fall, we would spread straw there first* FINLAND

6 *Someone with a watch knows what time it is; someone with two watches is never sure* FRANCE

7 *If it were not for the night, we could never know the stars* GERMANY

8 *Only those who have travelled the road know where the holes are deep* CHINA

9 *You may know a carpenter by his chips* ENGLAND

10 *One must measure to know which is longer* KOREA

11 *Those in love always know the time* GERMANY

12   *One needn't devour the whole chicken to know the flavour of the bird*   CHINA

13   *Those who live in the attic know where the roof leaks*
      NIGERIA

14   *Every pumpkin is known by its stem*   USA

15   *If two people tell you you are blind, shut one eye*
      GEORGIA

16   *Proverbs are the children of experience*   ENGLAND

17   *A proverb characterizes nations, but must first dwell among them*   SWITZERLAND

18   *If we would know what we are, let us anger our neighbours*   GERMANY

19   *To wish to know is to wish to doubt*   FRANCE

20   *It is difficult to recognize a fool who is also a proprietor*
      SOUTH AFRICA

21   *In crooked wood one recognizes the artist*   TOGO

22   *Experience is the mistress of fools*   ENGLAND

23   *At birth we cry – at death we see why*   BULGARIA

24   *Don't tell all of your jokes on one program*   USA

      See also: **296 KNOWLEDGE**

312 DISCLOSURE

1 *The beauty of the corn cob is apparent on the inside only*
KENYA

2 *A card that never appears neither wins nor loses* BRAZIL

3 *Mad folks and proverbs reveal many truths* USA

4 *Actions speak louder than words* ENGLAND

5 *To tell the truth is dangerous, to listen to it is annoying*
DENMARK

6 *Daisies won't tell* USA

7 *Dead men tell no tales* ENGLAND

313 CONCEALMENT

1 *Darkness conceals the hippopotamus* SOUTH AFRICA

2 *Art is the concealment of art* LATIN

3 *Black sheep hide mighty easy in the dark* USA

4 *The bait hides the hook* ENGLAND

5 *Give your love to your wife and your secret to your mother* IRELAND

6 *Don't cough in a hiding place* SUDAN

7 *Who is able to wipe off what is written on the forehead?*
INDIA

314 BOOKS

1   *A book holds a house of gold*   CHINA

2   *It is better to be entirely without a book than to believe it entirely*   CHINA

3   *Many books do not use up words; many words do not use up thoughts*   CHINA

4   *Scholars talk books; butchers talk pigs*   CHINA

5   *If you want to be acquainted with the past and the present, you must read five cartloads of books*   CHINA

6   *One is happy when one has books, but happier still when one has no need of them*   CHINA

7   *To read a book for the first time is to make the acquaintance of a new friend; to read it a second time is to meet an old one*   CHINA

8   *The head is older than the book*   BELGIUM

9   *Other people's books are difficult to read*   NETHERLANDS

10   *There is no worse robber than a bad book*   ITALY

11   *Teachers die, but books live on*   NETHERLANDS

12   *You can't judge a book by its cover*   USA

13   *It is not healthy to swallow books without chewing*
     GERMANY

315 NEWS – ADVERTISING

1 *No news is good news* ENGLAND

2 *Go abroad and you'll hear news of home* ENGLAND

3 *Those who bring good news knock hard* ENGLAND

4 *Good things sell themselves; bad things have to be advertised* ETHIOPIA

5 *It pays to advertise* USA

316 TEACHING – LEARNING

1 *Who teaches me for a day is my father for a lifetime* CHINA

2 *Love teaches asses to dance* FRANCE

3 *The belly teaches all arts* ENGLAND

4 *Necessity teaches new arts* NORWAY

5 *You do not teach the paths of the forest to an old gorilla* REPUBLIC OF CONGO

6 *You can't teach an old dog new tricks* ENGLAND

7 *Teachers open the door; you enter by yourself* CHINA

8 *Teachers die, but books live on* NETHERLANDS

9 *A child learns quicker to talk than to be silent* NORWAY

10 *By trying often, the monkey learns to jump from the tree* CAMEROON

* * * * * * * * * * * * * * * * * *

23 PROVERBS IN SHAKESPEARE'S SCHOOL

Proverbs played a major part in the education of a child in Elizabethan schools. They were seen as a means of providing moral advice as well as a technique for facilitating learning, especially in relation to Latin. John Withals' *Dictionarie in English and Latin* was the most popular Latin/English dictionary of the time. In its later editions it includes a large number of proverbial expressions. Because children would know many of the proverbs from their first-language background, they would be able to use this knowledge to recognize and memorize the corresponding Latin expressions.

Other books of proverbs were known in the schools, such as Richard Taverner's *Prouerbes or Adagies* – a collection of proverbs from Erasmus – and Nicholas Udall's *Floures of Terence* (the Latin poet). The children would have learned many of them by heart, when they arrived in grammar school, at the age of seven; and by the time they left, at fifteen, they would have acquired a repertoire of hundreds.

The contemporary audience at a Shakespeare play would have had little difficulty recognizing proverbial allusions when they occurred. When Lady Macbeth criticizes her husband for his tardiness, she says:

Letting 'I dare not' wait upon 'I would',
Like the poor cat i'th' adage.

Which adage? The proverb collections tell us: 'The cat would eat fish, and would not wet her feet'. Today, the allusion needs an editorial gloss.

* * * * * * * * * * * * * * * * * *

11 *Learn to handle a writing-brush, and you'll never handle a begging-bowl* CHINA

12 *By writing we learn to write* FRANCE

13 *Those who wish to learn to pray must go to sea* ENGLAND

14 *To learn costs you one effort, to unlearn, two* BULGARIA

15 *An old cat will not learn how to dance* MOROCCO

16 *Ploughing, we learn to plough; mowing, we learn to mow* LITHUANIA

17 *One must learn to be bored* FRANCE

18 *Learn, so that you may have something to forget* GERMANY

19 *Someone may learn and learn and yet remain a fool* GREECE

20 *One learns manners from the mannerless* IRAN

21 *You have to learn to crawl before you can walk* ENGLAND

22 *Learning is treasure a thief cannot touch* CHINA

23 *Not even a schoolteacher notices bad grammar in a compliment* USA

24 *If you would understand men, study women* FRANCE

25 *One can study calligraphy at eighty* JAPAN

26 *Leave women alone, and go and study mathematics* ITALY

27 *Experience is the mistress of fools* ENGLAND

28 *Even a mole may instruct a philosopher on the art of digging* CHINA

29 *Education don't come by bumping against the school-house* USA

317 LIES

1 *It is easy to lie about a far-off country* ETHIOPIA

2 *Old sayings contain no lies* SPAIN: BASQUE

3 *A lie has no legs, but a scandal has wings* ENGLAND

4 *Poets are fathers of lies* LATIN

5 *A lie becomes true when one believes it* GERMANY

6 *Those who speak much must either know a lot or lie a lot*
   GERMANY

7 *A lie stands upon one leg, but truth upon two* ENGLAND

8 *Those who do not lie never grow up* UGANDA

9 *A proverb never lies, it is only its meaning which deceives*
   GERMANY

10 *Ask no questions and you'll hear no lies* ENGLAND

11 *The end of an ox is beef, and the end of a lie is grief*
    MADAGASCAR

318 DECEPTION

1 *Doubt, and you'll not be deceived*   FRANCE

2 *A proverb never lies, it is only its meaning which deceives*
   GERMANY

3 *Every deceiver's eyes are full of tears*   BELGIUM

4 *If there is falsity in a proverb, then milk can be sour*
   INDIA

5 *Feigned laughter ruins the teeth*   INDIA

6 *The bait hides the hook*   ENGLAND

7 *The fish does not go after the hook, but after the bait*
   CZECH REPUBLIC

8 *A big fish is caught with big bait*   SIERRA LEONE

9 *They that think no ill are soonest beguiled*   ENGLAND

10 *Those who cheat me once, shame fall them; those who
   cheat me twice, shame fall me*   SCOTLAND

11 *The wise person is cheated only once*   FINLAND

12 *Full of courtesy, full of craft*   ENGLAND

13 *Eggs and vows are easily broken*   JAPAN

14 *New laws, new frauds*   ENGLAND

319 SIGNS – SYMBOLS

1   *Signposts only show the road, they don't go along it*
SWITZERLAND

2   *The sign-board brings the custom*   FRANCE

3   *The village that can be seen needs no signpost*   ALBANIA

4   *Any wood will do to make a signpost*   GREECE

5   *The postage stamp's usefulness lies in the ability to stick*
USA

6   *When a blind person carries the banner, woe to those who follow*   FRANCE

7   *Where the minute-hand suffices the hour-hand is not needed*   NETHERLANDS

8   *The label is bigger than the package*   GREECE

9   *Don't rely on the label of the bag*   FRANCE

10   *A nod's as good as a wink to a blind horse*   ENGLAND

11   *Don't snap your fingers at the dogs before you are outside the village*   FRANCE

12   *The steam that blows the whistle never turns the wheel*
USA

13   *A good deed is written on snow*   ESTONIA

14   *Who is able to wipe off what is written on the forehead?*
INDIA

15   *A debt is like a hippo's footprints*   NIGERIA

16   *The face came before the photograph*   USA

320   ART – ARTS

1   *Every art requires the whole person*   FRANCE

2   *A beautiful disorder is an effect of art*   FRANCE

3   *Fortune lifts up art, but not art fortune*   GREECE

4   *If pride were an art, how many graduates we should have*   ITALY

5   *Art is the concealment of art*   LATIN

6   *Good painters need not give a name to their pictures; bad ones must*   POLAND

7   *You cannot fill your belly by painting pictures of bread*   CHINA

8   *Add legs to the snake after you have finished drawing it*   CHINA

9   *Painting the pump will not clean out the well*   ENGLAND

10   *A blind man's wife needs no painting*   SCOTLAND

11   *One can paint the fur of a tiger but not his joints*   KOREA

12   *One must not shoot a glass arrow into a painted deer*   EGYPT

13   *Rotten wood cannot be carved*   CHINA

14   *Carve good deeds in stone, bad ones in sand*   ESTONIA

15   *If you engrave it too much it will become a hole*   INDIA

16   *An artist lives everywhere*   ENGLAND

17   *In crooked wood one recognizes the artist*   TOGO

321   LANGUAGES

1   *You are as many a person as languages you know*
     ARMENIA

2   *Who knows the language is at home everywhere*
     NETHERLANDS

3   *The eyes have one language everywhere*   ENGLAND

4   *A nation without a language is a nation without a heart*
     WALES

5   *The echo knows all languages*   FINLAND

6   *Don't talk Latin in front of the Franciscans*   FRANCE

7   *God is better pleased with adverbs than with nouns*
     ENGLAND

8   *Not even a schoolteacher notices bad grammar in a
compliment*   USA

322 WORDS

1   *Words will pay for most things*   SPAIN

2   *Many speak a word which if it were a florin they would put back in their purse*   GERMANY

3   *Words shake but examples attract*   SERBIA

4   *'Tis a good word that can better a good silence*
    NETHERLANDS

5   *Good words make us laugh; good deeds make us silent*
    FRANCE

6   *Small cares make many words, great ones are mute*
    GERMANY

7   *Words do not make flour*   ITALY

8   *Words are good, but fowls lay eggs*   GERMANY

9   *An ox is bound with ropes and a person with words*
    ITALY

10 *A proverb places the words in one's mouth*
    SWITZERLAND

11 *A kind word warms for three winters*   CHINA

12 *Where hands are needed words and letters are useless*
    GERMANY

13 *A true word is not beautiful and a beautiful word is not true*   JAPAN

14 *A word flies away like a sparrow and returns to the house like a crow*   GERMANY

15   *Many books do not use up words; many words do not use up thoughts*   CHINA

16   *Actions speak louder than words*   ENGLAND

17   *Better one living word than a hundred dead ones*   GERMANY

18   *A word and a stone let go cannot be called back*   ENGLAND

19   *A good word never broke a tooth*   IRELAND

20   *A bad word whispered will echo a hundred miles*   CHINA

21   *To kill with words is also murder*   GERMANY

22   *Every word has three explanations and three interpretations*   IRELAND

23   *Say kind words to hear kind words*   KOREA

24   *Promise is a bridge of words, unsafe to walk across*   GERMANY

25   *Many a true word is spoken in jest*   ENGLAND

26   *The second word makes the fray*   JAPAN

27   *Words and feathers are taken by the wind*   SPAIN: BASQUE

28   *Who does not understand half a word will not be wiser for a whole word*   FINLAND

323 NAMES – TITLES

1   *Those who own the boat should give it a name*
NORWAY

2   *Good painters need not give a name to their pictures; bad ones must*   POLAND

3   *A good child has several names*   ESTONIA

4   *A name doesn't harm us if we don't harm the name*
ESTONIA

5   *Call out a name in a crowd and somebody is sure to answer*   CHINA

6   *No nickname, no wealth*   CHINA

7   *A dog with money is addressed 'Mr Dog'*   USA

8   *Don't call the alligator a big-mouth till you have crossed the river*   BELIZE

9   *You come with a cat and call it a rabbit*   CAMEROON

10   *The beginning of wisdom is to call things by their right names*   CHINA

11   *Bad is called good when worse happens*   NORWAY

12   *Good silence is called saintliness*   PORTUGAL

13   *When you are chased by a wolf you call the boar your uncle*   SLOVENIA

14   *Proverbs are so called because they are proved*   ITALY

15   *If he calls it a silly and childish game, that means his wife can beat him at it*   USA

16   *Call a spade a spade*   ENGLAND

324   SPEECH

1   *It is easier to speak than to say something*   UKRAINE

2   *They that love most speak least*   SCOTLAND

3   *Speak of the miracle, but don't mention the saint*
    PHILIPPINES

4   *Turn your tongue seven times before speaking*   FRANCE

5   *Those who have a great nose think everyone speaks of it*
    SCOTLAND

6   *When everyone speaks, no one hears*   SCOTLAND

7   *Wine and children speak the truth*   ROMANIA

8   *Where paper speaks, beards are silent*   FRANCE

9   *Those who speak much must either know a lot or lie a lot*
    GERMANY

10   *Those who have not seen a hare run, must not speak of fear*   ITALY

11   *Who speaks of it commits it not*   ITALY

12   *Speak, lest tomorrow you be prevented*   KENYA

13   *An untouched drum does not speak*   LIBERIA

14 *Many a true word is spoken in jest* ENGLAND

15 *The meaning is best known to the speaker* FRANCE

16 *Speech is silver; silence is golden* ENGLAND

17 *Many speak a word which if it were a florin they would put back in their purse* GERMANY

18 *A child learns quicker to talk than to be silent* NORWAY

19 *Money talks* ENGLAND

20 *When gold talks, speech is useless* LATIN

21 *Beware the husband who talks* GREECE

22 *The tongue talks at the head's cost* ENGLAND

23 *A crow in a cage won't talk like a parrot* USA

24 *Talk of the devil and he will appear* ENGLAND

25 *The frightened person has many voices* FINLAND

26 *There is nothing so eloquent as a rattlesnake's tail* USA

27 *Example is a great orator* CZECH REPUBLIC

28 *A lie has no legs, but a scandal has wings* ENGLAND

29 *Slander by the stream will be heard by the frogs*
MOZAMBIQUE

30 *Death and proverbs love brevity* GERMANY

31 *The town that parleys is half surrendered* FRANCE

32 *Dead men tell no tales* ENGLAND

325 CONVERSATION

1   *An hour of play discovers more than a year of conversation*   PORTUGAL

2   *Conversation is a ladder for a journey*   SRI LANKA

3   *A good conversation is better than a good bed*   ETHIOPIA

4   *Too much discussion will lead to a row*   CÔTE D'IVOIRE

5   *Everybody talks about the weather, but nobody does anything about it*   USA

6   *It is possible to talk to cattle if you have common sense*   SWITZERLAND

7   *Scholars talk books; butchers talk pigs*   CHINA

8   *After three days without reading, talk becomes flavourless*   CHINA

9   *Birds hear talk in daytime, rats hear talk at night*   KOREA

10   *Don't talk Latin in front of the Franciscans*   FRANCE

11   *Don't tell all of your jokes on one program*   USA

12   *Never argue with someone who buys ink by the barrel*   CHINA

13   *Gossip needs no carriage*   RUSSIA

14   *Empty gossip jumps with one leg*   ESTONIA

15   *Gossip lasts but seventy-five days*   JAPAN

16   *Those who gossip about their relatives have no luck and no blessing*   NETHERLANDS

17   *Gossips always suspect that others are talking about them*   NIGERIA

18   *Lovers have much to relate – but it is always the same thing*   GERMANY

19   *What is said over the dead lion's body could not be said to him alive*   REPUBLIC OF CONGO

20   *The person who says it cannot be done should not interrupt the one doing it*   CHINA

21   *Think much, say little, write less*   FRANCE

22   *Hunger doesn't say, 'Stale bread,' and cold doesn't say 'Old coat.'*   GEORGIA

23   *'If I rest, I rust', says the key*   GERMANY

24   *'Virtue in the middle,' said the devil as he sat between two lawyers*   NORWAY

25   *The fish said, 'I have much to say, but my mouth is full of water.'*   GEORGIA

26   *Don't holler before you're hurt*   USA

27   *Before going to war say one prayer; before going to sea, two; before getting married, three*   POLAND

28   *That which you would say to another, say to yourself first*   ESTONIA

29   *That which is said at table should be wrapped up in the tablecloth*   ITALY

30   *Those who are silent do not say nothing*   SPAIN

31   *One may say what one has kept silent, but not keep silent what one has said*   SWITZERLAND

32   *Least said, soonest mended*   ENGLAND

33   *Little said is easy mended; nothing said needs no mending*   IRELAND

34   *Everyone who says goodbye is not gone*   USA

35   *Never say 'whoopee' before you jump*   CANADA

36   *Say kind words to hear kind words*   KOREA

37   *A weasel comes to say Happy New Year to the chickens*   CHINA

38   *It may be true what some say; it must be true what all say*   SCOTLAND

39   *When everybody says you are drunk, go to sleep*   ITALY

40   *People who do what they say are not cowards*   NIGERIA

41   *Don't quote your proverb until you bring your ship to port*   SCOTLAND

42   *A fault denied is twice committed*   FRANCE

43   *Put up or shut up*   USA

44   *The story is only half told when one side tells it*   ICELAND

45   *If you don't hear the story clearly, don't carry it off with you under your arm*   THAILAND

46   *An old story does not open the ear as a new one does*
NIGERIA

326   READING – WRITING

1   *After three days without reading, talk becomes flavourless*
CHINA

2   *Other people's books are difficult to read*   NETHERLANDS

3   *Those who read many epitaphs, lose their memory*
LATIN

4   *The wise read a letter backwards*   GERMANY

5   *To read a book for the first time is to make the acquaintance of a new friend; to read it a second time is to meet an old one*   CHINA

6   *By writing we learn to write*   FRANCE

7   *What one writes remains*   NETHERLANDS

8   *Wise silence has never been written down*   ITALY

9   *Good scribes are not those who write well, but who erase well*   RUSSIA

10   *Think much, say little, write less*   FRANCE

11   *Learn to handle a writing-brush, and you'll never handle a begging-bowl*   CHINA

12   *Those who can read and write have four eyes*   ALBANIA

13 *A love-letter sometimes costs more than a three-cent stamp* USA

14 *The heart's letter is read in the eyes* ENGLAND

15 *Never argue with someone who buys ink by the barrel* CHINA

16 *The best memory is not so firm as faded ink* CHINA

17 *In our alphabet, B comes after A* USA

18 *One can study calligraphy at eighty* JAPAN

19 *Where hands are needed words and letters are useless* GERMANY

20 *Ideas start with 'I'* USA

21 *When in anger, say the alphabet* USA

327 LITERATURE

1 *Life without literature is death* LATIN

2 *It is not good to be the poet of a village* GERMANY

3 *There dies a poet in everyone* ENGLAND

4 *Poets are fathers of lies* LATIN

5 *Poets and pigs are appreciated only after their death* ITALY

6 *Slowly but surely the excrement of foreign poets will come to your village* MALI

* * * * * * * * * * * * * * * * * *

24 A PROVERB POEM

Michael Drayton (1563–1631) wrote a sonnet which reflected the role played by proverbs in Elizabethan society:

> As Love and I late harbour'd in one inn,
> With proverbs thus each other entertain:
> 'In love there is no luck,' thus I begin;
> 'Fair words make fools,' replieth he again;
> 'Who spares to speak doth spare to speed,' quoth I;
> 'As well,' saith he, 'too forward as too slow;'
> 'Fortune assists the boldest,' I reply;
> 'A hasty man,' quoth he, 'ne'er wanted woe;'
> 'Labour is light,' quoth I, 'where love doth pay;'
> Saith he, 'Light burden's heavy, if far borne;'
> Quoth I, 'The main lost, cast the by away;'
> 'Y'have spun a fair thread,' he replies in scorn.
> And having thus awhile each other thwarted,
> Fools as we met, so fools again we parted.

* * * * * * * * * * * * * * * * * *

7   *The dog may be wonderful prose, but only the cat is poetry* FRANCE

8   *One actor cannot make a play* USA

9   *Those that begin the play must continue it* TURKEY

10   *Those who have free seats at a play hiss first* CHINA

328 ENDURANCE – PATIENCE

1 *Endurance pierces marble* MOROCCO

2 *The show must go on* USA

3 *Heroism consists in hanging on one minute longer*
NORWAY

4 *Genius means patience* FRANCE

5 *Rhubarb and patience work wonders* GERMANY

6 *With patience and saliva, the elephant swallows an ant*
COLOMBIA

7 *Have patience, fleas, the night is long* NICARAGUA

8 *Indolence is often taken for patience* FRANCE

9 *The string of our sack of patience is generally tied with a
slip knot* JAPAN

10 *The loom that's awry is best handled patiently*
SCOTLAND

11 *The boot must put up with the dirt* GERMANY

12 *We must take the crop as it grows* SCOTLAND

13 *Take the ball as it bounces* FRANCE

14 *Faint heart never won fair lady* ENGLAND

15 *It takes little effort to watch someone carry a load*
CHINA

16 *To learn costs you one effort, to unlearn, two* BULGARIA

17 *Needs must when the devil drives* ENGLAND

18 *Virtue is its own reward* ENGLAND

19 *Where there's a will there's a way* ENGLAND

20 *Where there's a will, there's a lawsuit* USA

329 CHOICE

1 *Of all the thirty-six alternatives, running away is the best*
CHINA

2 *The first in the boat has the choice of oars* ENGLAND

3 *An ulcer and a boil do not choose where to appear*
JAPAN

4 *It is a silly sheep that makes the wolf her confessor*
FRANCE

5 *They are fools who make their doctor their heir* FRANCE

6 *Beggars can't be choosers* ENGLAND

330 HABIT – PRACTICE

1 *Habit hardens the feet* NETHERLANDS

2 *Those who are not in the habit of riding forget the spurs*
IRELAND

3 *To be in the habit of no habit is the worst habit in the world* WALES

4   *Habit is a shirt that we wear till death*   RUSSIA

5   *A habit is first cobwebs, then cables*   USA

6   *Without practice one cannot even clean one's teeth*
     SRI LANKA

7   *Practice makes perfect*   ENGLAND

8   *Practice with the left hand while the right hand is still
     there*   LIBERIA

9   *Regularity is the best medicine*   INDIA

10   *You can't teach an old dog new tricks*   ENGLAND

11   *You can get used to anything except a rock in your shoe*
     USA

331 GOOD

1   *Money is a good passport*   FRANCE

2   *What is bad luck for one is good luck for another*
     GHANA

3   *A reasonable amount of fleas is good for a dog; they keep
     him from broodin' on being a dog*   USA

4   *No news is good news*   ENGLAND

5   *Those who bring good news knock hard*   ENGLAND

6   *Good medicine is bitter to the taste*   KOREA

7   *All good salt stings*   SPAIN

8   *It's an ill wind that blows nobody good*   ENGLAND

9   *Words are good, but fowls lay eggs*   GERMANY

10   *Good luck is the guardian of the stupid*   SWEDEN

11   *Good scribes are not those who write well, but who erase well*   RUSSIA

12   *A change is as good as a rest*   ENGLAND

13   *Those who cannot cut the bread evenly cannot get on well with people*   CZECH REPUBLIC

14   *If rivals are annoying you by playing well, consider adopting their strategy*   CHINA

15   *Whose presence does no good, their absence does no harm*   ENGLAND

16   *There is always something to be cut off young trees if they are to grow well*   GERMANY

17   *If you know the beginning well, the end will not trouble you*   SENEGAL

18   *All good things come to an end*   ENGLAND

19   *It is a fine thing to die for one's fatherland, but a still finer thing to live for it*   HUNGARY

20   *Golden bishop, wooden crozier; wooden bishop, golden crozier*   FRANCE

21   *Speech is silver; silence is golden*   ENGLAND

22   *Good things sell themselves; bad things have to be advertised*   ETHIOPIA

23 *Only when all contribute their firewood can they build up a good fire*   CHINA

24 *That which is to become a good nettle must sting early*   SWEDEN

25 *A good question is like one beating a bell*   CHINA

26 *Hope is a good breakfast but a bad supper*   ENGLAND

27 *A crooked log makes a good fire*   FRANCE

28 *Sweat makes good mortar*   GERMANY

29 *A borrowed drum never makes good dancing*   HAITI

30 *Bread is the staff of life, but the pudding makes a good crutch*   SCOTLAND

31 *Good painters need not give a name to their pictures; bad ones must*   POLAND

32 *A good song can be sung twice*   ESTONIA

33 *There is no price for good advice*   SPAIN

34 *There is no such thing as a pretty good omelette*   FRANCE

35 *A good buttock finds a bench for itself*   ESTONIA

36 *Good juice from fruit comes without squeezing*   IRAN

37 *Fire is a good slave, but a bad master*   ALBANIA

38 *Enough is as good as a feast*   ENGLAND

39 *Example is a great orator*   CZECH REPUBLIC

40 *The spectator is a great hero*   AFGHANISTAN

41   *Economy is itself a great income* LATIN

42   *It's a great life if you don't weaken* USA

43   *In vinegar, sharpness is a virtue* RUSSIA

44   *Good is good, but better is better* NETHERLANDS

332 BETTER

1   *Better go than send* CHINA

2   *Better an egg today than a hen tomorrow* ALBANIA

3   *Better the devil you know than the devil you don't* ENGLAND

4   *Better ask twice than go wrong once* GERMANY

5   *Better a crease in the shoe than a blister on the toe* ESTONIA

6   *Better a free meal of acorns than a honey feast on trust* WALES

7   *Better keep under an old hedge than creep under a new furze-bush* ENGLAND

8   *Better to drink and be unwell than not to drink and be unwell* MONTENEGRO

9   *Better one living word than a hundred dead ones* GERMANY

10   *Better be stung by a nettle than pricked by a rose* ENGLAND

11 *Better a diamond with a flaw than a pebble without one*
CHINA

12 *It is better to warn than to be warned*   BELGIUM

13 *It is better to be once in the church sleigh than always in the back runners*   FINLAND

14 *It is better to be entirely without a book than to believe it entirely*   CHINA

15 *It is better to follow no saint than six*   INDIA

16 *A courageous foe is better than a cowardly friend*
CHINA

17 *No doctor is better than three*   GERMANY

18 *Any excuse is better than none*   ENGLAND

19 *Making money selling manure is better than losing money selling musk*   EGYPT

20 *A sparrow in the hand is better than a crane on the wing*
FRANCE

21 *One bird in the dish is better than a hundred in the air*
GERMANY

22 *Honour is better than honours*   BELGIUM

23 *An ounce of luck is better than a pound of knowledge*
BELGIUM

24 *A full cabin is better than an empty castle*   IRELAND

25 *Be on a horse when you're searching for a better one*
CHINA

26   *The better the lawyer, the worse the Christian*
NETHERLANDS

27   *There is no better looking-glass than an old friend*
ENGLAND

28   *If you drink you die, if you don't drink you die, so it is better to drink*   RUSSIA

333   BEST

1   *Regularity is the best medicine*   INDIA

2   *The best neighbors are vacant lots*   USA

3   *Of all the thirty-six alternatives, running away is the best*
CHINA

4   *Of soup and love, the first is the best*   PORTUGAL

5   *The best time to plant a tree was twenty years ago; the second-best time is now*   CHINA

6   *The meaning is best known to the speaker*   FRANCE

7   *The best things in life are free*   USA

8   *Attack is the best defence*   ENGLAND

9   *They that get the next best are not ill off*   SCOTLAND

10   *Cabbage is the best invalid, it needs only a little water*
SERBIA

11   *There are dregs in the best bottle of wine*   FRANCE

12   *The best memory is not so firm as faded ink*   CHINA

334 BAD

1   *A bad thing never dies*   ENGLAND

2   *Whoever holds the ladder is as bad as the thief*
   GERMANY

3   *Carve good deeds in stone, bad ones in sand*   ESTONIA

4   *Three glasses of wine drive away the evil spirits, but with the fourth they return*   GERMANY

5   *Whose presence does no good, their absence does no harm*
   ENGLAND

6   *In rivers and bad government, the lightest things swim at the top*   USA

7   *Angels gave the gift of song, and while one sings one thinks no wrong*   ITALY

8   *They that think no ill are soonest beguiled*   ENGLAND

9   *A bad thing that does no harm is the same as a good one that does no good*   GERMANY

10   *A good lawyer is a bad neighbour*   FRANCE

11   *Fire is a good slave, but a bad master*   ALBANIA

12   *Hope is a good breakfast but a bad supper*   ENGLAND

13   *A bad word whispered will echo a hundred miles*
   CHINA

14 *It ain't half so bad if you can afford it*   USA

15 *It is hard to swim between two stretches of bad water*
NETHERLANDS

16 *A man's hat in his hand never did him any harm*
SCOTLAND

17 *Where there is music, there can be no harm*   SPAIN

18 *A name doesn't harm us if we don't harm the name*
ESTONIA

19 *Labour warms, sloth harms*   NETHERLANDS

20 *No harm in trying*   USA

21 *Aching teeth are ill tenants*   ENGLAND

22 *Women in mischief are wiser than men*   ENGLAND

23 *It's an ill wind that blows nobody good*   ENGLAND

24 *It's a poor mouse that has but one hole*   NETHERLANDS

25 *It's a poor rule that doesn't work both ways*   ENGLAND

26 *It's a poor crust that can't grease its own plate*   USA

335 WORSE

1 *The more servants, the worse service*   NETHERLANDS

2 *Bad is called good when worse happens*   NORWAY

3 *It's not so bad to fall in the gutter, but it's worse to lay there*   USA

4   *The soup would be none the worse for more meat*
    SUDAN

5   *Overdone is worse than underdone*   CANADA

6   *There is no worse robber than a bad book*   ITALY

7   *The better the lawyer, the worse the Christian*
    NETHERLANDS

8   *There is no worse abbot than the one who has been a
    monk*   SPAIN

336 WORST

1   *The cobbler always wears the worst shoes*   FRANCE

2   *Those who sing worst, let them begin first*   ENGLAND

3   *To be in the habit of no habit is the worst habit in the
    world*   WALES

337 BUSINESS

1   *Those who have no thirst have no business at the
    fountain*   NETHERLANDS

2   *If you suspect people, don't employ them; if you employ
    them, don't suspect them*   CHINA

3   *Errands are small on a spring day*   ICELAND

4   *New officials introduce strict measures*   CHINA

5   *Sunday plans never stand*   CANADA

6   *Better go than send*   CHINA

7   *Honesty is the best policy*   ENGLAND

8   *A bet's a bet*   USA

9   *Too many affairs are like pumpkins in water; one pops up while you try to hold down the other*   CHINA

338   PURSUIT

1   *When you are chased by a wolf you call the boar your uncle*   SLOVENIA

2   *When an elephant chases you, you climb a prickly tree*   KENYA

3   *A cow that has no tail should not try to chase away flies*   GUINEA

4   *If you catch fish you're a fisherman*   USA

5   *Those who know how to bend the fish-hook know how to straighten it*   TANZANIA

6   *The one who hunts two hares will catch neither*   FRANCE

7   *The one who hunts two rats will catch neither*   UGANDA

8   *If you follow a crow long enough you light on carrion*   ALBANIA

9   *Follow love and it will flee thee; flee love and it will follow thee*   SCOTLAND

10   *Never follow a beast into its lair*   SOUTH AFRICA

11   *All are not hunters who blow the horn*   FRANCE

12   *The one who seeks revenge should remember to dig two graves*   CHINA

339   AVOIDANCE

1   *Misfortune is not that which can be avoided, but that which cannot*   CHINA

2   *Some have been thought brave because they were afraid to run away*   ENGLAND

3   *A scalded cock runs away from the rain*   BULGARIA

4   *If you run away from a mosquito the sharper will its sting be*   SLOVENIA

5   *Those who run away will fight again*   GREECE

6   *Of all the thirty-six alternatives, running away is the best*   CHINA

7   *There's nothing like being bespattered for making someone defy the gutter*   FRANCE

8   *Follow love and it will flee thee; flee love and it will follow thee*   SCOTLAND

9   *Prevention is better than cure*   ENGLAND

10   *On going into a church leave the world behind the door*
     SPAIN

11   *The candle is put into the lantern and the moth is left*
     outside fluttering   IRAN

12   *Will the crocodile reject the carcass?*   MALAYSIA

13   *Once bitten, twice shy*   ENGLAND

14   *Those who tremble to hear a leaf fall should keep out of*
     the wood   FRANCE

340   PASSAGEWAY

1   *Knock before crossing even a stone bridge*   KOREA

2   *Let everyone praise the bridge they go over*   ENGLAND

3   *There is no bridge without a place the other side of it*
    WALES

4   *Promise is a bridge of words, unsafe to walk across*
    GERMANY

5   *Don't cross a bridge until you come to it*   ENGLAND

6   *Conversation is a ladder for a journey*   SRI LANKA

7   *It is no use lifting your leg until you come to the stile*
    ENGLAND

341 ROADS – STREETS

1   *To know the road ahead, ask those coming back*   CHINA

2   *Who marches fast remains on the road*   ALBANIA

3   *Only those who have travelled the road know where the holes are deep*   CHINA

4   *What is the use of running when we are not on the right road?*   GERMANY

5   *The other side of the road always looks cleanest*   ENGLAND

6   *There never was a five-pound note but there was a ten-pound road for it*   SCOTLAND

7   *Every road has two directions*   UKRAINE

8   *On a level road a small stone upsets the cartload*   ESTONIA

9   *Signposts only show the road, they don't go along it*   SWITZERLAND

10   *If you want to go fast, go the old road*   MYANMAR

11   *There is no light burden on a long road*   CHINA

12   *The broth from a distance grows cool on the road*   KENYA

13   *A road has no shadow*   SENEGAL

14   *All roads lead to Rome*   ENGLAND

15   *Every alley has its own tin can*   USA

16   *Beware of old streets and new inns*   GERMANY

17   *The crossroads always confuse the stranger*   NIGERIA

342   NEED

1   *Needs must when the devil drives*   ENGLAND

2   *Gossip needs no carriage*   RUSSIA

3   *Be always a little afraid so that you never have need of being much afraid*   FINLAND

4   *A head without a brain has no need of a hat*   SPAIN

5   *One is happy when one has books, but happier still when one has no need of them*   CHINA

6   *Where the finger-nail will enter, there is no need of iron*   INDIA

7   *Honour physicians before you have need of them*   ENGLAND

8   *Cabbage is the best invalid, it needs only a little water*   SERBIA

9   *A blind person needs no looking glass*   SCOTLAND

10   *A blind man's wife needs no painting*   SCOTLAND

11   *The village that can be seen needs no signpost*   ALBANIA

12   *It don't need a genius to spot a goat in a flock of sheep*   USA

13 *A hundred men may make an encampment, but it needs a woman to make a home*   CHINA

14 *Clumsy birds need early flight*   CHINA

15 *Empty barns need no thatch*   ENGLAND

16 *Never ask a barber if you need a haircut*   USA

17 *Little said is easy mended; nothing said needs no mending*   IRELAND

18 *Many donkeys need much straw*   SPAIN: BASQUE

19 *The bald need no comb*   POLAND

20 *The shell is needed till the bird is hatched*   RUSSIA

21 *Tangled hair needs a wide comb*   SERBIA

22 *A clean face needs no water*   BOHEMIA

23 *Fools need no passport*   DENMARK

24 *Those who are carried down the stream need not row*   ENGLAND

25 *Where the minute-hand suffices the hour-hand is not needed*   NETHERLANDS

26 *Where hands are needed words and letters are useless*   GERMANY

27 *A tree with ripe fruit needs little shaking*   SWITZERLAND

28 *Friendship does not need pepper to cry*   REPUBLIC OF CONGO

29 *Desperate diseases need desperate remedies*   ENGLAND

30 *A village in sight does not require a guide* TURKEY

31 *Every art requires the whole person* FRANCE

32 *The impossible requires no excuse* NETHERLANDS

33 *A vineyard does not require prayers, but a hoe* TURKEY

34 *Hasty questions require slow answers* NETHERLANDS

35 *It takes little effort to watch someone carry a load*
CHINA

36 *It takes two hands to clap* INDIA

37 *It takes a whole village to raise one child* NIGERIA

38 *It takes one to know one* ENGLAND

39 *Is it necessary to add acid to the lemon?* INDIA

40 *Necessity teaches new arts* NORWAY

41 *Necessity is the mother of invention* ENGLAND

42 *Ability and necessity dwell in the same cabin*
NETHERLANDS

43 *A dog in desperation will leap over a wall* CHINA

44 *Necessity knows no law* ENGLAND

45 *An indispensable thing never has much value* GEORGIA

343 MANNER – MEANS

1 *A boat does not go forward if everyone rows their own way* KENYA

2   *Everyone buckles their belt their own way*   SCOTLAND

3   *It's a poor rule that doesn't work both ways*   ENGLAND

4   *It is not the one way everyone goes mad*   IRELAND

5   *Not even a bell always rings the same way*   SERBIA

6   *Where there's a will there's a way*   ENGLAND

7   *Shut your door in such a way that you can open it again*
    DENMARK

8   *When it rains, the roof always drips the same way*
    LIBERIA

9   *The easiest way to get a divorce is to be married*   USA

10 *If you want to catch a wild horse, find a tight corral*
    HAITI

11 *There are more ways than one to kill a cat*   ENGLAND

12 *We each have our own way of killing fleas*   SPAIN

13 *Even a young foot finds ease in an old slipper*
    SCOTLAND

14 *A good buttock finds a bench for itself*   ESTONIA

344 TOOLS

1   *Without tools no handicraft*   SLOVAKIA

2   *A bad workman quarrels with his tools*   ENGLAND

3   *A handleless axe does not scare the forest*   BULGARIA

* * * * * * * * * * * * * * * * * *

25 PROVERBIAL SOFTWARE

If proverbs reflect daily experience, we would expect the world of the Internet to provide us with a fresh supply. But it will take time. By their nature, proverbs don't appear overnight.

A single software proverb in this book represents what I am sure will be a huge domain one day: 'Garbage in, garbage out.' I might have added 'What you see is what you get', but that has a curious history (see p. 380). Browsing through web pages brings to light a number of other candidates, though it is as yet unclear how widespread they are. There is sometimes a thin dividing line between a quotation and a proverb. Have these achieved proverbial status yet?

> *One test is worth a thousand opinions.*
> *If you didn't write it down, it didn't happen.*
> *To go faster, slow down.*
> *If you didn't measure it, you didn't do it.*
> *If something is worth doing once, it's worth building a tool to do it.*
> *If you've found three bugs in a program, best estimate is that there are three more.*

SEE ALSO Adults play with proverbs (p. 541)

* * * * * * * * * * * * * * * * * *

4   *An axe with a loose head is the bane of a man up a tree*
     NIGERIA

5   *The axe forgets, but the cut log does not*   ZIMBABWE

6   *Don't monkey with the buzz saw*   USA

7   *Even a drill goes in from the tip*   KOREA

8   *If you have fire-tongs, why use your hands?*   ESTONIA

9   *A hasty person drinks tea with a fork*   CHINA

10   *Fingers were made before forks*   ENGLAND

11   *Big hammers don't play with little nails*   GERMANY

12   *When the only thing you have is a hammer, everything looks like a nail*   FRANCE

13   *It takes a long time to sharpen a hammer made of wood*
     NETHERLANDS

14   *From the midst of the wood the hatchet gets its handle*
     GERMANY

15   *Do not remove a fly from your friend's forehead with a hatchet*   CHINA

16   *A vineyard does not require prayers, but a hoe*   TURKEY

17   *Let the cobbler stick to his last*   ENGLAND

18   *Don't buy a left-hand monkey-wrench*   CANADA

19   *To get out a rusty nail you must take away a piece of the wall*   MALTA

20 *A worn-out boat still has three thousand nails in it*
CHINA

21 *The nail suffers as much as the hole*   NETHERLANDS

22 *Every time we laugh a nail is removed from our coffin*
ITALY

23 *The protruding nail will be pounded down*   JAPAN

24 *If you are building a house and a nail breaks, do you stop building or do you change the nail?*
RWANDA AND BURUNDI

25 *Call a spade a spade*   ENGLAND

26 *A smith has tongs to save his hands*   SERBIA

27 *Don't keep all your tongs in one fire*   CANADA

28 *Those who have the tongs do not burn their fingers*
ALBANIA

345 PROVIDING – KEEPING

1 *A father is a banker provided by nature*   FRANCE

2 *God gives birds their food, but they must fly for it*
NETHERLANDS

3 *Do not blame God for having created the tiger, but thank Him for not having given it wings*   ETHIOPIA

4 *Thunder-clouds do not always give rain*   ARMENIA

5 *Black cows give white milk*   GERMANY

6   *Cast no dirt into the well that has given you water*
    ENGLAND

7   *Those who own the boat should give it a name*
    NORWAY

8   *Good painters need not give a name to their pictures; bad
    ones must*   POLAND

9   *The fly will never leave the confectioner's shop*   INDIA

10 *A river is filled by its tributaries*   ZIMBABWE

11 *No sow so dirty but finds a boar to kiss her*   GERMANY

12 *Even the bottom of a basket finds something to hold*
    MADAGASCAR

13 *The devil finds work for idle hands*   ENGLAND

14 *The lame goat has no siesta*   SPAIN

15 *Love yourself, then you will have no rivals*   ESTONIA

16 *Learn, so that you may have something to forget*
    GERMANY

17 *If pride were an art, how many graduates we should
    have*   ITALY

18 *Those who will have a cake out of the wheat must tarry
    the grinding*   ENGLAND

19 *Those who lie on the ground have no place from which to
    fall*   LATIN

20 *When the bee comes to your house, let her have beer; you*

may want to visit the bee's house some day
REPUBLIC OF CONGO

21 *Those who have once had luck cannot always call themselves unlucky* BELGIUM

22 *The first in the boat has the choice of oars* ENGLAND

23 *Chop, and you will have splinters* DENMARK

24 *A smith has tongs to save his hands* SERBIA

25 *A dog's mouth yields no ivory* CHINA

26 *Those who do not know how to squander their money – buy some porcelain and drop it* NETHERLANDS

27 *Don't keep all your tongs in one fire* CANADA

28 *Two swords cannot be kept in one sheath* INDIA

29 *Keep your broken arm inside your sleeve* CHINA

30 *Keep your hurry in your fist* IRELAND

31 *A good day is that in which to lay by cold porridge* MALAWI

32 *Waste not, want not* ENGLAND

33 *The most wasted of all days is the day when we have not laughed* FRANCE

346 SUFFICIENT

1 *The junk capsizes and the shark has its bellyful* MALAYSIA

2   *Any wood will do to make a signpost*   GREECE

3   *Want a thing long enough, and you don't*   CHINA

4   *It is not enough to run; one must start in time*   FRANCE

5   *People have enough to do weeding their own garden*
    BELGIUM

6   *It is not enough for people to know how to ride; they
    must know how to fall*   MEXICO

7   *You cannot fill your belly by painting pictures of bread*
    CHINA

8   *A blessing does not fill the belly*   IRELAND

9   *If you are looking for a fly in your food, it means you are
    full*   SOUTH AFRICA

10 *A sponge sucks itself full, but when it has to yield
    anything one has to squeeze it*   GERMANY

11 *The stomach never becomes full with licking*   ESTONIA

12 *Why should the cow trouble to think if she has plenty of
    hay?*   SLOVAKIA

13 *One bell serves a parish*   ITALY

14 *Where the minute-hand suffices the hour-hand is not
    needed*   NETHERLANDS

15 *Abundance does not spread, famine does*   SOUTH AFRICA

347 IMPORTANCE

1 *At a round table every seat is first*   GERMANY

2 *The bigger they come, the harder they fall*   USA

3 *What greater crime than loss of time?*   GERMANY

4 *A fox knows much; a hedgehog one great thing*   GREECE

5 *Those who steal a pin will steal an ox*   KOREA

6 *Small cares make many words, great ones are mute*
   GERMANY

7 *It's a poor thing that's not worth asking*   SCOTLAND

348 NO MATTER

1 *No matter how hard you throw a dead fish in the water,
it still won't swim*   REPUBLIC OF CONGO

2 *What matter what blossom it is if there is no fruit?*
   SERBIA

3 *No matter how long a log floats on the river it will never
be a crocodile*   MALI

4 *No matter how you slice it, it's still baloney*   USA

5 *No matter how full the river, it still wants to grow*
   REPUBLIC OF CONGO

6 *No matter how much the world changes, cats will never
lay eggs*   MALI

349 USEFUL

1 *The postage stamp's usefulness lies in the ability to stick*
USA

2 *If familiarity were useful, water wouldn't cook fish*
CAMEROON

3 *Those who would enter paradise must have a good key*
ENGLAND

4 *Better to light a candle than to curse the darkness*
CHINA

5 *Better a neighbour over the wall than a brother over the sea* ALBANIA

6 *The cat who frightens the mice away is as good as the cat who eats them* GERMANY

7 *When rats infest the palace a lame cat is better than the swiftest horse* CHINA

8 *What's the use of consulting a dead person's horoscope?*
SENEGAL

9 *What is the use of running when we are not on the right road?* GERMANY

10 *It's the tortoise that discounts the value of a pair of fast legs* JAPAN

11 *A nod's as good as a wink to a blind horse* ENGLAND

12 *One foot is better than two stilts* FRANCE

350 USELESS

1. *If it were not for the hands the clock would be useless*
   POLAND

2. *The miser and the pig are useless unless they are dead*
   FRANCE

3. *Where hands are needed words and letters are useless*
   GERMANY

4. *When gold talks, speech is useless*   LATIN

5. *A basket with its bottom burst is useless*   NIGERIA

6. *Do not fill your basket with useless shells of coconuts*
   KENYA

7. *Garbage in, garbage out*   USA

8. *When you have trodden on the cat, what help is it to stroke her back?*   SWITZERLAND

9. *You won't help shoots grow by pulling them up higher*
   CHINA

10. *A fifth wheel in the wagon hinders more than helps*
    FRANCE

11. *What's the good of a spoon after the meal is over?*
    LATVIA

12. *What good is the hay if the horse is dead?*   PHILIPPINES

13. *Until the soup boils over, the ladle has no value*
    TURKEY

14. *Music unheard has no value*   GREECE

15 *It is no use lifting your leg until you come to the stile*
    ENGLAND

16 *It is no use throwing water on a drowned rat* IRELAND

17 *It is no use standing with an open mouth in front of an oven* DENMARK

18 *It is no use applying eye-medicine from a two-storey window* JAPAN

19 *It is no use trying to tug the glacier backwards* CHINA

20 *There's no use in having a dog and barking yourself*
    ENGLAND

21 *Advice that ain't paid for ain't no good* USA

22 *It's no good locking the stable door after the horse is stolen* ENGLAND

23 *A well without a bucket is no good* USA

24 *Who sieves too much, keeps the rubbish* BELGIUM

25 *It is in vain to look for yesterday's fish in the house of the otter* INDIA

26 *It is no advantage for someone in a fever to change their bed* ENGLAND

27 *It's a poor thing that's not worth asking* SCOTLAND

351 PERFECT – IMPERFECT

1 *Practice makes perfect* ENGLAND

2 *A gem cannot be polished without friction, nor a person perfected without trials* CHINA

3 *The evening crowns the day* SWEDEN

4 *Old purses shut badly* NETHERLANDS

5 *Adam must have an Eve, to blame for his own faults* GERMANY

6 *Better a diamond with a flaw than a pebble without one* CHINA

7 *One bad pipe ruins the entire organ* NETHERLANDS

8 *The circumstances of people will appear from the condition of their hat* SRI LANKA

9 *In every family's cooking-pot is one black spot* CHINA

10 *One spot spots the whole dress* BELGIUM

11 *Even in the sun there are spots* HUNGARY

352 CLEAN

1 *Cleanliness is next to godliness* ENGLAND

2 *New brooms sweep clean* ENGLAND

3 *A new broom sweeps clean, but the old brush knows the corners* IRELAND

4   *An old broom still sweeps the room*   ESTONIA

5   *The other side of the road always looks cleanest*
       ENGLAND

6   *A clean face needs no water*   BOHEMIA

7   *They must have clean fingers who would blow another's
nose*   DENMARK

8   *Without practice one cannot even clean one's teeth*
       SRI LANKA

9   *Sparrows clean their beaks against the branch on which
they sit*   ESTONIA

10   *Eating pears always cleans one's teeth*   KOREA

11   *If you haven't much to do, start cleaning your own
backyard*   USA

12   *Sweep off your own back porch first*   USA

13   *Let everyone sweep before their own door*   GERMANY

14   *Painting the pump will not clean out the well*   ENGLAND

15   *A north-easterly wind is heaven's broom*   ESTONIA

16   *Never feed a dog with corn, nor attempt to pick your teeth
with a pair of scissors*   CHINA

17   *The night washes what the day has soaped*
       SWITZERLAND

18   *One is usually at a loss to know how to sweep the ground
in a market-place*   NIGERIA

19　*When you sweep the stairs, you start at the top*
GERMANY

20　*The stairs are swept downwards, not upwards*
ROMANIA

21　*Only the sweep knows what is up the chimney*　ITALY

353　DIRTY

1　*The boot must put up with the dirt*　GERMANY

2　*Cast no dirt into the well that has given you water*
ENGLAND

3　*Dirt will not stain unless you touch it*　POLAND

4　*The lazy ox drinks dirty water*　COLOMBIA

5　*Dirty water cannot be washed*　TOGO

6　*No sow so dirty but finds a boar to kiss her*　GERMANY

7　*There's nothing like being bespattered for making someone defy the gutter*　FRANCE

8　*One buffalo brings mud and all the herd are smeared with it*　MALAYSIA

9　*The rhinoceros which has no calf takes itself to the muddy pool*　SOUTH AFRICA

10　*Do not fear a stain that disappears with water*　SPAIN

11　*If you pound palm-nuts, some will stain your cloth*
CÔTE D'IVOIRE

12   *A white cloth and a stain never agree*   NIGERIA

354   HEALTH – ILL HEALTH

1   *A nation's health is a nation's wealth*   USA

2   *It is not healthy to swallow books without chewing*
     GERMANY

3   *Desperate diseases need desperate remedies*   ENGLAND

4   *When a severe illness comes, eat bread and onions*
     INDIA

5   *Every invalid is a physician*   IRELAND

6   *Cabbage is the best invalid, it needs only a little water*
     SERBIA

7   *It is no advantage for someone in a fever to change their
     bed*   ENGLAND

8   *It is the sick duck that is worried by the weasel*   CHINA

9   *A rich person's sickness and a poor person's pancake are
     smelt a long way off*   BELGIUM

10 *Sickness comes riding on horseback and goes away on
     foot*   BELGIUM

11 *Better to drink and be unwell than not to drink and be
     unwell*   MONTENEGRO

355 DISEASES

1 *Desperate diseases need desperate remedies* ENGLAND

2 *Never confuse asthma with passion* USA

3 *Better a crease in the shoe than a blister on the toe*
ESTONIA

4 *An ulcer and a boil do not choose where to appear*
JAPAN

5 *Sparrows who aspire to be peacocks are likely to break a thigh* MYANMAR

6 *The tongue has no bones, yet breaks its own skull*
ALBANIA

7 *Don't be breaking your shin on a stool that's not in your way* IRELAND

8 *The hyena of your own country does not break your bones*
KENYA

9 *Keep your broken arm inside your sleeve* CHINA

10 *An elephant does not die from one broken rib* KENYA

11 *A good word never broke a tooth* IRELAND

12 *Even a fly has a cough* ITALY

13 *Two barrels of tears will not heal a bruise* CHINA

14 *If one finger is gashed, all the fingers are covered with blood* REPUBLIC OF CONGO

15 *A big head, a big headache* BULGARIA

16   *When rats infest the palace a lame cat is better than the swiftest horse* CHINA

17   *The lame goat has no siesta* SPAIN

18   *Reform a gambler? Cure leprosy* CHINA

19   *Justice becomes injustice when it makes two wounds on a head which only deserves one* REPUBLIC OF CONGO

20   *You cannot tie up another's wound while your own is still bleeding* ESTONIA

21   *When a severe illness comes, eat bread and onions* INDIA

22   *Who suffers from diarrhoea is not afraid of the dark* SOUTH AFRICA

356 MENDING – RESTORING

1   *Least said, soonest mended* ENGLAND

2   *Little said is easy mended; nothing said needs no mending* IRELAND

3   *You must go behind the door to mend old breeches* ENGLAND

4   *Where the drum is burst is the place to mend it* REPUBLIC OF CONGO

5   *Do not tear down the east wall to repair the west* CHINA

6   *Love takes away the sight and matrimony restores it*
GERMANY

7   *They wouldn't make erasers if we didn't make mistakes*
USA

357 HEALING – MEDICINE

1   *Two barrels of tears will not heal a bruise*   CHINA

2   *God heals and the doctor gets the money*   BELGIUM

3   *Time heals all wounds*   ENGLAND

4   *The mouth is the healer and executioner of the body*
DENMARK

5   *Don't take the antidote before the poison*   LATIN

6   *An apothecary ought not to be long a cuckold*   FRANCE

7   *It is no use applying eye-medicine from a two-storey
window*   JAPAN

8   *What butter or whiskey will not cure, there is no cure for*
IRELAND

9   *What can't be cured must be endured*   ENGLAND

10   *Reform a gambler? Cure leprosy*   CHINA

11   *Prevention is better than cure*   ENGLAND

12   *Ignorance is a medicine*   KOREA

13   *Good medicine is bitter to the taste*   KOREA

14   *Time is anger's medicine* GERMANY

15   *Regularity is the best medicine* INDIA

16   *Insults and pills must not be chewed* GERMANY

17   *Desperate diseases need desperate remedies* ENGLAND

358 DOCTORS – DENTISTS

1   *A young doctor makes a full graveyard* CHINA

2   *An apple a day keeps the doctor away* ENGLAND

3   *An apple at night puts the dentist to flight* ENGLAND

4   *God heals and the doctor gets the money* BELGIUM

5   *They are fools who make their doctor their heir* FRANCE

6   *Physician, heal thyself* ENGLAND

7   *No doctor is better than three* GERMANY

8   *Honour physicians before you have need of them*
     ENGLAND

9   *Every invalid is a physician* IRELAND

10   *Those who physic themselves poison a fool* ENGLAND

11   *The medicine man is not esteemed in his own village*
     KENYA

359 DETERIORATION

1   *The cobbler always wears the worst shoes* FRANCE

2   *Sharp acids corrode their own containers* ALBANIA

3   *You cannot damage a wrecked ship* ITALY

4   *The best memory is not so firm as faded ink* CHINA

5   *Hunger doesn't say, 'Stale bread,' and cold doesn't say 'Old coat.'* GEORGIA

6   *A worn-out boat still has three thousand nails in it* CHINA

360 POISON

1   *Why use poison when you can kill with honey?* BELGIUM

2   *Don't take the antidote before the poison* LATIN

3   *A guest and a fish after three days are poison* FRANCE

4   *Those who physic themselves poison a fool* ENGLAND

361 SAFETY – DANGER

1   *Those who ring the bell are quite safe* SPAIN

2   *Better be safe than sorry* ENGLAND

3   *Good luck is the guardian of the stupid* SWEDEN

4   *Do not protect yourself by a fence, but by your friends*
CZECH REPUBLIC

5   *A protector is like a cloak*   HAITI

6   *Those who wait for a dead person's shoes are in danger of going barefoot*   FRANCE

7   *A fallen lighthouse is more dangerous than a reef*
CHINA

8   *Don't monkey with the buzz saw*   USA

9   *To tell the truth is dangerous, to listen to it is annoying*
DENMARK

10   *Every definition is dangerous*   LATIN

11   *Promise is a bridge of words, unsafe to walk across*
GERMANY

12   *When the mouse laughs at the cat, there is a hole*
GAMBIA

13   *It's a poor mouse that has but one hole*   NETHERLANDS

14   *Forewarned is forearmed*   ENGLAND

15   *It is better to warn than to be warned*   BELGIUM

16   *Walls hear without warnings*   ENGLAND

362   PRESERVATION

1   *God preserve us from pitch-forks, for they make three holes*   SWITZERLAND

2   *If you want to keep your milk sweet, leave it in the cow*
      LIBERIA

3   *God saves the moon from the wolves*   POLAND

4   *A smith has tongs to save his hands*   SERBIA

5   *Save your bottles; it may rain whiskey*   USA

6   *A stitch in time saves nine*   ENGLAND

363   TRYING

1   *No harm in trying*   USA

2   *It is no use trying to tug the glacier backwards*   CHINA

3   *By trying often, the monkey learns to jump from the tree*
      CAMEROON

4   *If you get to thinking you're someone of influence, try
ordering around someone else's dog*   USA

5   *Do not try to borrow combs from shaven monks*   CHINA

6   *A cow that has no tail should not try to chase away flies*
      GUINEA

7   *Never try to catch two frogs with one hand*   CHINA

8   *If you try to sit on two chairs, you'll sit on the floor*   USA

9   *Too many affairs are like pumpkins in water; one pops up
while you try to hold down the other*   CHINA

10   *Nothing venture, nothing gain*   ENGLAND

11   *Never feed a dog with corn, nor attempt to pick your teeth with a pair of scissors* CHINA

364 USING – NOT USING

1   *When you want to test the depth of a stream, don't use both feet* CHINA

2   *When you buy, use your eyes not your ears*
      CZECH REPUBLIC

3   *Why use poison when you can kill with honey?*
      BELGIUM

4   *If you have fire-tongs, why use your hands?* ESTONIA

5   *Use a thorn to extract a thorn* INDIA

6   *Many books do not use up words; many words do not use up thoughts* CHINA

7   *The used key is always bright* ENGLAND

8   *If rivals are annoying you by playing well, consider adopting their strategy* CHINA

9   *Learn to handle a writing-brush, and you'll never handle a begging-bowl* CHINA

10   *It is not economical to go to bed early to save the candles if the result is twins* CHINA

11   *Spare the rod and spoil the child* ENGLAND

12   *If you don't want the gun to go off, don't cock the trigger*
REPUBLIC OF CONGO

365   DEEDS

1   *Actions speak louder than words*   ENGLAND

2   *Better do a good deed near at home than go far away to burn incense*   CHINA

3   *Do a good deed and throw it into the sea*   BULGARIA

4   *A good deed is written on snow*   ESTONIA

5   *Carve good deeds in stone, bad ones in sand*   ESTONIA

6   *Good words make us laugh; good deeds make us silent*
FRANCE

7   *The better the day, the better the deed*   ENGLAND

8   *The person who says it cannot be done should not interrupt the one doing it*   CHINA

9   *Nothing should be done in a hurry except catching fleas*
GERMANY

10   *Do what you will, but be the first*   BELGIUM

11   *People have enough to do weeding their own garden*
BELGIUM

12   *People who do what they say are not cowards*   NIGERIA

13   *If you haven't much to do, start cleaning your own backyard*   USA

14 *Friendly is as friendly does* USA

15 *Everybody talks about the weather, but nobody does anything about it* USA

16 *What is done cannot be undone* ENGLAND

17 *When in Rome do as the Romans do* ENGLAND

18 *Never put off till tomorrow what can be done today* ENGLAND

19 *Those who make the first bad move always lose the game* JAPAN

20 *The game's not over until the last man strikes out* USA

21 *One good turn deserves another* ENGLAND

22 *A hug a day keeps the demons at bay* GERMANY

23 *Put up or shut up* USA

24 *Pride goes before a fall* ENGLAND

25 *Hanging and wiving go by destiny* ENGLAND

26 *Laws catch flies but let hornets go free* ENGLAND

27 *Who sieves too much, keeps the rubbish* BELGIUM

28 *A full cup must be carried steadily* ENGLAND

29 *For the diligent, a week has seven days; for the slothful, seven tomorrows* GERMANY

30 *Leave women alone, and go and study mathematics* ITALY

31 *Forewarned is forearmed* ENGLAND

32   *Making preparations does not spoil the trip*   GUINEA

366   WORK – PAY – LEISURE

1   *Quick work – double work*   MONTENEGRO

2   *The devil finds work for idle hands*   ENGLAND

3   *Too many hands spoil the pie*   USA

4   *A hundred men may make an encampment, but it needs a woman to make a home*   CHINA

5   *Every work revenges itself on its master*   GERMANY

6   *A bad workman quarrels with his tools*   ENGLAND

7   *No one is a blacksmith at birth*   NAMIBIA

8   *To be a smith you must work at the forge*   LATIN

9   *A smith has tongs to save his hands*   SERBIA

10   *Even the best smith sometimes hits his thumb*
     NETHERLANDS

11   *The loom that's awry is best handled patiently*
     SCOTLAND

12   *Labour warms, sloth harms*   NETHERLANDS

13   *Sweat makes good mortar*   GERMANY

14   *Mediocrity is climbing molehills without sweating*
     ICELAND

15   *A change is as good as a rest*   ENGLAND

16 *Why should the cow trouble to think if she has plenty of hay?* SLOVAKIA

17 *A quick nickel is better than a slow dollar* USA

18 *A quick sixpence is better than a slow shilling* ENGLAND

19 *Give your tongue more holidays than your head* SCOTLAND

20 *Holidays come like kings and go like beggars* ESTONIA

367 ENERGY

1 *All rivers do what they can for the sea* ENGLAND

2 *The postage stamp's usefulness lies in the ability to stick* USA

3 *The higher the castle the nearer to the lightning* RUSSIA

4 *Lightning never strikes twice in the same place* ENGLAND

5 *Sharp acids corrode their own containers* ALBANIA

6 *The steam that blows the whistle never turns the wheel* USA

7 *A sponge sucks itself full, but when it has to yield anything one has to squeeze it* GERMANY

8 *Good juice from fruit comes without squeezing* IRAN

9 *The energy of the dung-beetle is put into rolling its ball of dung* CHINA

* * * * * * * * * * * * * * * * * * *

26 'PROVERBS' IN SHAKESPEARE

Shakespeare uses the words *proverb* or *proverbs* twenty times in the plays (not at all in the poems). On two occasions he has fun with the word. In *The Merry Wives of Windsor* (III.i.96) the Host asks:

> Shall I lose my doctor? No; he gives me the potions and the motions. Shall I lose my parson? My priest? My Sir Hugh? No; he gives me the proverbs and the no-verbs.

And in *Romeo and Juliet* (I.iv.37), Romeo turns the noun into a verb, to mean 'provided with worldly wisdom':

> For I am proverbed with a grandsire phrase –
> I'll be a candle-holder and look on.

In *Henry V* (III.vii.110), the characters engage in a spontaneous proverb contest:

> *Orleans*: Ill will never said well.
> *Constable*: I will cap that proverb with 'There is flattery in friendship.'
> *Orleans*: And I will take up that with 'Give the devil his due!'
> *Constable*: Well placed. There stands your friend for the devil. Have at the very eye of that proverb with 'A pox of the devil.'
> *Orleans*: You are the better at proverbs by how much 'A fool's bolt is soon shot.'

Constable: You have shot over.

Orleans: 'Tis not the first time you were overshot.

The arrival of a Messenger stops the contest.

SEE ALSO Proverbs in Shakespeare (p. 76)

* * * * * * * * * * * * * * * * * *

10 *Insects do not nest in a busy door-hinge* CHINA

11 *The dust raised by the sheep does not choke the wolf*
ENGLAND

12 *If the grass is mown it is not uprooted* BULGARIA

13 *A stone is never uprooted by the wind*
REPUBLIC OF CONGO

368 OPERATION

1 *It's a poor rule that doesn't work both ways* ENGLAND

2 *Rhubarb and patience work wonders* GERMANY

3 *A cask of wine works more miracles than a church full of saints* ITALY

4 *The exception proves the rule* ENGLAND

5 *Not even Apollo keeps his bow always at full stretch*
LATIN

6   *God works in moments*   FRANCE

7   *The saints of the home work no miracles*   ITALY

8   *Rules are made to be broken*   ENGLAND

9   *If rivals are annoying you by playing well, consider
adopting their strategy*   CHINA

369   INACTIVITY

1   *When in doubt, do nothing*   ENGLAND

2   *When the sun shines the moon has nothing to do*
FRANCE

3   *Don't stand by the water and long for fish; go home and
weave a net*   CHINA

4   *It is no use standing with an open mouth in front of an
oven*   DENMARK

5   *A stationary stone gathers moss*   RUSSIA

6   *Procrastination is the thief of time*   ENGLAND

7   *'If I rest, I rust', says the key*   GERMANY

8   *Nothing kills like doing nothing*   DENMARK

9   *It is not clever to play but to stop playing*   USA

370 LAZINESS

1 *Indolence is often taken for patience*   FRANCE

2 *Idle curiosity sometimes fills the mousetrap*
   NETHERLANDS

3 *The idle person will put the cat in the fire*   SCOTLAND

4 *The devil finds work for idle hands*   ENGLAND

5 *The lazy ox drinks dirty water*   COLOMBIA

6 *Lazy people think their hands and feet were lent them*
   GEORGIA

7 *Labour warms, sloth harms*   NETHERLANDS

8 *For the diligent, a week has seven days; for the slothful,
   seven tomorrows*   GERMANY

9 *There is time enough to yawn in the grave*   ESTONIA

10 *Yawning is king*   NIGERIA

371 AWAKE – ASLEEP

1 *Dawn does not come twice to wake us*   SOUTH AFRICA

2 *The more one sleeps the less one lives*   PORTUGAL

3 *Those who wake up and find themselves famous haven't
   been asleep*   CHINA

4 *The eyes close in sleep, but the pillow remains awake*
   MALAYSIA

5   *All are not asleep who have their eyes shut*   GERMANY

6   *Don't praise a cottage in which you haven't yet slept*
     SOUTH AFRICA

7   *When everybody says you are drunk, go to sleep*   ITALY

8   *Wake not a sleeping cat*   FRANCE

9   *Let sleeping dogs lie*   ENGLAND

10   *Those who sleep with dogs must rise with fleas*
     SCOTLAND

11   *The shrimp that sleeps is carried away by the current*
     CHILE

12   *There's no rest for the wicked*   ENGLAND

13   *Chickens come home to roost*   ENGLAND

14   *The lame goat has no siesta*   SPAIN

372   BEDS

1   *It is not economical to go to bed early to save the candles
     if the result is twins*   CHINA

2   *Bed is the poor person's opera*   EGYPT

3   *A long beard does not prevent a house going to bed
     hungry*   CAMEROON

4   *You have no wisdom if you go to sleep before you make
     your bed*   UGANDA

5 *It is no advantage for someone in a fever to change their
bed*   ENGLAND

6 *Bed is your brother*   ZANZIBAR

7 *When the bed is small lie in the centre*   SPAIN

8 *A good conversation is better than a good bed*   ETHIOPIA

9 *A small bed will not hold two persons*   NIGERIA

10 *Generals die in bed*   USA

373 HASTE

1 *A hasty person drinks tea with a fork*   CHINA

2 *Hasty questions require slow answers*   NETHERLANDS

3 *More haste, less speed*   ENGLAND

4 *God did not create hurry*   FINLAND

5 *Nothing should be done in a hurry except catching fleas*
GERMANY

6 *Keep your hurry in your fist*   IRELAND

7 *Error is always in a hurry*   ENGLAND

8 *Dress slowly when you are in a hurry*   FRANCE

9 *Those who are in a hurry are always late*   GEORGIA

374 ADVICE

1   *There is no price for good advice*   SPAIN

2   *Advice should be viewed from behind and not from in front*   SWEDEN

3   *Advice that ain't paid for ain't no good*   USA

4   *Advisers are not givers*   NETHERLANDS

5   *Consult anyone, even your knees*   JAPAN

6   *When you have no companion, consult your walking-stick*   ALBANIA

7   *What's the use of consulting a dead person's horoscope?*
    SENEGAL

8   *A gladiator only takes counsel in the arena*   LATIN

9   *Adversity comes with instruction in its hand*   WALES

375 ABILITY – SKILL – CUNNING

1   *Ability and necessity dwell in the same cabin*
    NETHERLANDS

2   *Ability is the poor person's wealth*   USA

3   *Who is able to wipe off what is written on the forehead?*
    INDIA

4   *Accomplishments remain with oneself*   JAPAN

5   *To open a shop is easy; to keep it open is an art*   CHINA

6   *The art of being a merchant consists more in getting paid
    than in making sales*   SPAIN

7   *To have is to have, but the art is to get*   NETHERLANDS

8   *Even a mole may instruct a philosopher on the art of
    digging*   CHINA

9   *The belly teaches all arts*   ENGLAND

10 *Necessity teaches new arts*   NORWAY

11 *Even the best smith sometimes hits his thumb*
    NETHERLANDS

12 *A good driver turns in a small space*   FRANCE

13 *A good cat deserves a good rat*   ENGLAND

14 *A good lawyer is a bad neighbour*   FRANCE

15 *Dogs do not know how to swim until the water reaches
    their ears*   UKRAINE

16 *Those who know how to bend the fish-hook know how to
    straighten it*   TANZANIA

17 *One is usually at a loss to know how to sweep the ground
    in a market-place*   NIGERIA

18 *It is not enough for people to know how to ride; they
    must know how to fall*   MEXICO

19 *A bad workman blames his tools*   ENGLAND

20 *Don't show a hyena how well you can bite*   KENYA

21 *Those who make the first bad move always lose the game*
    JAPAN

22   *Those who sing worst, let them begin first*   ENGLAND

23   *Clumsy birds need early flight*   CHINA

24   *Every art requires the whole person*   FRANCE

25   *It is a cunning mouse which nests in the cat's ear*
      ENGLAND

26   *A sly rabbit will have three openings to its den*   CHINA

376   DIFFICULT

1   *All things are difficult before they are easy*   SPAIN

2   *Other people's books are difficult to read*   NETHERLANDS

3   *It is difficult to recognize a fool who is also a proprietor*
     SOUTH AFRICA

4   *It is very difficult to beat a drum with a sickle*   NIGERIA

5   *It is hard to catch wolves with sheep*   NETHERLANDS

6   *Once on a tiger's back, it is hard to alight*   CHINA

7   *It is a hard job to make old monkeys pull faces*
     BELGIUM

8   *When an old barn begins to burn, it is hard to put out*
     NETHERLANDS

9   *A fifth wheel in the wagon hinders more than helps*
     FRANCE

10   *When the going is rough, big potatoes come to the top*
     USA

11 *It is hard to swim between two stretches of bad water*
NETHERLANDS

12 *The toughest broncs is always them you've rode some other place* USA

13 *The hippo blocked up the ford, and no one could cross*
NIGERIA

377 EASY

1 *It is easy to lie about a far-off country* ETHIOPIA

2 *It is easy to keep the castle that was never besieged*
CHINA

3 *It's easy to hold the fort when it's not attacked* USA

4 *Wood half-burnt is easily kindled* ENGLAND

5 *Those who place their ladder too steeply will easily fall backwards* CZECH REPUBLIC

6 *Carrying-poles which bend easily do not break* CHINA

7 *The one who has put an egg into a bottle can easily take it out* NIGERIA

8 *When someone's coat is threadbare, it is easy to pick a hole in it* ENGLAND

9 *Little said is easy mended; nothing said needs no mending* IRELAND

10 *Eggs and vows are easily broken* JAPAN

11   *Black sheep hide mighty easy in the dark*   USA

12   *To open a shop is easy; to keep it open is an art*   CHINA

13   *It is easy to steal from a cut loaf*   ENGLAND

14   *It is easier to throw the load off the cart than to put it on*   CZECH REPUBLIC

15   *It is easier to speak than to say something*   UKRAINE

16   *It is easy to drive a frog into the water*   SERBIA

17   *All things are difficult before they are easy*   SPAIN

18   *It is easy to make pipes sitting amongst bulrushes*   CZECH REPUBLIC

19   *It is easy to hurt yourself on a stone that has sharp corners*   KOREA

20   *On a slimy shore it is easy to push a canoe*   CAMEROON

21   *The easiest way to get a divorce is to be married*   USA

22   *Easy come, easy go*   ENGLAND

23   *It is easier to rule a nation than a son*   CHINA

378 HELP

1   *The biggest help is help, and even the smallest help is help*   IRELAND

2   *Heaven helps those who help themselves*   ENGLAND

3   *Only God helps the ill-dressed*   SPAIN

4   *Every little helps*   ENGLAND

5   *Assistance conquers a lion*   MOROCCO

6   *One good turn deserves another*   ENGLAND

379   TAKING SIDES

1   *The story is only half told when one side tells it*
    ICELAND

2   *If you can't beat 'em, join 'em*   USA

3   *If rivals are annoying you by playing well, consider
    adopting their strategy*   CHINA

4   *Love yourself, then you will have no rivals*   ESTONIA

5   *United we stand; divided we fall*   USA

380   QUARRELLING

1   *A quarrel in a neighbouring house is refreshing*   INDIA

2   *Those who wish to live at Rome must not quarrel with
    the pope*   FRANCE

3   *An heir also inherits quarrels*   NAMIBIA

4   *It takes two to make a quarrel*   ENGLAND

5   *Too much discussion will lead to a row*   CÔTE D'IVOIRE

381 ATTACK – FIGHTING

1   *Ants can attack with a grain of rice*   MADAGASCAR

2   *Attack is the best defence*   ENGLAND

3   *One must not shoot a glass arrow into a painted deer*
EGYPT

4   *If you had not been among the crows, you would not
have been shot*   SCOTLAND

5   *Never show your teeth unless you can bite*   IRELAND

6   *Don't show a hyena how well you can bite*   KENYA

7   *If you want an audience, start a fight*   CHINA

8   *One does not distribute sweetmeats in a fight*   INDIA

9   *The one who will fight will find a cudgel in every hedge*
ENGLAND

10   *One dog can't fight*   IRELAND

11   *Those who run away will fight again*   GREECE

12   *It takes two blows to make a battle*   ENGLAND

13   *Don't lead with your chin*   USA

14   *The second word makes the fray*   JAPAN

* * * * * * * * * * * * * * * * * *

27 BEING BILINGUAL

Some 'English' proverbs are known in their original language. In these Latin examples, the original version is often preferred over the translation.

Caveat emptor.	Let the buyer beware.
In vino veritas.	In wine there is truth.
Per ardua ad astra.	Through hardship to the stars.
Festina lente.	Make haste slowly.

* * * * * * * * * * * * * * * * * *

382 DEFENCE – CASTLES

1 *The higher the castle the nearer to the lightning* RUSSIA

2 *A full cabin is better than an empty castle* IRELAND

3 *It is easy to keep the castle that was never besieged* CHINA

4 *It's easy to hold the fort when it's not attacked* USA

5 *Attack is the best defence* ENGLAND

6 *Those who cannot build the dyke should hand over the land* NETHERLANDS

7 *Three brothers, three fortresses* PORTUGAL

8   *Do not tear down the east wall to repair the west*
CHINA

9   *United we stand; divided we fall*   USA

10 *Courteous asking breaks even city walls*   UKRAINE

11 *A hug a day keeps the demons at bay*   GERMANY

383   WAR – PEACE

1   *Let those who do not know what war is go to war*
CHINA

2   *While in battle you cannot lend your sword*   BELGIUM

3   *No one wages war with ghosts*
DEMOCRATIC REPUBLIC OF CONGO

4   *Before going to war say one prayer; before going to sea,
two; before getting married, three*   POLAND

5   *Proverbs are constantly warring against each other*
SWITZERLAND

6   *All is fair in love and war*   ENGLAND

7   *The town that parleys is half surrendered*   FRANCE

8   *The peace-maker gets two-thirds of the blows*
MONTENEGRO

9   *Peace makes money and money makes war*   FRANCE

384 SOLDIERS

1 *An army marches on its stomach* FRANCE

2 *A gladiator only takes counsel in the arena* LATIN

3 *Away from the battle all are soldiers* GERMANY

4 *Three sorts of people are always to be found, soldiers, professors, and women* GERMANY

5 *Old soldiers never die* ENGLAND

385 WEAPONS

1 *A featherless arrow does not travel very far* ZANZIBAR

2 *Not every sort of wood is fit to make an arrow* FRANCE

3 *Beware of a returning arrow* JAPAN

4 *One must not shoot a glass arrow into a painted deer* EGYPT

5 *The one who carries the bludgeon owns the buffalo* INDIA

6 *Not even Apollo keeps his bow always at full stretch* LATIN

7 *Do not lift the club too high, it may fall on your head* FINLAND

8 *The one who will fight will find a cudgel in every hedge* ENGLAND

9   *Have a mouth as sharp as a dagger, but a heart as soft as tofu*   CHINA

10   *Dynamite comes in small packages*   USA

11   *A loaded gun frightens one; an unloaded one two*
     MONTENEGRO

12   *God, what things we see when we go out without a gun!*
     SOUTH AFRICA

13   *If you don't want the gun to go off, don't cock the trigger*
     REPUBLIC OF CONGO

14   *Beware the man with only one gun*   USA

15   *Even in the sheath the knife must be sharp*   FINLAND

16   *The spear of kinship soon pierces the eye*   CAMEROON

17   *While in battle you cannot lend your sword*   BELGIUM

18   *Two swords cannot be kept in one sheath*   INDIA

19   *Good nature is stronger than tomahawks*   USA

386 COMPLETE – INCOMPLETE

1   *When one starts the song too high it isn't finished*
     GERMANY

2   *A borrowed fiddle does not finish a tune*   ZIMBABWE

3   *Add legs to the snake after you have finished drawing it*
     CHINA

4   *Do a good deed and throw it into the sea*   BULGARIA

5   *Friday begun, never done*   USA

6   *Sooner begun, sooner done*   ENGLAND

7   *Every song has its end*   SLOVENIA

8   *The end of separation is meeting again*   TURKEY

9   *The longest chant has an end*   SCOTLAND

10   *The final lead weights are the heaviest*   NETHERLANDS

387 SUCCESS – FAILURE

1   *The world will not conquer him who is always rubbing his beard*   INDIA

2   *Assistance conquers a lion*   MOROCCO

3   *Do what you will, but be the first*   BELGIUM

4   *The only victory over love is flight*   FRANCE

5   *A card that never appears neither wins nor loses*   BRAZIL

6   *Many lose when they win, and others win when they lose*   GERMANY

7   *If you play alone, you will win*   SYRIA

8   *Three kinds of men fail to understand women – young men, old men, and middle-aged men*   IRELAND

9   *United we stand; divided we fall*   USA

10 *To always win brings suspicion, to always lose brings contempt* GERMANY

11 *Pride goes before a fall* ENGLAND

12 *One may as well lose the game by a card too much as a card too few* SPAIN

13 *None but the bashful lose* FRANCE

14 *One does not lose by asking the way* CHINA

15 *Those who make the first bad move always lose the game* JAPAN

16 *Failures are the pillars of success* WALES

388 FORTUNE – MISFORTUNE

1 *When a donkey is well off he goes dancing on ice* CZECH REPUBLIC

2 *Easy street never leads anywhere* USA

3 *A big crop is best, but a little crop will do* SCOTLAND

4 *Adversity comes with instruction in its hand* WALES

5 *Bad is called good when worse happens* NORWAY

6 *Whether the stone bumps the jug, or the jug bumps the stone, it is bad for the jug* USA

7 *Ambassadors suffer no penalty* ITALY

8 *When two elephants struggle, it is the grass that suffers* ZANZIBAR

9   *Misfortunes come by forties*   WALES

10   *Misfortune is not that which can be avoided, but that which cannot*   CHINA

389   LUCK – BAD LUCK

1   *Those who have once had luck cannot always call themselves unlucky*   BELGIUM

2   *An ounce of luck is better than a pound of knowledge*   BELGIUM

3   *What is bad luck for one is good luck for another*   GHANA

4   *Luck and bad luck are driving in the same sledge*   RUSSIA

5   *Those who gossip about their relatives have no luck and no blessing*   NETHERLANDS

390   POWER

1   *If power can be bought, then sell your mother to get it; you can always buy her back later*   GHANA

2   *A friend in power is a friend lost*   USA

3   *It is easier to rule a nation than a son*   CHINA

4   *Only with a new ruler do you appreciate the value of the old*   MYANMAR

5   *Men hold the buffalo by its rope, a ruler by his word*
    INDONESIA

6   *Those who have no authority will not have ceremonial drums*   CAMEROON

7   *Parents who are afraid to put their foot down will have children who step on their toes*   CHINA

8   *In rivers and bad government, the lightest things swim at the top*   USA

9   *A word and a stone let go cannot be called back*
    ENGLAND

10 *We cannot direct the wind, but we can adjust the sails*
    GERMANY

11 *Money is a good passport*   FRANCE

12 *There is always a boss above the boss*   NETHERLANDS

13 *If you look in a chief's bag you will always find something*   UGANDA

14 *If you get to thinking you're someone of influence, try ordering around someone else's dog*   USA

15 *I gave an order to a cat, and the cat gave it to its tail*
    CHINA

16 *A cat may look at a king*   ENGLAND

17 *Whoever is king, tea is queen*   IRELAND

18 *In chess the fools are nearest the kings* FRANCE

19 *Loved by a king is not loved* SERBIA

20 *Holidays come like kings and go like beggars* ESTONIA

21 *Yawning is king* NIGERIA

22 *New lords, new laws* FRANCE

23 *New officials introduce strict measures* CHINA

24 *Fire is a good slave, but a bad master* ALBANIA

25 *The clock must be the master in the house* SWEDEN

26 *Generals die in bed* USA

27 *Before you beat a dog, find out who its master is* CHINA

28 *A little dog is really brave in front of his master's house*
    HAITI

391 OBEDIENCE – DISOBEDIENCE

1 *Obey the customs of the village you enter* JAPAN

2 *Neither break a law nor make one* IRELAND

3 *Rules are made to be broken* ENGLAND

4 *Revolutions are not made by men in spectacles* USA

5 *It is easy to drive a frog into the water* SERBIA

6 *Loving and singing are not to be forced* GERMANY

7   *It is a hard job to make old monkeys pull faces*
BELGIUM

392 SERVICE

1   *The more servants, the worse service*   NETHERLANDS

2   *It is better to follow no saint than six*   INDIA

3   *One servant is a servant; two servants are half a servant; three servants are no servant at all*   POLAND

4   *Children regard their father's guest as a slave*
REPUBLIC OF CONGO

5   *Fire is a good slave, but a bad master*   ALBANIA

6   *People are not trodden on unless they lie down first*
GERMANY

7   *A wild goose never lays a tame egg*   ENGLAND

393 FREEDOM

1   *Law is a spider's web; big flies break through but the little ones are caught*   HUNGARY

2   *Laws catch flies but let hornets go free*   ENGLAND

3   *Proverbs are like butterflies; some are caught and some fly away*   GERMANY

4   *Before marrying live wildly for three years*   POLAND

5   *Walk as your shoes will let you*   SCOTLAND

6   *Your liberty ends where my nose begins*   USA

394   CATCHING

1   *It is not the thief that is hanged, but the one who was caught stealing*   CZECH REPUBLIC

2   *A bee was never caught in a shower*   ENGLAND

3   *Never try to catch two frogs with one hand*   CHINA

4   *Eagles do not catch flies*   HUNGARY

5   *You can't catch trout with dry trousers*   USA

6   *A closed mouth catches no flies*   ENGLAND

7   *If you want to catch a wild horse, find a tight corral*
      HAITI

8   *Don't value a badger skin before catching the badger*
      JAPAN

9   *You cannot catch a tiger cub unless you enter the tiger's den*   JAPAN

10   *The early bird catches the worm*   ENGLAND

11   *The one who hunts two rats will catch neither*   UGANDA

12   *The one who hunts two hares will catch neither*
       FRANCE

13   *If you catch fish you're a fisherman*   USA

14   *Proverbs are like butterflies; some are caught and some fly away*   GERMANY

15   *Laws catch flies but let hornets go free*   ENGLAND

16   *Law is a spider's web; big flies break through but the little ones are caught*   HUNGARY

17   *The cat does not catch mice for God*   INDIA

18   *Foxes are caught with foxes*   FINLAND

19   *You never know how a cow catches a rabbit*
      NETHERLANDS

20   *A big fish is caught with big bait*   SIERRA LEONE

21   *Time to catch bears is when they're out*   USA

22   *It is hard to catch wolves with sheep*   NETHERLANDS

23   *A cat with mittens won't catch mice*   SCOTLAND

24   *Cows can't catch no rabbits*   USA

25   *Set a thief to catch a thief*   ENGLAND

26   *Nothing should be done in a hurry except catching fleas*
      GERMANY

395   RESTRAINT

1   *A beautiful bird is the only kind we cage*   CHINA

2   *A crow in a cage won't talk like a parrot*   USA

3   *Men hold the buffalo by its rope, a ruler by his word*
INDONESIA

4   *Idle curiosity sometimes fills the mousetrap*
NETHERLANDS

5   *Rein in the horse at the edge of the cliff*   CHINA

6   *The horse must graze where it is tethered*   BELGIUM

7   *An ox is bound with ropes and a person with words*
ITALY

396   PERMISSION

1   *Let sleeping dogs lie*   ENGLAND

2   *When the bee comes to your house, let her have beer; you may want to visit the bee's house some day*
REPUBLIC OF CONGO

3   *Let those who do not know what war is go to war*
CHINA

4   *Laws catch flies but let hornets go free*   ENGLAND

5   *Sometimes one must let turnips be pears*   GERMANY

6   *Don't let the sideshow run away with the circus*   USA

7   *Live and let live*   ENGLAND

8   *Fools need no passport*   DENMARK

9   *If you don't have a ticket, you don't ride*   USA

397 PREVENTION

1   *A pretty basket does not prevent worries*
    REPUBLIC OF CONGO

2   *You cannot prevent the birds of sadness from flying over your head, but you can prevent them from nesting in your hair* CHINA

3   *A long beard does not prevent a house going to bed hungry* CAMEROON

4   *Speak, lest tomorrow you be prevented*   KENYA

5   *The tortoise breathes; it is only its shell that prevents our noticing it* NIGERIA

6   *Going slowly doesn't stop one arriving*   GUINEA

7   *However much the beetle is afraid, it will not stop the lizard swallowing it* CAMEROON

398 ACQUIRING

1   *To have is to have, but the art is to get*   NETHERLANDS

2   *You never accumulate if you don't speculate*   USA

3   *A greyhound finds its food in its feet*   IRELAND

4   *A smile will gain you ten more years of life*   CHINA

5   *Nothing venture, nothing gain*   ENGLAND

6   *One can't get beans out of wild melons*   NAMIBIA

7   *What you lose on the swings you gain on the roundabouts*   ENGLAND

8   *If power can be bought, then sell your mother to get it; you can always buy her back later*   GHANA

9   *After a typhoon there are pears to gather up*   CHINA

10   *You can't get dollars by pinching nickels*   USA

11   *Many kiss the child for the nurse's sake*   ENGLAND

12   *When an ant gets wings it perishes*   SERBIA

13   *Economy is itself a great income*   LATIN

14   *Making money selling manure is better than losing money selling musk*   EGYPT

15   *In buying horses and in taking a wife, shut your eyes tight and commend yourself to God*   ITALY

16   *Strike a flint and you get fire*   USA

17   *Faint heart never won fair lady*   ENGLAND

399   LOSING

1   *Goods held in common mostly get lost*   GERMANY

2   *Count not what is lost but what is left*   CHINA

3   *Making money selling manure is better than losing money selling musk*   EGYPT

4   *Who lends to a friend loses twice*   FRANCE

5 *While the sheep bleats it loses its mouthful*   BELGIUM

6 *The cry of the hyena and the loss of the goat are one*
NIGERIA

7 *All's lost that's put in a broken dish*   SCOTLAND

8 *Don't start economizing when you are down to your last
dollar*   USA

9 *Those who look fixedly at gold lose their sight*
NETHERLANDS

10 *Those who lose Monday lose all the week*   GEORGIA

11 *Those who read many epitaphs, lose their memory*
LATIN

12 *Those who have lost their oxen are always hearing bells*
SPAIN

13 *Friends are lost by calling often and calling seldom*
SCOTLAND

14 *Better lose the anchor than the whole ship*
NETHERLANDS

15 *The brook would lose its song if you removed the rocks*
USA

16 *Generally one loses less by being known too little than by
being known too much*   LATIN

17 *What you lose on the swings you gain on the
roundabouts*   ENGLAND

18 *The rose that is smelt by many loses its fragrance*
SPAIN

19 *What greater crime than loss of time?* GERMANY

20 *You may light another's candle at your own without loss*
DENMARK

21 *A friend in power is a friend lost* USA

22 *One is usually at a loss to know how to sweep the ground
in a market-place* NIGERIA

23 *A head without a brain has no need of a hat* SPAIN

24 *Those who lose dreaming are lost*
ABORIGINAL AUSTRALIA

400 HAVING POSSESSIONS

1 *Those who have two garments do not wear one only*
ZANZIBAR

2 *Those who have free seats at a play hiss first* CHINA

3 *It is difficult to recognize a fool who is also a proprietor*
SOUTH AFRICA

4 *What you can't have, abuse* ITALY

5 *Goods held in common mostly get lost* GERMANY

6 *Those who own the boat should give it a name*
NORWAY

7 *Row with the oars you have* NETHERLANDS

8 *One is happy when one has books, but happier still when
one has no need of them* CHINA

* * * * * * * * * * * * * * * * * * *

28 AUTHORIAL CREATIONS

Many authors have provided English with proverbs.

> *Kind hearts are more than coronets* (Tennyson's poem 'Lady
> Clara Vere de Vere')
> *Laugh and the world laughs with you; weep and you weep alone*
> (Ella Wheeler Wilcox's poem 'Solitude')
> *A thing of beauty is a joy for ever* (John Keats' poem
> 'Endymion')
> *There's no accounting for tastes* (Ann Radcliffe's novel *The
> Mysteries of Udolpho*)
> *Fools rush in where angels fear to tread* (Alexander Pope's
> poem 'An Essay on Criticism')
> *A little learning is a dangerous thing* (Alexander Pope, as
> above)

SEE ALSO Proverbs in Shakespeare (p. 488)

* * * * * * * * * * * * * * * * * *

9   *Those who have the tongs do not burn their fingers*
     ALBANIA

10   *Those who have only one bow should be content with one
fiddle* GERMANY

11   *If you have fire-tongs, why use your hands?* ESTONIA

12   *Those who have the frying-pan in their hand turn it at
will* NETHERLANDS

13 *Those who would enter paradise must have a good key*
ENGLAND

14 *They must stoop who have a low door*   SCOTLAND

15 *When the only thing you have is a hammer, everything looks like a nail*   FRANCE

16 *To build, one must have two purses*   BELGIUM

17 *Those who wish to barter do not like their belongings*
NIGERIA

18 *Those who have an egg in their pocket do not dance*
GABON

19 *If you don't have a ticket, you don't ride*   USA

20 *You can't have your cake and eat it*   ENGLAND

21 *They are fools who make their doctor their heir*   FRANCE

22 *If you have two loaves of bread, sell one and buy a lily*
CHINA

23 *No one boasts of what belongs to another*
CÔTE D'IVOIRE

24 *Folks is mighty generous with money what they ain't got*
USA

25 *Sell not your bearskin until you have the bear*   USA

26 *The only insurance against fire is to have two houses*
NIGERIA

27 *The one who carries the bludgeon owns the buffalo*
INDIA

28 *To have is to have, but the art is to get*   NETHERLANDS

401 HAVING A MIND

1 *Some guys got it, and some guys ain't got it*   USA

2 *It is possible to talk to cattle if you have common sense*
   SWITZERLAND

3 *Those who have no authority will not have ceremonial
   drums*   CAMEROON

4 *None sigh deeper than those who have no troubles*
   NORWAY

5 *If you have strings, pull them*   USA

6 *We each have our own way of killing fleas*   SPAIN

7 *A ten-dollar dude may have a two-dollar salary*   USA

8 *No nickname, no wealth*   CHINA

9 *You have no wisdom if you go to sleep before you make
   your bed*   UGANDA

10 *A good child has several names*   ESTONIA

11 *Cleverness eats its owner*   SOUTH AFRICA

402 HAVING A BODY

1 *Beware of those who squint or have red hair*   SERBIA

2 *If you had teeth of steel, you could eat iron coconuts*
   SENEGAL

3 *He who has a beard has also a comb*   ALBANIA

4 *Have a mouth as sharp as a dagger, but a heart as soft as tofu*   CHINA

5 *They must have clean fingers who would blow another's nose*   DENMARK

6 *The frightened person has many voices*   FINLAND

7 *Who has no head has legs*   ALBANIA

8 *Those who have a great nose think everyone speaks of it*
   SCOTLAND

403 HAVING RELATIVES AND PETS

1 *If you have no relatives, get married*   EGYPT

2 *Those who have no children do not understand love*
   ITALY

3 *Many have bees and buy wax*   GERMANY

4 *Happy owner, happy cat; indifferent owner, reclusive cat*
   CHINA

5   *There's no use in having a dog and barking yourself*
ENGLAND

6   *Those who have not bread to spare should not keep a dog*
CHINA

404   WHAT ANIMALS HAVE

1   *Flies have ears*   KENYA

2   *Even a fly has a cough*   ITALY

3   *In a cat's eye, all things belong to cats*   ENGLAND

4   *A bull does not enjoy fame in two herds*   ZAMBIA

5   *Every owl has its olive-tree*   CUBA

6   *It is not common for hens to have pillows*   SCOTLAND

7   *Every dog has its day*   ENGLAND

8   *A bird does not sing because it has an answer; it sings because it has a song*   CHINA

9   *Little crows have the largest beaks*   BELGIUM

10   *The cow which has the loudest bellowing has the slenderest tail*   IRELAND

11   *A cow that has no tail should not try to chase away flies*
GUINEA

12   *Why should the cow trouble to think if she has plenty of hay?*   SLOVAKIA

13 *The junk capsizes and the shark has its bellyful*
MALAYSIA

14 *The rhinoceros which has no calf takes itself to the muddy pool* SOUTH AFRICA

15 *It's a poor mouse that has but one hole* NETHERLANDS

405 WHAT THINGS AND NOTIONS HAVE

1 *An indispensable thing never has much value* GEORGIA

2 *Everything has two handles* GREECE

3 *My banjo has no bells on it* NIGERIA

4 *A road has no shadow* SENEGAL

5 *The fruit must have a stem before it grows* LIBERIA

6 *Happy nations have no history* BELGIUM

7 *A lie has no legs, but a scandal has wings* ENGLAND

8 *Every word has three explanations and three interpretations* IRELAND

9 *Music unheard has no value* GREECE

406 OFFERS – PROMISES – REFUSALS

1 *Those who plant a hedge round their garden invite it to be jumped* RUSSIA

2 *When luck offers a finger one must take the whole hand* SWEDEN

3 *Never trust your back to a slap* SCOTLAND

4 *In buying horses and in taking a wife, shut your eyes tight and commend yourself to God* ITALY

5 *A careless watch bids the thief come in* SCOTLAND

6 *A promise is a debt* ZANZIBAR

7 *Promise is a bridge of words, unsafe to walk across* GERMANY

8 *Eggs and vows are easily broken* JAPAN

9 *Men hold the buffalo by its rope, a ruler by his word* INDONESIA

10 *Who refuses, muses* FRANCE

407 RETAINING

1 *Who sieves too much, keeps the rubbish* BELGIUM

2 *If I keep a green bough in my heart, a singing-bird will come* CHINA

3 *One may say what one has kept silent, but not keep silent what one has said* SWITZERLAND

4 *A word and a stone let go cannot be called back* ENGLAND

5 *The best memory is not so firm as faded ink* CHINA

6 *A sponge sucks itself full, but when it has to yield anything one has to squeeze it* GERMANY

7 *A bit of fragrance always clings to the hand that gives you roses* CHINA

408 GIVING – GIFTS

1 *They give twice who give quickly* TURKEY

2 *Advisers are not givers* NETHERLANDS

3 *Only when all contribute their firewood can they build up a good fire* CHINA

4 *A padded jacket is an acceptable gift, even in summer* JAPAN

5 *Angels gave the gift of song, and while one sings one thinks no wrong* ITALY

6 *Fear the Greeks even when they bring gifts* LATIN

7 *Give with discretion, accept with memory* CZECH REPUBLIC

8 *When you give a child a nut, give it also something to break it with*   GEORGIA

9 *Give to no one the end of the thread*   TURKEY

10 *A bit of fragrance always clings to the hand that gives you roses*   CHINA

11 *Give your tongue more holidays than your head*
   SCOTLAND

12 *Give your love to your wife and your secret to your mother*   IRELAND

13 *Give credit where credit is due*   ENGLAND

14 *I gave an order to a cat, and the cat gave it to its tail*
   CHINA

15 *To the pig a carrot is a present*   GERMANY

16 *An onion shared with a friend tastes like roast lamb*
   EGYPT

17 *Those who have not bread to spare should not keep a dog*
   CHINA

18 *One does not distribute sweetmeats in a fight*   INDIA

19 *There is no grace in a benefit that sticks to the fingers*
   ENGLAND

20 *God gives the wideness of the mouth according to the bigness of the spoon*   POLAND

21 *Those who cannot build the dyke should hand over the land*   NETHERLANDS

22   *Leave a good name behind in case you return*   KENYA

23   *Be it an onion, let it be given graciously*   AFGHANISTAN

409   RECEIVING

1   *It is with its own face that the plate receives the soup*
NIGERIA

2   *It is the pot that boils, but the dish gets the credit*
CAMEROON

3   *If you laugh at your mother-in-law, you'll get dirt in your eye*   KENYA

4   *The easiest way to get a divorce is to be married*   USA

5   *Ask a silly question, get a silly answer*   ENGLAND

6   *One generation plants the trees; another gets the shade*
CHINA

7   *Those who blow in the fire will get sparks in their eyes*
GERMANY

8   *God heals and the doctor gets the money*   BELGIUM

9   *Every blade of grass gets its own drop of dew*
SCOTLAND

10   *A gladiator only takes counsel in the arena*   LATIN

11   *The peace-maker gets two-thirds of the blows*
MONTENEGRO

12 *Give with discretion, accept with memory*
    CZECH REPUBLIC

13 *Who goes around the village long enough will get either a
    dog-bite or a dinner*   SERBIA

14 *The wheel that does the squeaking is the one that gets the
    grease*   USA

15 *Those who want the last drop out of the can get the lid
    on their nose*   NETHERLANDS

16 *From the midst of the wood the hatchet gets its handle*
    GERMANY

17 *Grapes get their colour from grapes*   IRAN

18 *When luck offers a finger one must take the whole hand*
    SWEDEN

19 *You must take the little potato with the big potato*
    IRELAND

20 *Don't take the antidote before the poison*   LATIN

21 *They that get the next best are not ill off*   SCOTLAND

22 *You get what you pay for*   USA

410 LENDING – BORROWING

1 *While in battle you cannot lend your sword*   BELGIUM

2 *Lazy people think their hands and feet were lent them*
   GEORGIA

3 *The beauty of a loan is repayment* RUSSIA

4 *Do not try to borrow combs from shaven monks* CHINA

5 *A borrowed drum never makes good dancing* HAITI

6 *The borrowed cloak never warms* SYRIA

7 *A borrowed fiddle does not finish a tune* ZIMBABWE

8 *Who lends to a friend loses twice* FRANCE

9 *Better a free meal of acorns than a honey feast on trust*
   WALES

10 *A debt is always new* ESTONIA

11 *A promise is a debt* ZANZIBAR

12 *A debt is like a hippo's footprints* NIGERIA

411 TAKING .

1 *Those who want the rose must also take the thorns*
   GERMANY

2 *When the leopard moves away, it takes its tail with it*
   NIGERIA

3 *You cannot take one part of a fowl for cooking and leave
   the other part to lay eggs* INDIA

4 *Take a second look; it costs you nothing* CHINA

5 *Words and feathers are taken by the wind*
   SPAIN: BASQUE

6 *One cannot grab a bald man by the hair*   NETHERLANDS

7 *Don't let the sideshow run away with the circus*   USA

8 *You need not take someone else's hand to crush a sand-fly*   NIGERIA

9 *To get out a rusty nail you must take away a piece of the wall*   MALTA

10 *Love takes away the sight and matrimony restores it*   GERMANY

11 *Take away the wife of a strong man only when he is out*   UGANDA

12 *Public money is like holy water, one helps oneself to it*   ITALY

13 *Do not remove a fly from your friend's forehead with a hatchet*   CHINA

14 *The brook would lose its song if you removed the rocks*   USA

15 *Every time we laugh a nail is removed from our coffin*   ITALY

412   STEALING

1 *Steal a bell with your ears covered*   CHINA

2 *Those who steal a pin will steal an ox*   KOREA

3   *It's no good locking the stable door after the horse is stolen*   ENGLAND

4   *Those who steal the egg will also steal the hen*   MALTA

5   *The person who steals once is always a thief*   SPAIN

6   *If you love, love the moon; if you steal, steal a camel*   EGYPT

7   *A howlin' coyote ain't stealin' no chickens*   USA

8   *It is easy to steal from a cut loaf*   ENGLAND

9   *The existence of the sea means the existence of pirates*   MALAYSIA

10   *Procrastination is the thief of time*   ENGLAND

11   *There is no worse robber than a bad book*   ITALY

12   *You can't get dollars by pinching nickels*   USA

13   *If you kill, kill an elephant; if you rob, rob a treasury*   INDIA

14   *Fair exchange is no robbery*   ENGLAND

15   *Whoever holds the ladder is as bad as the thief*   GERMANY

16   *A careless watch bids the thief come in*   SCOTLAND

17   *It is not the thief that is hanged, but the one who was caught stealing*   CZECH REPUBLIC

18   *Learning is treasure a thief cannot touch*   CHINA

19   *Set a thief to catch a thief*   ENGLAND

20 *No annual fair without a thief* NETHERLANDS

413 BUYING – SELLING

1 *Let the buyer beware* LATIN

2 *When you buy, use your eyes not your ears*
CZECH REPUBLIC

3 *If you have two loaves of bread, sell one and buy a lily*
CHINA

4 *Everyone is foolish until they buy land* IRELAND

5 *Those who do not know how to squander their money –
buy some porcelain and drop it* NETHERLANDS

6 *Many have bees and buy wax* GERMANY

7 *Never argue with someone who buys ink by the barrel*
CHINA

8 *In buying horses and in taking a wife, shut your eyes
tight and commend yourself to God* ITALY

9 *If power can be bought, then sell your mother to get it;
you can always buy her back later* GHANA

10 *You don't have to buy a dairy just because you want a
glass of milk* USA

11 *Don't buy a left-hand monkey-wrench* CANADA

12 *Money cannot buy time* CHINA

13 *The art of being a merchant consists more in getting paid than in making sales* SPAIN

14 *Making money selling manure is better than losing money selling musk* EGYPT

15 *Never look an auto bargain under the hood* USA

16 *Those who must die must die in the dark, even though they sell candles* COLOMBIA

17 *The woman who sells fans often shades her eyes with her hands* CHINA

18 *Why feed a bullock after it is sold?* INDIA

19 *Good things sell themselves; bad things have to be advertised* ETHIOPIA

20 *Sell not your bearskin until you have the bear* USA

21 *Scholars talk books; butchers talk pigs* CHINA

22 *Let every pedlar carry his own pack* GERMANY

23 *Don't put all your goods in your shop window* USA

24 *No melon-seller cries: Bitter melons!* CHINA

25 *The bazaar knows neither father nor mother* TURKEY

26 *People sell their rags in their own market* EGYPT

27 *One is usually at a loss to know how to sweep the ground in a market-place* NIGERIA

28 *You never accumulate if you don't speculate* USA

29 *Priests return to the temple; merchants to the shop*
CHINA

30 *Goods held in common mostly get lost*   GERMANY

31 *The fly will never leave the confectioner's shop*   INDIA

32 *Those who change their trade make soup in a basket*
ENGLAND

33 *The morning is the mother of trades and the evening the mother of thoughts*   ITALY

34 *An anchored ship doesn't carry much cargo*   USA

35 *They are your enemies who are of your trade*   SPAIN

36 *Those who wish to barter do not like their belongings*
NIGERIA

37 *The sign-board brings the custom*   FRANCE

38 *Who knows when death or a customer will come?*
INDIA

39 *Those who deal in onions no longer smell them*
GERMANY

40 *Fair exchange is no robbery*   ENGLAND

41 *To open a shop is easy; to keep it open is an art*   CHINA

414 MONEY

1 *Money is a good passport* FRANCE

2 *Money is never old-fashioned* NETHERLANDS

3 *Money makes the world go round* USA

4 *Money talks* ENGLAND

5 *Money cannot buy time* CHINA

6 *Money cries in one's pocket* ESTONIA

7 *Brotherly love for brotherly love, but cheese for money*
   ALBANIA

8 *Making money selling manure is better than losing
   money selling musk* EGYPT

9 *God heals and the doctor gets the money* BELGIUM

10 *Those who do not know how to squander their money –
   buy some porcelain and drop it* NETHERLANDS

11 *Peace makes money and money makes war* FRANCE

12 *Public money is like holy water, one helps oneself to it*
   ITALY

13 *Where there is most mind there is least money* LATIN

14 *Jesting costs money* SPAIN

15 *No money, no friends* NETHERLANDS

16 *A dog with money is addressed 'Mr Dog'* USA

17 *Proverbs are the coins of the people* RUSSIA

18 *Gaming money won't get cold* SCOTLAND

19 *A fool and his money are soon parted* ENGLAND

20 *Folks is mighty generous with money what they ain't got*
    USA

21 *To build, one must have two purses* BELGIUM

22 *Old purses shut badly* NETHERLANDS

23 *A blow on the purse of another is like a blow on a sand-hill* EGYPT

24 *Much treasure, many moths* ESTONIA

25 *Scholars are the treasure of a nation* CHINA

26 *Learning is treasure a thief cannot touch* CHINA

27 *Sadness is a valuable treasure, only discovered in people you love* MADAGASCAR

28 *If you kill, kill an elephant; if you rob, rob a treasury*
    INDIA

29 *The miser and the pig are useless unless they are dead*
    FRANCE

415 TYPES OF MONEY

1 *Another day, another dollar* USA

2 *Don't hold the dime so near your eye that you can't see the dollar* USA

3 *A dollar in the bank is worth two in the hand*   USA

4 *You can't get dollars by pinching nickels*   USA

5 *Don't start economizing when you are down to your last dollar*   USA

6 *A ten-dollar dude may have a two-dollar salary*   USA

7 *A quick nickel is better than a slow dollar*   USA

8 *A quick sixpence is better than a slow shilling*   ENGLAND

9 *All that glitters is not gold*   ENGLAND

10 *A book holds a house of gold*   CHINA

11 *That is gold which is worth gold*   ENGLAND

12 *Those who look fixedly at gold lose their sight*
   NETHERLANDS

13 *There is no dust so blinding as gold dust*   USA

14 *Speech is silver; silence is golden*   ENGLAND

15 *When gold talks, speech is useless*   LATIN

16 *Seconds are the gold dust of time*   USA

17 *There never was a five-pound note but there was a ten-pound road for it*   SCOTLAND

18 *Don't spoil the ship for a ha'porth of tar*   ENGLAND

19 *A love-letter sometimes costs more than a three-cent stamp*   USA

20 *Many speak a word which if it were a florin they would put back in their purse*   GERMANY

416 RICH – POOR

1 *A rich person's sickness and a poor person's pancake are smelt a long way off* BELGIUM

2 *A father is a banker provided by nature* FRANCE

3 *The only insurance against fire is to have two houses* NIGERIA

4 *It ain't half so bad if you can afford it* USA

5 *Fortune lifts up art, but not art fortune* GREECE

6 *If you want one year of prosperity, grow grain. If you want ten years of prosperity, grow trees. If you want a hundred years of prosperity, grow people* CHINA

7 *No nickname, no wealth* CHINA

8 *A nation's health is a nation's wealth* USA

9 *The circumstances of people will appear from the condition of their hat* SRI LANKA

10 *Holidays come like kings and go like beggars* ESTONIA

11 *Beggars can't be choosers* ENGLAND

12 *Learn to handle a writing-brush, and you'll never handle a begging-bowl* CHINA

13 *They that get the next best are not ill off* SCOTLAND

14 *The forest is the poor person's fur-coat* ESTONIA

15 *Bed is the poor person's opera* EGYPT

417 PAYMENT

418 COST

2   *The tongue talks at the head's cost*   ENGLAND

3   *Take a second look; it costs you nothing*   CHINA

4   *To learn costs you one effort, to unlearn, two*   BULGARIA

5   *Jesting costs money*   SPAIN

6   *What costs nothing is worth nothing*   NETHERLANDS

7   *A love-letter sometimes costs more than a three-cent stamp*   USA

8   *There is no price for good advice*   SPAIN

9   *Don't value a badger skin before catching the badger*   JAPAN

10   *That is gold which is worth gold*   ENGLAND

11   *Only an owl knows the worth of an owl*   INDIA

419   CHEAP – DEAR

1   *Cheap soup has no taste*   TURKESTAN

2   *You can't make a cheap palace*   USA

3   *Those who have free seats at a play hiss first*   CHINA

4   *Better a free meal of acorns than a honey feast on trust*   WALES

5   *The best things in life are free*   USA

6   *Precious ointments are put in small boxes*   FRANCE

* * * * * * * * * * * * * * * * * *

29 ADULTS PLAY WITH PROVERBS

Everyone plays with language or enjoys language play. This 'ludic' function of language always involves taking a normal usage and manipulating it to create a special effect. We see it operating in such genres as puns, riddles, jokes, advertising slogans, newspaper headlines, and all the domains of literature.

Proverbs, by their nature, are fixed expressions. Quite a minor change is therefore very noticeable, and can have a strong effect, as in these examples from the world of computing:

Too many clicks spoil the browse.
What boots up, must come down.
The email of the species is more deadly than the mail.
A journey of a thousand sites begins with a single click.
Give a man a fish and you feed him for a day; teach him to use
    the Net and he won't bother you for weeks.
The modem is the message.
The geek shall inherit the earth.
You can't teach a new mouse old clicks.
Windows will never cease.
There's no place like your home page.

SEE ALSO Children play with proverbs (p. 136)

* * * * * * * * * * * * * * * * * *

7   *A diamond on a dunghill is a precious diamond still*
USA

8   *An indispensable thing never has much value*   GEORGIA

9   *Sadness is a valuable treasure, only discovered in people you love*   MADAGASCAR

10   *It is only the first bottle that is dear*   FRANCE

420 ECONOMIZING

1   *It is not economical to go to bed early to save the candles if the result is twins*   CHINA

2   *Don't start economizing when you are down to your last dollar*   USA

3   *Economy is itself a great income*   LATIN

421 HAPPINESS – JOY

1   *What makes one abbot glad makes another abbot sad*
SCOTLAND

2   *Happy nations have no history*   BELGIUM

3   *Two happy days are seldom brothers*   BULGARIA

4   *Happy owner, happy cat; indifferent owner, reclusive cat*
CHINA

5   *Joy and courage make a handsome face*   FRANCE

6   *Grief and joy are a revolving wheel*   INDIA

7   *A day of sorrow is longer than a month of joy*   CHINA

8   *Those who have only one bow should be content with one fiddle*   GERMANY

9   *A contented mind is a continual feast*   ENGLAND

10   *A satisfied heart will often sigh*   FRANCE

11   *One is happy when one has books, but happier still when one has no need of them*   CHINA

12   *If ignorance is bliss, why be otherwise?*   USA

13   *Great consolation may grow out of the smallest saying*   SWITZERLAND

14   *A weasel comes to say Happy New Year to the chickens*   CHINA

15   *Even a young foot finds ease in an old slipper*   SCOTLAND

16   *A bald-headed man cannot grow hair by getting excited about it*   REPUBLIC OF CONGO

422 PLEASURE

1   *A good conversation is better than a good bed*   ETHIOPIA

2   *Politeness pleases even a cat*   CZECH REPUBLIC

3   *Variety is the spice of life*   ENGLAND

4   *Where one was born, every blade of grass pleases*   ITALY

5   *God is better pleased with adverbs than with nouns*
ENGLAND

6   *One family builds the wall; two families enjoy it*   CHINA

7   *Enough is as good as a feast*   ENGLAND

8   *Cats love fish but fear to wet their paws*   CHINA

9   *Misery loves company*   ENGLAND

10   *A lobster loves water, but not when he's being cooked in it*   SENEGAL

11   *A contented mind is a continual feast*   ENGLAND

12   *A quarrel in a neighbouring house is refreshing*   INDIA

423   SADNESS – GRIEF

1   *Small cares make many words, great ones are mute*
GERMANY

2   *What can't be cured must be endured*   ENGLAND

3   *Grief and joy are a revolving wheel*   INDIA

4   *Misery loves company*   ENGLAND

5   *The end of an ox is beef, and the end of a lie is grief*
MADAGASCAR

6   *What the eye cannot see, the heart cannot grieve about*
ENGLAND

7   *To the jaundiced all things seem yellow*   FRANCE

8   *What makes one abbot glad makes another abbot sad*
    SCOTLAND

9   *You cannot prevent the birds of sadness from flying over
    your head, but you can prevent them from nesting in your
    hair*   CHINA

10 *Sadness is a valuable treasure, only discovered in people
    you love*   MADAGASCAR

11 *The saddest dog sometimes wags its tail*   ENGLAND

12 *A day of sorrow is longer than a month of joy*   CHINA

13 *The nail suffers as much as the hole*   NETHERLANDS

14 *When a blind person carries the banner, woe to those who
    follow*   FRANCE

15 *Woe to the house where there is no chiding*   ENGLAND

16 *A pretty basket does not prevent worries*
    REPUBLIC OF CONGO

17 *Time heals all wounds*   ENGLAND

18 *An axe with a loose head is the bane of a man up a tree*
    NIGERIA

19 *A reasonable amount of fleas is good for a dog; they keep
    him from broodin' on being a dog*   USA

20 *A satisfied heart will often sigh*   FRANCE

21 *Better be safe than sorry*   ENGLAND

424 PAIN

1 *Whichever finger you bite, every one hurts* RUSSIA

2 *Aching teeth are ill tenants* ENGLAND

3 *The tongue always goes to the aching tooth* BULGARIA

4 *Their mosquito won't bite me* CÔTE D'IVOIRE

5 *A hungry louse bites hard* USA

6 *Once bitten, twice shy* ENGLAND

7 *Pride feels no pain* EGYPT

8 *A handsome shoe often pinches the feet* FRANCE

9 *Those who go barefoot aren't pinched by their shoes*
    GERMANY

10 *Better be stung by a nettle than pricked by a rose*
    ENGLAND

11 *When an elephant chases you, you climb a prickly tree*
    KENYA

12 *If the panther knew how much it is feared, it would do much more harm* CAMEROON

13 *If you know what hurts yourself, you know what hurts others* MADAGASCAR

14 *The first blow does not hurt like the second* ZANZiBAR

15 *A broken glass can't be hurt* ENGLAND

16 *Falling hurts least those who fly low* CHINA

17 *It is easy to hurt yourself on a stone that has sharp corners* KOREA

18 *Be like the mouth and hand: when the hand is hurt the mouth blows on it; when the mouth is hurt the hand rubs it* MADAGASCAR

19 *Don't holler before you're hurt* USA

20 *Never scald your lips with someone else's porridge* IRELAND

21 *Those who have been scalded with hot soup blow on cold water* UKRAINE

22 *A scalded cock runs away from the rain* BULGARIA

23 *If you run away from a mosquito the sharper will its sting be* SLOVENIA

24 *They dread a moth, who have been stung by a wasp* ALBANIA

25 *The more you squeeze a nettle the less it stings* GERMANY

26 *All good salt stings* SPAIN

27 *That which is to become a good nettle must sting early* SWEDEN

28 *Warm a frozen serpent, and it will sting you first* ARMENIA

425 **TROUBLES**

1 *None sigh deeper than those who have no troubles*
NORWAY

2 *Troubles never come singly* ENGLAND

3 *If rivals are annoying you by playing well, consider adopting their strategy* CHINA

4 *To tell the truth is dangerous, to listen to it is annoying*
DENMARK

5 *The big toe never does the ear any harm* NIGERIA

6 *Pelt a dog with a bone and you will not offend him*
ITALY

7 *A gem cannot be polished without friction, nor a person perfected without trials* CHINA

8 *With silence we irritate the devil* BULGARIA

9 *If you know the beginning well, the end will not trouble you* SENEGAL

10 *It is the sick duck that is worried by the weasel* CHINA

11 *It is not good to be the poet of a village* GERMANY

12 *One must learn to be bored* FRANCE

13 *If you are worried by the rain you can always plunge into the sea* CHINA

14 *Today is the tomorrow that you worried about yesterday*
USA

426 LAUGHING – JESTING

1 *Good words make us laugh; good deeds make us silent*
FRANCE

2 *Those who laugh last laugh loudest* ENGLAND

3 *There is no marriage where there is no weeping, and no funeral where there is no laughing* ITALY

4 *A smile will gain you ten more years of life* CHINA

5 *Look the other way when the girl in the tea-house smiles*
JAPAN

6 *Those who tickle themselves laugh when they like*
GERMANY

7 *The most wasted of all days is the day when we have not laughed* FRANCE

8 *Every time we laugh a nail is removed from our coffin*
ITALY

9 *Anyone may laugh on a hillside* SCOTLAND

10 *Feigned laughter ruins the teeth* INDIA

11 *A true jest is no jest* SCOTLAND

12 *Many a true word is spoken in jest* ENGLAND

13 *Jesting costs money* SPAIN

14 *Don't tell all of your jokes on one program* USA

427 CRYING

1 *At birth we cry – at death we see why* BULGARIA

2 *The baby who does not cry does not get fed*
PHILIPPINES

3 *Two barrels of tears will not heal a bruise* CHINA

4 *Money cries in one's pocket* ESTONIA

5 *Friendship does not need pepper to cry*
REPUBLIC OF CONGO

6 *Rather once cry your heart out than always sigh* CHINA

7 *Nothing wipes your tears away but your own hand*
EGYPT

8 *Shed no tears until seeing the coffin* CHINA

9 *Every deceiver's eyes are full of tears* BELGIUM

10 *Nothing dries sooner than a tear* LATIN

11 *There is no marriage where there is no weeping, and no funeral where there is no laughing* ITALY

428 AMUSEMENTS

1 *An amuser is not amused* ZANZIBAR

2 *The game is not worth the candle* ENGLAND

3 *If rivals are annoying you by playing well, consider adopting their strategy* CHINA

4   *An hour of play discovers more than a year of conversation*   PORTUGAL

5   *If he calls it a silly and childish game, that means his wife can beat him at it*   USA

6   *Big hammers don't play with little nails*   GERMANY

7   *If you play alone, you will win*   SYRIA

8   *While the cat's away, the mice will play*   ENGLAND

9   *Never say 'whoopee' before you jump*   CANADA

10   *Don't let the sideshow run away with the circus*   USA

11   *Those who make the first bad move always lose the game*   JAPAN

12   *If the string is long the kite will fly high*   CHINA

13   *Strong people can spin their top in the sand*   JAPAN

14   *No annual fair without a thief*   NETHERLANDS

15   *Don't get off the merry-go-round before it stops*   USA

16   *What you lose on the swings you gain on the roundabouts*   ENGLAND

17   *If the swing goes forward it will go backward too*   SRI LANKA

18   *Without tools no handicraft*   SLOVAKIA

429 PERFORMING ARTS

1 *When a donkey is well off he goes dancing on ice*
CZECH REPUBLIC

2 *Love teaches asses to dance* FRANCE

3 *An old cat will not learn how to dance* MOROCCO

4 *When the music changes, so does the dance* NIGERIA

5 *Those who have an egg in their pocket do not dance*
GABON

6 *You can't dance at two weddings with one pair of feet*
USA

7 *Those who hear not the music think the dancers mad*
CHINA

8 *A borrowed drum never makes good dancing* HAITI

9 *The show must go on* USA

430 GAMBLING – CARDS

1 *Reform a gambler? Cure leprosy* CHINA

2 *Gaming money won't get cold* SCOTLAND

3 *One may as well lose the game by a card too much as a card too few* SPAIN

4 *A card that never appears neither wins nor loses* BRAZIL

431 SPORTS – GAMES

1 *The game's not over until the last man strikes out* USA

2 *One cannot ski so softly that the traces cannot be seen* FINLAND

3 *Who plays at bowls must expect the ball returned* NETHERLANDS

4 *In chess the fools are nearest the kings* FRANCE

5 *They are truly superior who can look upon a game of chess in silence* CHINA

6 *After the game the king goes into the sack like the pawn* ITALY

432 BEAUTY

1 *Beauty does not make the pot boil* IRELAND

2 *Beauty is an empty calabash* CAMEROON

3 *Beauty is in the oleander and the oleander is bitter* MOROCCO

4 *Beauty draws more than oxen* ENGLAND

5 *A pig won't spare even the most beautiful fruit* ALBANIA

6 *A beautiful maiden is a devil's pocket* PHILIPPINES

7 *A beautiful bird is the only kind we cage* CHINA

8 *A beautiful disorder is an effect of art* FRANCE

9   *A true word is not beautiful and a beautiful word is not true*   JAPAN

10   *A bird with a beautiful plumage doesn't sit in the corner*   CAMEROON

11   *One cannot make soup out of beauty*   ESTONIA

12   *A handsome shoe often pinches the feet*   FRANCE

13   *Faint heart never won fair lady*   ENGLAND

14   *The beauty of a loan is repayment*   RUSSIA

15   *The beauty of the corn cob is apparent on the inside only*   KENYA

16   *A big nose never spoiled a handsome face*   FRANCE

17   *Age before beauty*   USA

18   *In the choicest vase are found the ugliest cracks*   CHINA

19   *Handsome is as handsome does*   ENGLAND

20   *Joy and courage make a handsome face*   FRANCE

21   *A dog's mouth yields no ivory*   CHINA

22   *The worm don't see nothing pretty in the robin's song*   USA

23   *A pretty basket does not prevent worries*   REPUBLIC OF CONGO

433 BEAUTIFICATION

1 *Never ask a barber if you need a haircut* USA

2 *He who has a beard has also a comb* ALBANIA

3 *Do not try to borrow combs from shaven monks* CHINA

4 *The bald need no comb* POLAND

5 *Tangled hair needs a wide comb* SERBIA

6 *Wash a dog, comb a dog: still a dog* USA

7 *A bald head is soon shaved* SCOTLAND

8 *God does not shave – why should I?* BULGARIA

9 *You cannot shave a man's head in his absence* NIGERIA

10 *The leopard cannot change its spots* ENGLAND

434 JEWELLERY – ORNAMENT

1 *Better a diamond with a flaw than a pebble without one*
CHINA

2 *A diamond on a dunghill is a precious diamond still*
USA

3 *A gem cannot be polished without friction, nor a person perfected without trials* CHINA

4 *The wife of the amber-turner wears pearls of glass* IRAN

5 *A single bracelet doesn't jingle* GUINEA

6   *The house with an old grandparent harbours a jewel*
CHINA

435 SPOILING

1   *The vulture's foot spoils the soup*   NIGERIA

2   *One rotten egg spoils the whole pudding*   GERMANY

3   *One rotten apple spoils the whole barrel*   ENGLAND

4   *Making preparations does not spoil the trip*   GUINEA

5   *Too many hands spoil the pie*   USA

6   *Spare the rod and spoil the child*   ENGLAND

7   *Don't spoil the ship for a ha'porth of tar*   ENGLAND

8   *The sweeter the perfume, the uglier the flies which gather round the bottle*   CHINA

9   *Too many cooks spoil the broth*   ENGLAND

10   *In the choicest vase are found the ugliest cracks*   CHINA

436 RIDICULE

1   *One camel does not make fun of another camel's hump*   GUINEA

2   *Those who have free seats at a play hiss first*   CHINA

3   *When the mouse laughs at the cat, there is a hole*
    GAMBIA

4   *If he calls it a silly and childish game, that means his
    wife can beat him at it*   USA

5   *If you laugh at your mother-in-law, you'll get dirt in
    your eye*   KENYA

6   *Custom is rust that mocks at every file*   BOHEMIA

7   *When the date-crop is over, everyone mocks at the palm-
    tree*   ETHIOPIA

8   *Don't call the alligator a big-mouth till you have crossed
    the river*   BELIZE

437   HOPE

1   *Those who live with hope die with desire*   BELGIUM

2   *The smaller the lizard, the greater its hope of becoming a
    crocodile*   ETHIOPIA

3   *Ambition and fleas jump high*   GERMANY

4   *Hope is a good breakfast but a bad supper*   ENGLAND

5   *A pessimist is a person who has lived with an optimist*
    USA

6   *Every cloud has a silver lining*   ENGLAND

7   *Those who lose dreaming are lost*
    ABORIGINAL AUSTRALIA

438 FEAR

1   *Be not afraid of growing slowly, be afraid only of standing still*   CHINA

2   *Who sits on the floor, is not afraid of a fall*
CZECH REPUBLIC

3   *Be always a little afraid so that you never have need of being much afraid*   FINLAND

4   *A blind mule ain't afraid of darkness*   USA

5   *Parents who are afraid to put their foot down will have children who step on their toes*   CHINA

6   *However much the beetle is afraid, it will not stop the lizard swallowing it*   CAMEROON

7   *Who suffers from diarrhoea is not afraid of the dark*
SOUTH AFRICA

8   *A burnt bairn dreads the fire*   SCOTLAND

9   *They dread a moth, who have been stung by a wasp*
ALBANIA

10   *Those who have not seen a hare run, must not speak of fear*   ITALY

11   *A clear conscience never fears midnight knocking*   CHINA

12   *A clear conscience fears no accusation*   ENGLAND

13   *Who has been almost drowned fears not the rain*
ALBANIA

14 *Those who fear wild cranes should not sow beans*
MALTA

15 *Conscience is like tickling, some fear it and some don't*
ITALY

16 *Fear the Greeks even when they bring gifts* LATIN

17 *An old horse doesn't fear the whip* SWITZERLAND

18 *New-born calves don't fear tigers* CHINA

19 *If the panther knew how much it is feared, it would do much more harm* CAMEROON

20 *Fools rush in where angels fear to tread* ENGLAND

21 *A loaded gun frightens one; an unloaded one two*
MONTENEGRO

22 *The cat who frightens the mice away is as good as the cat who eats them* GERMANY

23 *The frightened person has many voices* FINLAND

24 *A pessimist is a person who has lived with an optimist*
USA

25 *A handleless axe does not scare the forest* BULGARIA

26 *If love be timid, it is not true* SPAIN

27 *To the timorous all leaves seem to rustle* SWITZERLAND

28 *Do not fear a stain that disappears with water* SPAIN

29 *Those who tremble to hear a leaf fall should keep out of the wood* FRANCE

30   *Some have been thought brave because they were afraid to run away*   ENGLAND

31   *A coward's fear makes a brave man braver*   SCOTLAND

32   *A courageous foe is better than a cowardly friend*
      CHINA

33   *People who do what they say are not cowards*   NIGERIA

439   COURAGE

1   *Joy and courage make a handsome face*   FRANCE

2   *A courageous foe is better than a cowardly friend*
     CHINA

3   *Adventures are to the adventurous*   ENGLAND

4   *Boldness, and again boldness, and always boldness*
     FRANCE

5   *A coward's fear makes a brave man braver*   SCOTLAND

6   *A little dog is really brave in front of his master's house*
     HAITI

7   *An old rat is a brave rat*   FRANCE

8   *Some have been thought brave because they were afraid to run away*   ENGLAND

9   *If bravery is ten, nine is strategy*   TURKEY

10   *The spectator is a great hero*   AFGHANISTAN

11   *Heroism consists in hanging on one minute longer*
    NORWAY

12   *Discretion is the better part of valour*   ENGLAND

13   *There are old pilots, and there are bold pilots, but there are no old, bold pilots*   USA

440   CAUTION

1   *Add caution to caution*   JAPAN

2   *Beware of a person's shadow and a bee's sting*
    MYANMAR

3   *Beware of people who dislike cats*   IRELAND

4   *Beware of those who squint or have red hair*   SERBIA

5   *Beware of old streets and new inns*   GERMANY

6   *Beware the husband who talks*   GREECE

7   *Beware of the door which has several keys*   INDIA

8   *Beware of a returning arrow*   JAPAN

9   *Beware the man with only one gun*   USA

10   *Let the buyer beware*   LATIN

11   *Hasty questions require slow answers*   NETHERLANDS

12   *Fools rush in where angels fear to tread*   ENGLAND

* * * * * * * * * * * * * * * * * *

30 COUNTRY VARIATIONS – BELIEFS AND BEHAVIOUR

It is relatively easy to find distinctive proverbial expression in relation to such 'concrete' entities as artefacts, plants, and animals. More difficult to identify are proverbs which reflect the specific beliefs and behaviour of the people of a country, region, or cultural tradition.

However long the procession, it always returns to the church
    (PHILIPPINES)
Every priest praises his convent (PHILIPPINES)
Better do a good deed near at home than go far away to burn
    incense (CHINA)
Golden bishop, wooden crozier; wooden bishop, golden crozier
    (FRANCE)
Not even Apollo keeps his bow always at full stretch (LATIN)
Right church but wrong pew (USA)
Do not try to borrow combs from shaven monks (CHINA)
Those who wish to live at Rome must not quarrel with the pope
    (FRANCE)
When one sheep is over the dam, the rest will follow
    (NETHERLANDS)
Those who have no authority will not have ceremonial drums
    (CAMEROON)
If you bow at all, bow low (CHINA)
One can study calligraphy at eighty (JAPAN)
A borrowed drum never makes good dancing (HAITI)
Don't talk Latin in front of the Franciscans (FRANCE)
One cannot ski so softly that the traces cannot be seen
    (FINLAND)

You may read Pompeii in some people's faces (ITALY)

A gladiator only takes counsel in the arena (LATIN)

If you look in a chief's bag you will always find something
  (UGANDA)

People carrying elephant's flesh on their head should not look for
  crickets underground (NIGERIA)

Don't tell all of your jokes on one program (USA)

SEE ALSO Country variations – climate (p. 90); artefacts
(p. 151); animals (p. 302); plants (p. 323)

* * * * * * * * * * * * * * * * * *

441 DESIRE

1   *Those who live with hope die with desire*   BELGIUM

2   *Never confuse asthma with passion*   USA

3   *There's no accounting for tastes*   ENGLAND

4   *If you don't want the gun to go off, don't cock the trigger*
    REPUBLIC OF CONGO

5   *If you want to keep your milk sweet, leave it in the cow*
    LIBERIA

6   *Why should someone without a head want a hat?*
    CHILE

7   *If you want one year of prosperity, grow grain. If you*
    want ten years of prosperity, grow trees. If you want a
    hundred years of prosperity, grow people   CHINA

8 *A padded jacket is an acceptable gift, even in summer*
  JAPAN

9 *A drowning man will clutch at a straw* ENGLAND

10 *Those who tickle themselves laugh when they like*
  GERMANY

11 *One should not light a fire unless one wants to cook*
  DENMARK

12 *Those who want the last drop out of the can get the lid on their nose* NETHERLANDS

13 *Those who want the rose must also take the thorns*
  GERMANY

14 *If you want to go fast, go the old road* MYANMAR

15 *No matter how full the river, it still wants to grow*
  REPUBLIC OF CONGO

16 *If you want to be acquainted with the past and the present, you must read five cartloads of books* CHINA

17 *Those who have the frying-pan in their hand turn it at will* NETHERLANDS

18 *Do what you will, but be the first* BELGIUM

19 *Those who wish to live at Rome must not quarrel with the pope* FRANCE

20 *When the bee comes to your house, let her have beer; you may want to visit the bee's house some day*
  REPUBLIC OF CONGO

21 *Those who do not wish little things do not deserve big things* BELGIUM

22 *If you want an audience, start a fight* CHINA

23 *Those who wish to learn to pray must go to sea* ENGLAND

24 *To wish to know is to wish to doubt* FRANCE

25 *If you wish to be angry, pay for something in advance* MONTENEGRO

26 *Those who wish to barter do not like their belongings* NIGERIA

27 *Sparrows who aspire to be peacocks are likely to break a thigh* MYANMAR

28 *Death and proverbs love brevity* GERMANY

29 *To want to forget something is to remember it* FRANCE

30 *Want a thing long enough, and you don't* CHINA

442 WONDERS

1 *Rhubarb and patience work wonders* GERMANY

2 *Admiration is the daughter of ignorance* SPAIN

3 *Speak of the miracle, but don't mention the saint* PHILIPPINES

4 *Miracles come to those who believe in them* FRANCE

5   *The saints of the home work no miracles*   ITALY

6   *A cask of wine works more miracles than a church full of saints*   ITALY

7   *The dog may be wonderful prose, but only the cat is poetry*   FRANCE

443   FAME – SHAME

1   *It is the pot that boils, but the dish gets the credit*   CAMEROON

2   *Fame is a gull floating on water*   CHINA

3   *A bull does not enjoy fame in two herds*   ZAMBIA

4   *Those who wake up and find themselves famous haven't been asleep*   CHINA

5   *Eat not cherries with the great*   ENGLAND

6   *Generally one loses less by being known too little than by being known too much*   LATIN

7   *Leave a good name behind in case you return*   KENYA

8   *A dog with money is addressed 'Mr Dog'*   USA

9   *Those who cheat me once, shame fall them; those who cheat me twice, shame fall me*   SCOTLAND

10   *To fall is no shame, but to remain fallen is*   SWEDEN

444 PRIDE – MODESTY

1 *Pride feels no pain* EGYPT

2 *If pride were an art, how many graduates we should have* ITALY

3 *Pride only goes the length one can spit*
 REPUBLIC OF CONGO

4 *Pride goes before a fall* ENGLAND

5 *Salt doesn't boast that it is salted* HAITI

6 *No one boasts of what belongs to another*
 CÔTE D'IVOIRE

7 *You cannot push yourself forward by patting yourself on the back* CHINA

8 *None but the bashful lose* FRANCE

9 *Lower your head modestly while passing, and you will harvest bananas* REPUBLIC OF CONGO

445 FRIENDS

1 *The friends of my friends are my friends* BELGIUM

2 *The enemies of my enemies are my friends* FRANCE

3 *Friendship is steps* KENYA

4 *Friendship does not need pepper to cry*
 REPUBLIC OF CONGO

5   *Friendly is as friendly does*   USA

6   *To read a book for the first time is to make the acquaintance of a new friend; to read it a second time is to meet an old one*   CHINA

7   *When you have no companion, consult your walking-stick*   ALBANIA

8   *Do not protect yourself by a fence, but by your friends*
CZECH REPUBLIC

9   *A courageous foe is better than a cowardly friend*
CHINA

10 *Who lends to a friend loses twice*   FRANCE

11 *Someone without a friend is like the right hand without the left*   BELGIUM

12 *There is no better looking-glass than an old friend*
ENGLAND

13 *Friends are lost by calling often and calling seldom*
SCOTLAND

14 *Those who seek a constant friend go to the cemetery*
RUSSIA

15 *You do not know who is your friend or who is your enemy until the ice breaks*   ICELAND

16 *Who has God for his friend has all the saints in his pocket*   ITALY

17 *Do not remove a fly from your friend's forehead with a hatchet*   CHINA

18 *No money, no friends* NETHERLANDS

19 *An onion shared with a friend tastes like roast lamb*
     EGYPT

20 *A stone from the hand of a friend is an apple*
     MAURITANIA

21 *A friend in power is a friend lost* USA

22 *'Tis a good word that can better a good silence*
     NETHERLANDS

23 *A good word never broke a tooth* IRELAND

24 *Say kind words to hear kind words* KOREA

25 *A kind word warms for three winters* CHINA

26 *Where they like you, do not go often* SPAIN

27 *A starving crocodile is never pleasant* MADAGASCAR

446 NEIGHBOURS

1 *If your neighbour is an early riser, you will become one*
    ALBANIA

2 *When walking through your neighbour's melon-patch,
    don't tie your shoe* CHINA

3 *If we would know what we are, let us anger our
    neighbours* GERMANY

4 *Love your neighbour, yet pull not down your hedge*
    ENGLAND

5   *Better a neighbour over the wall than a brother over the sea*   ALBANIA

6   *A good lawyer is a bad neighbour*   FRANCE

7   *The best neighbors are vacant lots*   USA

447   ENEMIES

1   *They are your enemies who are of your trade*   SPAIN

2   *The enemies of my enemies are my friends*   FRANCE

3   *You do not know who is your friend or who is your enemy until the ice breaks*   ICELAND

4   *A courageous foe is better than a cowardly friend*   CHINA

5   *Those who cannot cut the bread evenly cannot get on well with people*   CZECH REPUBLIC

6   *Translators, traitors*   ITALY

448   SOCIETY

1   *Obey the customs of the village you enter*   JAPAN

2   *Communities begin by building their kitchen*   FRANCE

3   *Community is as strong as water, and as stupid as a pig*   RUSSIA

4   *A ten-dollar dude may have a two-dollar salary*   USA

5   *No one can call again yesterday*   ENGLAND

6   *Friends are lost by calling often and calling seldom*
    SCOTLAND

7   *If familiarity were useful, water wouldn't cook fish*
    CAMEROON

8   *Every day cannot be a feast of lanterns*   CHINA

9   *When the bee comes to your house, let her have beer; you
    may want to visit the bee's house some day*
    REPUBLIC OF CONGO

10 *On going into a church leave the world behind the door*
    SPAIN

11 *All hillbillies don't live in the hills*   CANADA

12 *Ambassadors suffer no penalty*   ITALY

13 *Punctuality is the politeness of princes*   FRANCE

14 *Those who have no authority will not have ceremonial
    drums*   CAMEROON

15 *Send your charity abroad wrapped in blankets*
    ENGLAND

16 *Charity begins at home*   ENGLAND

17 *Charity covers a multitude of sins*   ENGLAND

449 POLITENESS

1 *Politeness pleases even a cat*   CZECH REPUBLIC

2 *Courteous asking breaks even city walls*   UKRAINE

3 *Full of courtesy, full of craft*   ENGLAND

4 *Too much courtesy is discourtesy*   JAPAN

5 *Be it an onion, let it be given graciously*   AFGHANISTAN

6 *Those who are always nice are not always nice*   POLAND

7 *The later in the evening, the nicer the people*
   NETHERLANDS

8 *Punctuality is the politeness of princes*   FRANCE

9 *One learns manners from the mannerless*   IRAN

10 *Insults and pills must not be chewed*   GERMANY

450 LOVE

1 *Love teaches asses to dance*   FRANCE

2 *Give your love to your wife and your secret to your
   mother*   IRELAND

3 *Follow love and it will flee thee; flee love and it will
   follow thee*   SCOTLAND

4 *The greatest love is mother-love; after that comes a dog's
   love; and after that the love of a sweetheart*   POLAND

5   *More precious than our children are the children of our children*   EGYPT

6   *Love and blindness are twin sisters*   UKRAINE

7   *Love is not blind, it merely doesn't see*   GERMANY

8   *Love takes away the sight and matrimony restores it*   GERMANY

9   *The boat of affection ascends even mountains*   BANGLADESH

10   *A gardener's flirtations take place outside the garden*   AFGHANISTAN

11   *Absence makes the heart grow fonder*   ENGLAND

12   *The only victory over love is flight*   FRANCE

13   *To understand your parents' love, bear your own children*   CHINA

14   *Never rely on love or the weather*   GERMANY

15   *Those who have no children do not understand love*   ITALY

16   *Sadness is a valuable treasure, only discovered in people you love*   MADAGASCAR

17   *If love be timid, it is not true*   SPAIN

18   *Love your neighbour, yet pull not down your hedge*   ENGLAND

19   *Love everyone except an attorney*   IRELAND

20   *They that love most speak least*   SCOTLAND

21 *Those in love always know the time* GERMANY

22 *Of soup and love, the first is the best* PORTUGAL

23 *Loved by a king is not loved* SERBIA

24 *Those who love the tree love the branch* ENGLAND

25 *Love yourself, then you will have no rivals* ESTONIA

26 *A fire in the heart makes smoke in the head* GERMANY

27 *One thread for the needle, one love for the heart* SUDAN

28 *Where there is love there is no darkness* BURUNDI

29 *If you love, love the moon; if you steal, steal a camel*
EGYPT

30 *Loving and singing are not to be forced* GERMANY

31 *Don't be so much in love that you can't tell when it's
raining* MADAGASCAR

32 *All is fair in love and war* ENGLAND

33 *When in love, a cliff becomes a meadow* ETHIOPIA

34 *A love-letter sometimes costs more than a three-cent
stamp* USA

35 *Everything will perish save love and music* SCOTLAND

36 *Lovers have much to relate – but it is always the same
thing* GERMANY

37 *Lovers, lunatics* LATIN

451 KISSES – CARESSES

1   *A kiss without a beard is like an egg without salt*
     NETHERLANDS

2   *A hug a day keeps the demons at bay*   GERMANY

3   *Many kiss the child for the nurse's sake*   ENGLAND

4   *No sow so dirty but finds a boar to kiss her*   GERMANY

5   *The more you stroke a cat, the more it lifts its tail*
     ESTONIA

6   *When you have trodden on the cat, what help is it to stroke her back?*   SWITZERLAND

7   *Gin caresses lungs and liver*   NETHERLANDS

452 DISLIKE – ANGER

1   *Beware of people who dislike cats*   IRELAND

2   *Happy owner, happy cat; indifferent owner, reclusive cat*
     CHINA

3   *Cats love fish but fear to wet their paws*   CHINA

4   *If you don't like my apples, don't shake my tree*   USA

5   *It is the hyenas of the same den that hate one another*
     KENYA

6   *If we would know what we are, let us anger our neighbours*   GERMANY

7   *A waiting appetite kindles many a spite*   ENGLAND

8   *When in anger, say the alphabet*   USA

9   *If you wish to be angry, pay for something in advance*
     MONTENEGRO

10   *Time is anger's medicine*   GERMANY

11   *A soft answer turns away wrath*   ENGLAND

12   *Better to light a candle than to curse the darkness*
     CHINA

13   *Every work revenges itself on its master*   GERMANY

14   *The one who seeks revenge should remember to dig two
     graves*   CHINA

453   MARRIAGE

1   *Before marrying live wildly for three years*   POLAND

2   *Beware the husband who talks*   GREECE

3   *There is no marriage where there is no weeping, and no
     funeral where there is no laughing*   ITALY

4   *Honest men marry soon; wise men never*   ENGLAND

5   *Before going to war say one prayer; before going to sea,
     two; before getting married, three*   POLAND

6   *If he calls it a silly and childish game, that means his
     wife can beat him at it*   USA

* * * * * * * * * * * * * * * * * * *

31 BIBLICAL PROVERBS

Any scriptural work is likely to be a fruitful and influential source of proverbs; the Old and New Testaments of the Bible contain several hundred. The first four verses of the Proverbs of Solomon (here cited in the Authorized Version) explain their significance:

> The Proverbs of Solomon, the son of David, king of Israel:
> To know wisdom and instruction; to perceive the words of understanding;
> To receive the instruction of wisdom, justice, and judgment, and equity;
> To give subtilty to the simple, to the young man knowledge and discretion.

And the following examples illustrate their acceptance:

10.2 *Treasures of wickedness profit nothing: but righteousness delivereth from death.*

10.10 *He that winketh with the eye causeth sorrow: but a prating fool shall fall.*

13.11 *Wealth gotten by vanity shall be diminished: but he that gathereth by labour shall increase.*

14.30 *A sound heart is the life of the flesh: but envy the rottenness of the bones.*

16.8 *Better is a little with righteousness than great revenues without right.*

16.18 *Pride goeth before destruction, and an haughty spirit before a fall.*

16.23 *The heart of the wise teacheth his mouth, and addeth learning to his lips.*

16.24 *Pleasant words are as an honeycomb, sweet to the soul, and health to the bones.*

* * * * * * * * * * * * * * * * * *

7 *If you have no relatives, get married* EGYPT

8 *Never marry a woman who has bigger feet than you* MOZAMBIQUE

9 *The easiest way to get a divorce is to be married* USA

10 *Love takes away the sight and matrimony restores it* GERMANY

11 *If you go to the wedding you cover up the sledge* ESTONIA

12 *You can't dance at two weddings with one pair of feet* USA

13 *A blind man's wife needs no painting* SCOTLAND

14 *Give your love to your wife and your secret to your mother* IRELAND

15 *In buying horses and in taking a wife, shut your eyes tight and commend yourself to God* ITALY

16 *The wife of the amber-turner wears pearls of glass* IRAN

17 *Take away the wife of a strong man only when he is out* UGANDA

18 *Hanging and wiving go by destiny* ENGLAND

19 *An apothecary ought not to be long a cuckold* FRANCE

454 TENDERNESS – FORGIVENESS

1 *In December and January have mercy on the poor*
LEBANON

2 *It is because the toad is too tenderhearted that he has no intelligence* HAITI

3 *A pig won't spare even the most beautiful fruit* ALBANIA

4 *The impossible requires no excuse* NETHERLANDS

5 *Any excuse is better than none* ENGLAND

6 *Transgressions should never be forgiven a third time*
CHINA

7 *If there were no fault, there would be no pardon* EGYPT

455 GOODNESS – EVIL

1 *Two wrongs do not make a right* ENGLAND

2 *A bad thing that does no harm is the same as a good one that does no good* GERMANY

3 *Justice becomes injustice when it makes two wounds on a head which only deserves one* REPUBLIC OF CONGO

4   *All is fair in love and war*   ENGLAND

5   *Who speaks of it commits it not*   ITALY

6   *What greater crime than loss of time?*   GERMANY

7   *Fair exchange is no robbery*   ENGLAND

8   *Carve good deeds in stone, bad ones in sand*   ESTONIA

9   *There's no crime in the blow that has not been struck*
    IRELAND

10   *Once a crook, always a crook*   USA

11   *The better the lawyer, the worse the Christian*
    NETHERLANDS

12   *A fault denied is twice committed*   FRANCE

13   *A barren sow was never good to pigs*   ENGLAND

14   *A clear conscience never fears midnight knocking*   CHINA

15   *A good deed is written on snow*   ESTONIA

16   *A clear conscience fears no accusation*   ENGLAND

17   *Conscience is like tickling, some fear it and some don't*
    ITALY

18   *If there were no fault, there would be no pardon*   EGYPT

19   *Transgressions should never be forgiven a third time*
    CHINA

20   *A young saint, an old devil*   ITALY

21   *Charity covers a multitude of sins*   ENGLAND

22 *The saints of the home work no miracles*   ITALY

23 *Good nature is stronger than tomahawks*   USA

24 *The better the day, the better the deed*   ENGLAND

25 *Do a good deed and throw it into the sea*   BULGARIA

26 *Good words make us laugh; good deeds make us silent*
        FRANCE

27 *Better do a good deed near at home than go far away to
    burn incense*   CHINA

28 *Bad is called good when worse happens*   NORWAY

29 *There's no rest for the wicked*   ENGLAND

30 *A good child has several names*   ESTONIA

31 *Honesty is the best policy*   ENGLAND

32 *Leave a good name behind in case you return*   KENYA

33 *That miller is honest who has hair on his teeth*
        GERMANY

34 *Honest men marry soon; wise men never*   ENGLAND

35 *Good silence is called saintliness*   PORTUGAL

36 *'Virtue in the middle,' said the devil as he sat between
    two lawyers*   NORWAY

37 *Virtue is its own reward*   ENGLAND

456 DESERVING

1   *A good cat deserves a good rat*   ENGLAND

2   *Those who do not wish little things do not deserve big things*   BELGIUM

3   *Justice becomes injustice when it makes two wounds on a head which only deserves one*   REPUBLIC OF CONGO

4   *One good turn deserves another*   ENGLAND

457 RESPECT – CONTEMPT

1   *If you bow at all, bow low*   CHINA

2   *Those who haven't seen a church bow before a fireplace*   POLAND

3   *The medicine man is not esteemed in his own village*   KENYA

4   *Honour is better than honours*   BELGIUM

5   *Honour physicians before you have need of them*   ENGLAND

6   *Everything ancient is to be respected*   GREECE

7   *To always win brings suspicion, to always lose brings contempt*   GERMANY

8   *There is no honour among thieves*   ENGLAND

9   *If you would climb into the saddle don't despise the stirrup*   GERMANY

10   *Familiarity breeds contempt*   ENGLAND

458 PRAISE – BLAME

1   *Every priest praises his convent*   PHILIPPINES

2   *Let everyone praise the bridge they go over*   ENGLAND

3   *Applause is the beginning of abuse*   JAPAN

4   *Don't praise a cottage in which you haven't yet slept*
     SOUTH AFRICA

5   *Give credit where credit is due*   ENGLAND

6   *It takes two hands to clap*   INDIA

7   *Only with a new ruler do you appreciate the value of
     the old*   MYANMAR

8   *Poets and pigs are appreciated only after their death*
     ITALY

9   *The spoon is prized when the soup is being eaten*
     CZECH REPUBLIC

10   *There is no grace in a benefit that sticks to the fingers*
     ENGLAND

11   *Paper does not blush*   ITALY

12   *To be in the habit of no habit is the worst habit in the
     world*   WALES

13   *Two things make one either greater or smaller, praise and
     shadows*   GERMANY

14   *Not even a schoolteacher notices bad grammar in a compliment*   USA

15   *What you can't have, abuse*   ITALY

16   *When people praise, few believe it, but when they blame, all believe it*   BELGIUM

17   *Woe to the house where there is no chiding*   ENGLAND

18   *She is a foolish woman who blames her own cabbage*   DENMARK

19   *The absent always bear the blame*   NETHERLANDS

20   *It's not so bad to fall in the gutter, but it's worse to lay there*   USA

21   *'Thank you' won't pay the fiddler*   SCOTLAND

22   *A bad workman blames his tools*   ENGLAND

23   *Do not blame God for having created the tiger, but thank Him for not having given it wings*   ETHIOPIA

24   *Adam must have an Eve, to blame for his own faults*   GERMANY

459   DRUNKENNESS

1   *It is only the first bottle that is dear*   FRANCE

2   *Drinking a little too much is drinking a great deal too much*   GERMANY

3 *Better to drink and be unwell than not to drink and be unwell*   MONTENEGRO

4 *If you drink you die, if you don't drink you die, so it is better to drink*   RUSSIA

5 *A red-nosed man may not be a drinker, but he will find nobody to believe it*   CHINA

6 *Bacchus has drowned more people than Neptune*   GERMANY

7 *When everybody says you are drunk, go to sleep*   ITALY

460 LAWS – LAWYERS

1 *Neither break a law nor make one*   IRELAND

2 *New lords, new laws*   FRANCE

3 *New laws, new frauds*   ENGLAND

4 *Laws catch flies but let hornets go free*   ENGLAND

5 *Law is a spider's web; big flies break through but the little ones are caught*   HUNGARY

6 *Necessity knows no law*   ENGLAND

7 *Laws have wax noses*   FRANCE

8 *Kick an attorney downstairs and he'll stick to you for life*   SCOTLAND

9 *Love everyone except an attorney*   IRELAND

10   *'Virtue in the middle,' said the devil as he sat between two lawyers*   NORWAY

11   *A good lawyer is a bad neighbour*   FRANCE

12   *The better the lawyer, the worse the Christian*   NETHERLANDS

13   *Where there's a will, there's a lawsuit*   USA

461   PUNISHMENT

1   *Before you beat a dog, find out who its master is*   CHINA

2   *Don't shout before the birch-rod falls*   LATVIA

3   *It is not the thief that is hanged, but the one who was caught stealing*   CZECH REPUBLIC

4   *Hanging and wiving go by destiny*   ENGLAND

5   *The rod that will hang him is still growing*   IRELAND

6   *Nobody is hanged for thinking*   HUNGARY

7   *Might as well be hanged for a sheep as a lamb*   ENGLAND

8   *Ambassadors suffer no penalty*   ITALY

9   *Spare the rod and spoil the child*   ENGLAND

10   *Both legs in the stocks or only one is all the same*   GERMANY

11   *An old horse doesn't fear the whip*   SWITZERLAND

462 GOD – GODS

1   *God did not create hurry*   FINLAND

2   *God heals and the doctor gets the money*   BELGIUM

3   *God is better pleased with adverbs than with nouns*
ENGLAND

4   *God does not shave – why should I?*   BULGARIA

5   *God gives the wideness of the mouth according to the
bigness of the spoon*   POLAND

6   *God saves the moon from the wolves*   POLAND

7   *God gives birds their food, but they must fly for it*
NETHERLANDS

8   *God, what things we see when we go out without a gun!*
SOUTH AFRICA

9   *God works in moments*   FRANCE

10 *God listens to short prayers*   ITALY

11 *God preserve us from pitch-forks, for they make three
holes*   SWITZERLAND

12 *God knows on which knee the camel will squat down*
AFGHANISTAN

13 *Before God and the bus-conductor we are all equal*
GERMANY

14 *The mills of God grind slowly*   ENGLAND

15 *When God made the rabbit He made bushes too*
HUNGARY

16 *Who has God for his friend has all the saints in his
pocket* ITALY

17 *Solitude is full of God* SERBIA

18 *In buying horses and in taking a wife, shut your eyes
tight and commend yourself to God* ITALY

19 *Only God helps the ill-dressed* SPAIN

20 *The cat does not catch mice for God* INDIA

21 *Do not blame God for having created the tiger, but thank
Him for not having given it wings* ETHIOPIA

22 *Slowness comes from God and quickness from the devil*
MOROCCO

23 *Cleanliness is next to godliness* ENGLAND

24 *If you believe, it is a deity; otherwise, a stone* INDIA

25 *Not even Apollo keeps his bow always at full stretch*
LATIN

463 ANGELS – SAINTS

1 *Angels gave the gift of song, and while one sings one
thinks no wrong* ITALY

2 *Fools rush in where angels fear to tread* ENGLAND

3   *Speak of the miracle, but don't mention the saint*
    PHILIPPINES

4   *Who has God for his friend has all the saints in his*
    pocket   ITALY

5   *Pilgrims seldom come home saints*   GERMANY

6   *A cask of wine works more miracles than a church full of*
    saints   ITALY

7   *It is better to follow no saint than six*   INDIA

464   DEVILS

1   *The devil makes pots, but not always lids*
    ITALY: SARDINIA

2   *Better the devil you know than the devil you don't*
    ENGLAND

3   *A hug a day keeps the demons at bay*   GERMANY

4   *The devil finds work for idle hands*   ENGLAND

5   *A beautiful maiden is a devil's pocket*   PHILIPPINES

6   *With silence we irritate the devil*   BULGARIA

7   *'Virtue in the middle,' said the devil as he sat between*
    two lawyers   NORWAY

8   *Talk of the devil and he will appear*   ENGLAND

9   *A young saint, an old devil*   ITALY

10   *Slowness comes from God and quickness from the devil*
MOROCCO

11   *Needs must when the devil drives*   ENGLAND

12   *Three glasses of wine drive away the evil spirits, but with the fourth they return*   GERMANY

465 HEAVEN

1   *A north-easterly wind is heaven's broom*   ESTONIA

2   *Heaven helps those who help themselves*   ENGLAND

3   *Even a hen, when it drinks, looks towards heaven*
TURKEY

4   *Those who would enter paradise must have a good key*
ENGLAND

5   *Only heaven can see the back of a sparrow*
SOUTH AFRICA

466 WORSHIP

1   *Proverbs are little gospels*   SPAIN

2   *Pray devoutly but hammer stoutly*   ENGLAND

3   *Pilgrims seldom come home saints*   GERMANY

4   *Pray to God, but continue to row to the shore*   RUSSIA

* * * * * * * * * * * * * * * * * * *

32 UNFINISHED PROVERBS

A sure sign that a proverb has been assimilated into a culture is when only its first part is used. The user knows that the listener or reader can complete it. Indeed, in some cases the truncated form is probably more widespread than the full form. Some examples:

> *Ask a silly question . . .*
> *What the eye cannot see . . .*
> *Those who laugh last . . .*
> *People who live in glass houses . . .*
> *The proof of the pudding . . .*

In its truncated form, a proverb may even be incorporated into a normal sentence, as in: 'That's the proof of the pudding, isn't it?'

* * * * * * * * * * * * * * * * * *

5   *Before going to war say one prayer; before going to sea, two; before getting married, three*   POLAND

6   *Those who wish to learn to pray must go to sea*
    ENGLAND

7   *God listens to short prayers*   ITALY

8   *A vineyard does not require prayers, but a hoe*   TURKEY

9   *The better the lawyer, the worse the Christian*
    NETHERLANDS

10   *When the fox starts preaching, look to the hens*
      SPAIN: BASQUE

11   *A maker of idols is never an idol-worshipper*   CHINA

12   *One bell serves a parish*   ITALY

13   *A blessing does not fill the belly*   IRELAND

14   *Those who gossip about their relatives have no luck and
      no blessing*   NETHERLANDS

15   *Public money is like holy water, one helps oneself to it*
      ITALY

16   *Better do a good deed near at home than go far away to
      burn incense*   CHINA

17   *However long the procession, it always returns to the
      church*   PHILIPPINES

18   *The broad-minded see the truth in different religions; the
      narrow-minded see only the differences*   CHINA

467 CLERGY

1   *A dog may look at a bishop*   FRANCE

2   *There is no worse abbot than the one who has been a
      monk*   SPAIN

3   *What makes one abbot glad makes another abbot sad*
      SCOTLAND

4   *It is a silly sheep that makes the wolf her confessor*
    FRANCE

5   *A cat may go to a monastery, but she still remains a cat*
    ETHIOPIA

6   *Do not try to borrow combs from shaven monks*   CHINA

7   *Those who wish to live at Rome must not quarrel with
    the pope*   FRANCE

8   *He who never leaves Paris will never be pope*   FRANCE

9   *Not everyone can be the pope of Rome*   NETHERLANDS

10 *Golden bishop, wooden crozier; wooden bishop, golden
    crozier*   FRANCE

11 *Every priest praises his convent*   PHILIPPINES

12 *Priests return to the temple; merchants to the shop*
    CHINA

13 *Don't talk Latin in front of the Franciscans*   FRANCE

14 *Priests and women never forget*   GERMANY

468 CHURCH

1   *Those who haven't seen a church bow before a fireplace*
    POLAND

2   *One bell serves a parish*   ITALY

3   *Let the church stand in the churchyard*   ENGLAND

4   *On going into a church leave the world behind the door*
SPAIN

5   *A cask of wine works more miracles than a church full of saints* ITALY

6   *It is better to be once in the church sleigh than always in the back runners* FINLAND

7   *Right church but wrong pew* USA

8   *Priests return to the temple; merchants to the shop*
CHINA

9   *However long the procession, it always returns to the church* PHILIPPINES

FURTHER READING

A classic collection of proverbs from many languages is Selwyn Gurney Champion, *Racial Proverbs* (London: Routledge, 1938).

Modern proverbs are included in Wolfgang Mieder, Stewart A Kingsbury, and Kelsie B Harder, *A Dictionary of American Proverbs* (New York: Oxford University Press, 1992) and Bartlett Jere Whiting, *Modern Proverbs and Proverbial Sayings* (Harvard University Press, 1989).

Examples of collections from specific languages include those published by Hippocrene Books, New York, such as: Marjorie Lin and Schalk Leonard, *Dictionary of 1000 Chinese Proverbs* (1998); Gerd de Ley, *Dictionary of 1000 Dutch Proverbs* (1998), and Gerd de Ley, *African Proverbs* (1999). For an older example of the genre, see Alexander Nicolson, *Gaelic Proverbs* (1881; Edinburgh: Birlinn, 1996).

Proverbium: Yearbook of International Proverb Scholarship, edited by Wolfgang Mieder, and published annually by the University of Vermont.

Paremia, edited by Julia Sevilla Muñoz, Universidad

Complutense de Madrid, published by Librería Sánchez-Cuesta, Madrid.

De Proverbio, a multilingual electronic journal of international proverb studies: http://www.deproverbio.com/

INDEXES

Index 1:

INDEX OF THEMES

This is an alphabetical index of the themes included in the proverb classification. The alphabetical order of the index is word-by-word.

Index 2:

BOOK TO ROGET

Use this index if you want to find out which proverb categories relate to which semantic categories in Roget's *Thesaurus*. Roget categories are identified by their number and description, as given in the Longman edition (Kirkpatrick, 1987).

Index 3:

ROGET TO BOOK

Use this index if you want to find out which of Roget's semantic categories relate to the lexemes and proverb sections in this book. Roget categories are identified by their number and description, as given in the Longman edition (Kirkpatrick, 1987). The alphabetical order of the lexemes is word-by-word.

1 *existence* be, come, consist, create, everything, existence, make, stand 1
2 *nonexistence* perish 1
11 *consanguinity* aunt, blood relation, brother, brotherly, family, father, grandparent, kinship, relative, sister, uncle 2
13 *identity* one, same, twin 3
16 *uniformity* same 3
17 *nonuniformity* exception, variety 4
18 *similarity* alike, another 3
19 *dissimilarity* difference 4
26 *quantity* lot, much, two-thirds 6
27 *degree* little, stage, step 7
28 *equality* equal, much, same, worth 3
32 *greatness* deal, great, most, much 6
33 *smallness* bit, drop, handful, little, piece, sip, small 5
34 *superiority* beat, better, beyond, boss, great, superior 17
35 *inferiority* bad, mediocrity, pretty 17
36 *increase* add, double, grow, gather 7
37 *decrease* less 7
38 *addition* another, more 7

41 *remainder* dregs, leave, rest 17
43 *mixture* mix, tangled 18
45 *union* bind, grow, marry, strap, tie 18
46 *disunion* break, burst, crack, cut, divided, leave, part, separation, skin (*verb*), slice, ungum 19
47 *bond* buckle, button, chain, coupled, gum, gummed, knot, link, mortar, rope, slip knot, stitch, string 18, 20
48 *coherence* stick, together 18
49 *noncoherence* loose, slip, slippery 19
50 *combination* add, put together 22
51 *decomposition* rotten, rust 17
52 *whole* entire, whole 21
53 *part* arm, back, belly, bone, buttock, cheek, chin, ear, elbow, eye, face, finger, fingernail, fist, foot, forehead, fragment, half, hand, head, heart, horn, joint, knee, leg, lip, liver, lung, mouth, neck, nose, palm, part, paw, piece, rib, shin, skull, splinter, stomach, tail, thigh, thumb, toe, tongue, tooth, trunk 21, 232–50

damage, faded, stale, worn-out 359

656 *restoration* heal, healer, repair, restore 356–7

658 *remedy* antidote, apothecary, apply, cure, dentist, doctor, medicine, medicine man, physic, physician, pill, remedy 357–8

659 *bane* poison 360

660 *safety* guardian, protect, protector, safe 361

661 *danger* danger, dangerous, unsafe 361

662 *refuge* hole 361

664 *warning* forewarned, warn, warning 361

666 *preservation* keep, preserve, save 362

667 *escape* break through, fly away 393

669 *preparation* cock, forearmed, preparations 364–5

671 *attempt* attempt, try, venture 363

672 *undertaking* make 365

673 *use* adopt, handle, put, use, use up, used 364, 366–7

674 *nonuse* save, spare 364

676 *action* ability, action, deed, do, energy, lightning, make, sharp, steam, strike out, turn 365, 367

677 *inaction* indolence 370

678 *activity* awake, busy, diligent, quick, sieve, steadily, wake, wake up 365–7, 371

679 *inactivity* asleep, bed, idle, lazy, leave alone, lie, procrastination, rest, sloth, slothful, stand, stationary, yawn, yawning 365, 369–72

680 *haste* haste, hasty, hurry 373

681 *leisure* holiday, rest 366

682 *exertion* effort, labour, sweat, trouble, work 328, 366

683 *repose* go to bed, go to sleep, rest, roost, siesta, sleep, sleeping 371–2

686 *agent* blacksmith, hand, I, make, master, smith, workman 326, 366

688 *conduct* mannerless, manners, strategy 368, 449

691 *advice* advice, adviser, consult, instruction 374

693 *precept* rule 368

694 *skill* ability, able, accomplishment, art, arts, good, know, well 297, 375

695 *unskilfulness* bad, clumsy 375

698 *cunning* cunning, move, sly 375

700 *difficulty* difficult, hard, job, rough, tough 376

701 *facility* easily, easy 377

702 *hindrance* block, burden, choke, hinder 170, 183, 376

703 *aid* assistance, help 378

705 *cooperation* join 379

706 *opponent* rival 379

708 *party* side 379

709 *dissension* quarrel, row 380

710 *concord* united 379

712 *attack* attack, besiege, shoot 381

713 *defence* at bay, castle, defence, dyke, fort, fortress, hold, keep, wall 382

715 *resistance* stand 382

716 *contention* bite, fight, fray 381

717 *peace* peace, peace-maker 383

718 *war* battle, wage war, war 381, 383

721 *submission* surrender 383

722 *combatant* army, gladiator, lead, soldier 381, 384

723 *arms* arrow, bludgeon, bow, club, cudgel, dagger, dynamite, gun, knife, loaded, spear, sword, tomahawk, trigger, unloaded 385

724 *arena* arena 59

Index 4:

LEXEMES

This is a word-by-word index which relates lexemes to the semantic fields recognized in the body of the book.

• A lexeme is a unit of sense, ignoring any grammatical variations. For example, the two words *ant* and *ants* both belong to the one lexeme 'ant'; the four words *walk, walks, walking*, and *walked* all belong to the one lexeme 'walk'.

• A semantic field is a group of lexemes which define a domain of meaning. For example, lexemes like 'apple' and 'lemon' belong to the field of FRUIT, 'boil' and 'fried' belong to the field of COOKING.

In this book, the salient lexemes in a proverb have been indexed in relation to the semantic fields to which they belong. For example, in the proverb *The sun shines on both sides of the hedge*, the salient lexemes are *sun, shine, both, side*, and *hedge*. This proverb will therefore be found in the following fields:

167 SUN – MOON – STARS

274 LIGHT

12 TWO – TWICE – BOTH

110 SIDES

108 ENCLOSURES

The index gives the section number and the item number relating to each usage. For example, 274.7 is the seventh item in section 274 LIGHT.

121.10, 122.10, 138.21, 222.1, 276.4, 295.11

hammer (*noun*) 31.7, 36.4, 83.2, 116.14, 165.4, 282.10, 344.11–13, 400.15, 428.6

hammer (*verb*) 54.7, 132.17, 466.2

hand (*noun*) 3.32, 33, 5.7, 9.1, 4–5, 20, 12.12, 21, 38, 15.4, 16.24, 18.4, 15, 21.5, 23.11, 18, 25.15, 28.33, 38.3, 52.16, 65.10, 77.7, 94.5, 99.8, 103.4, 110.11– 12, 118.9, 129.14, 130.9, 135.5, 136.15, 138.8, 143.19, 145.14, 42, 149.32, 162.4, 173.4, 182.22, 183.8, 188.11, 209.6, 210.2, 214.1, 215.17, 221.20, 225.1, 226.4, 229.9, 230.13, 239.3, 240.16, 242.2, 244.23, 246.1–28, 247.7, 12, 249.10–11, 251.2–3, 253.4, 258.16, 262.7, 295.19, 322.12, 326.19, 330.8, 332.20, 334.16, 342.26, 36, 344.8, 26, 345.13, 24, 350.1, 3, 362.4, 363.7, 364.4, 366.2–3, 9, 370.4, 6, 374.9, 388.4, 394.3, 400.11–12, 406.2, 407.7, 408.10, 409.18, 410.2, 411.8, 413.17, 415.3, 424.18, 427.7, 435.5, 441.17, 445.11, 20, 458.6, 464.4

hand over 111.6, 181.2, 382.6, 408.21

handful 5.3, 72.9, 218.6, 220.15

handicraft 344.1, 428.18

handle (*noun*) 12.20, 22, 26.19, 72.3, 87.3, 94.1–3, 124.8, 222.9, 344.14, 405.2, 409.16

handle (*verb*) 24.13, 104.1, 316.11, 326.11, 328.10, 364.9, 366.11, 416.12

handleless 94.4, 222.8, 344.3, 438.25

handsome 1.8, 81.3, 102.5, 239.4, 6, 249.2, 421.5, 424.8, 432.12, 16, 19–20, 439.1

hang 1.4, 8.17, 35.3, 36.14, 16, 63.8, 67.19, 95.4–6, 101.22, 206.9, 227.7, 251.8, 284.2, 328.3, 394.1, 412.17, 439.11, 461.3, 5–7

hanging (*noun*) 309.1, 365.25, 453.18, 461.4

ha'porth 126.12, 165.13, 415.18, 435.7

happen 52.1, 7, 323.11, 335.2, 388.5, 455.28

happy 2.10, 12.9, 32.1, 33.23, 48.11,

136.8, 193.10, 208.17, 211.8, 228.22, 306.1, 314.6, 325.37, 342.5, 400.8, 403.4, 405.6, 421.2–4, 11, 14, 452.2

harbour (*verb*) 2.16, 26.13, 46.25, 66.18, 434.6

hard (*adjective*) 12.3, 23.1, 39.5, 45.6, 10, 46.27, 59.3, 65.7, 105.4, 128.4, 146.31, 158.1, 171.2–3, 174.29, 201.5, 203.3, 206.8, 207.9, 208.18, 234.5, 237.25, 256.3, 282.4, 334.15, 376.5–8, 11, 391.7, 394.22

hard (*adverb*) 1.12, 57.1–2, 8–9, 124.17, 128.3, 134.3, 139.9, 158.22, 174.19, 186.2, 212.1, 221.13, 263.8, 315.3, 331.5, 347.2, 348.1, 424.5

harden 54.6, 249.6, 330.1

hare 12.37, 15.15, 130.11, 205.6–7, 277.26, 324.10, 338.6, 394.12, 438.10

harm (*noun*) 3.10, 53.2–3, 69.5, 81.4, 103.4, 201.4, 229.9, 243.4, 246.21, 249.20, 270.8, 296.27, 331.15, 334.5, 9, 16–17, 20, 363.1, 424.12, 425.5, 438.19, 455.2

harm (*verb*) 254.5, 323.4, 334.18–19, 366.12, 370.7

harmony 270.4

harvest (*verb*) 145.18, 156.6, 160.2, 227.14, 237.12, 444.9

haste 7.13, 130.17, 373.3

hasty 153.6, 287.13, 288.4, 342.34, 344.9, 373.1, 373.2, 440.11

hat 10.3, 23.17, 55.14, 103.1, 103.2, 103.3, 103.4, 103.5, 168.32, 229.9, 237.3, 237.4, 246.21, 282.1, 304.26, 334.16, 342.4, 351.8, 399.23, 416.9, 441.6

hatched 40.10, 98.5, 184.6, 184.7, 209.8, 211.11, 290.2, 342.20

hatchet 87.3, 94.2, 220.11, 222.9, 239.8, 344.14, 344.15, 409.16, 411.13, 445.17

hate 3.8, 65.8, 200.4, 452.5

have 2.1, 7, 22, 3.6, 4.6, 5.12–13, 20, 6.8, 17, 8.16, 23, 26, 9.2–3, 22, 10.10, 11.1, 8–12, 18–19, 12.4, 14, 20, 22, 34, 65, 13.1, 5, 14.1, 12, 34–6, 15.8, 16.12,

living (*adjective*) 10.2, 14.28, 187.5, 322.17, 332.9

lizard 51.17, 83.9, 141.6, 215.7–8, 221.2, 397.7, 437.2, 438.6

load (*noun*) 5.21, 59.18, 80.4–6, 124.1, 125.11, 134.8, 170.3, 188.10, 281.2, 328.15, 342.35, 377.14

loaded (*adjective*) 12.26, 385.11, 438.21

loaf 9.3, 15.17, 19.23, 149.7, 12, 15, 22, 226.2, 377.13, 400.22, 412.8, 413.3

loan 410.3, 417.8, 432.14

lobster 143.20, 174.34, 213.2, 422.10

lock (*verb*) 41.7, 67.20, 118.18, 199.17, 350.22, 412.3

log 19.27, 36.6, 53.38, 112.7, 127.9, 178.14, 215.5, 223.11–12, 255.25, 257.1, 307.7, 331.27, 344.5, 348.3

long (*adjective*) 14.18, 20.9, 11, 26.15, 28.29, 31.7, 11, 18, 32.17, 33.16, 32, 34.8, 36.4, 7–8, 12–13, 20, 43.3, 66.15, 80.1, 81.19, 82.1, 84.17, 86.1–3, 5–11, 14, 90.2, 114.4, 116.14, 125.21, 129.8, 11, 136.36, 139.8, 147.12, 149.31, 165.4, 170.7, 209.15, 211.16, 219.6, 238.2, 15, 240.12, 247.8, 252.4, 255.26, 258.2, 262.1, 271.8, 290.6, 292.1, 304.27, 308.7, 311.10, 328.7, 341.11, 344.13, 354.9, 372.3, 386.9, 397.3, 416.1, 421.7, 423.12, 428.12, 466.17, 468.9

long (*adverb*) 1.4, 8.17, 31.10, 35.3, 36.2, 5–6, 9–10, 14, 17–19, 21–22, 49.17, 64.16, 78.5, 119.2, 121.7, 125.23, 127.9, 20, 136.30, 138.24, 144.3, 156.3, 7, 174.30, 178.14, 185.3, 11, 190.3, 194.14, 195.33, 200.3, 210.6, 215.5, 223.12, 250.11, 267.10, 286.4, 328.3, 338.8, 346.3, 348.3, 357.6, 409.13, 439.11, 441.30, 453.19

long (*verb*) 62.15, 104.4, 121.17, 139.11, 174.21, 212.9, 369.3

look (*noun*) 12.27, 15.1, 277.4, 411.4, 418.3

look (*verb*) 3.15, 4.8, 12.61, 17.6, 19.36, 28.14, 22, 28, 34.3, 39.29, 40.20, 42.3, 47.7, 49.12, 66.11, 14, 70.6, 73.2, 84.2, 88.4, 90.22, 91.8–9, 108.5, 12, 110.7,

9, 112.3, 121.2, 124.9, 125.4, 133.11, 13, 19, 142.5, 145.7, 147.6, 153.2, 157.1, 158.20, 161.13, 164.8, 167.6, 193.11, 195.4, 196.6, 197.1, 198.2, 208.8, 211.23, 27, 212.13, 15, 220.18, 221.4, 223.18, 28, 224.9, 230.3–4, 237.16, 244.19, 258.12, 264.10, 275.10, 14, 277.1–3, 5–14, 279.12, 281.7, 282.6–10, 285.3, 289.1–4, 6, 294.6, 341.5, 342.9, 344.12, 346.9, 350.25, 352.5, 390.13, 16, 399.9, 400.15, 413.15, 415.12, 426.5, 431.5, 465.3, 466.10, 467.1

looking-glass 45.22, 277.44, 278.9, 332.27, 445.12

loom (*noun*) 24.13, 104.1, 328.10, 366.11

loose (*adjective*) 10.17, 19.34, 39.26, 54.19, 158.33, 182.28, 223.26, 237.19, 344.4, 423.18

loosen 6.22, 18.13, 54.15

lord 44.13, 390.22, 460.2

lose 5.19, 12.45, 16.9–10, 15, 17, 27, 17.16, 19.14, 21.11, 28.12, 39–40, 30.11, 32.20, 33.8, 39.17, 48.8, 49.12, 53.12, 56.8, 59.13, 75.2, 126.2, 133.16, 141.2, 178.1, 182.2, 190.6, 194.24, 206.2, 226.6, 227.16, 262.3, 8, 267.7, 268.8, 277.1, 287.8, 290.1, 292.12, 295.24, 306.5, 312.2, 326.3, 332.19, 365.19, 375.21, 387.5–6, 10, 12–15, 390.2, 398.7, 14, 399.1–5, 7, 9–18, 21, 24, 400.5, 410.8, 411.14, 413.14, 30, 414.8, 415.12, 428.11, 16, 430.3–4, 437.7, 443.6, 444.8, 445.10, 13, 21, 457.7, 448.6

loss 3.2, 22.22, 31.13, 181.5, 198.4, 200.2, 268.16, 275.4, 347.3, 352.18, 375.17, 399.6, 19–20, 22, 413.27, 455.6

lot ('fortune') 145.22, 160.12, 170.11, 182.5, 309.2

lot ('multitude') 6.18, 296.13, 317.6, 324.9

lot ('site') 23.9, 59.5, 333.2, 446.7

loud (*adjective*) 23.2, 88.8, 194.11, 250.5, 266.2, 4, 268.7, 272.4, 404.10

Index 5:

INDEX OF COUNTRIES

This index lists the sections in this book which include proverbs from a particular country. Latin is also included.